BIOHISTORY:
THE INTERPLAY BETWEEN
HUMAN SOCIETY AND
THE BIOSPHERE

Past and Present

MaB

MAN AND THE BIOSPHERE SERIES

Series Editor J.N.R. Jeffers

VOLUME 8

BIOHISTORY:
THE INTERPLAY BETWEEN
HUMAN SOCIETY AND
THE BIOSPHERE

Past and Present

S. Boyden

Centre for Resource and Environmental Studies
Australian National University

Illustrations by Jorge Bontes

PUBLISHED BY

PARIS

AND

The Parthenon Publishing Group

International Publishers in Science, Technology & Education

Published in 1992 by the United Nations Educational, Scientific and Cultural
Organization,
7 Place de Fontenoy, 75700 Paris, France—UNESCO ISBN 92-3-102747-6
and
The Parthenon Publishing Group Limited
Casterton Hall, Carnforth,
Lancs LA6 2LA, UK—ISBN 1-85070-371-X
and
The Parthenon Publishing Group Inc.
120 Mill Road,
Park Ridge
New Jersey, 07656, USA—ISBN 1-85070-371-X

Typeset by Lasertext Ltd, Stretford, Manchester
Printed and bound in Great Britain by
Butler and Tanner Ltd., Frome and London

British Library Cataloguing in Publication Data

Boyden, S.
Biohistory: the interplay between human society and the biosphere –
past and present
I. Title II. Series
304.5
ISBN 1-85070-371-X

Library of Congress Cataloging-in-Publication Data

Boyden, Stephen Vickers.
Biohistory : the interplay between human society and the biosphere /
Stephen Boyden.
p. cm. — (Man and the biosphere series : v. 8)
Includes bibliographical references and index.
ISBN 1-85070-371-X (Parthenon) : $68.00
1. Human ecology. 2. Biosphere. 3. Human evolution. 4. Geobiology.
5. Sociobiology. I. Title. II. Series.
GF50.867 1992
304.2—dc20
91-46009
CIP

PREFACE

UNESCO's Man and the Biosphere Programme

Improving scientific understanding of natural and social processes relating to man's interactions with his environment, providing information useful to decision-making on resource use, promoting the conservation of genetic diversity as an integral part of land management, enjoining the efforts of scientists, policy-makers and local people in problem-solving ventures, mobilizing resources for field activities, strengthening of regional co-operative frameworks: these are some of the generic characteristics of UNESCO's Man and the Biosphere (MAB) Programme.

The MAB Programme was launched in the early 1970s. It is a nationally based, international programme of research, training, demonstration and information diffusion. The overall aim is to contribute to efforts for providing the scientific basis and trained personnel needed to deal with problems of rational utilization and conservation of resources and resource systems, and problems of human settlements. MAB emphasizes research for solving problems: it thus involves research by interdisciplinary teams on the interactions between ecological and social systems; field training; and applying a systems approach to understanding the relationships between the natural and human components of development and environmental management.

MAB is a decentralized programme with field projects and training activities in all regions of the world. These are carried out by scientists and technicians from universities, academies of sciences, national research laboratories and other research and development institutions, under the auspices of more than a hundred MAB National Committees. Activities are undertaken in co-operation with a range of international governmental and non-governmental organizations.

Man and the Biosphere Book Series

The Man and the Biosphere Series was launched with the aim of communicating some of the results generated by the MAB Programme and is aimed primarily at upper level university students, scientists and resource managers, who are not necessarily specialists in ecology. The books are not normally suitable for undergraduate text books but rather provide additional resource material in the form of case studies based on primary data collection and written by the researchers involved; global and regional syntheses of comparative research conducted in several sites or countries; and state-of-the-art assessments of knowledge or methodological approaches based on scientific meetings, commissioned reports or panels of experts. The Series Editor is John Jeffers, formerly Director of the Institute of Terrestrial Ecology, in the United Kingdom, who has been associated with MAB since its inception.

Biohistory: The Interplay between Human Society and the Biosphere

The present volume provides an overview of biohistory – the broad sequence of happenings in the history of the biosphere and of civilization, from the beginning of life to the present day. The concern with the interplay of human culture, society, natural processes and biophysical systems is based on a conceptual approach which nearly two decades ago helped shape a MAB pilot project on the ecology of the city of Hong Kong and its hinterland.

The author of this book, Stephen Boyden, was instrumental in the early 1970s in the planning and setting-up of the Hong Kong Human Ecology Programme, a multi-disciplinary research initiative involving a range of different institutions and specialists from the natural and social sciences. It was perhaps the first attempt to describe the ecology of a large city in an integrative and holistic way. The study encompassed measurements of the changing patterns of flow and use of energy, nutrients and water, changes in housing and transport, as well as the life conditions and patterns of health and disease of the human population. The Hong Kong study was adopted by UNESCO as an initial pilot project in that part of the MAB Programme dealing with ecological studies on human settlements (MAB Project Area 11). The studies in Hong Kong gave rise to a large number of scientific publications, with the results being summarized in a MAB Technical Note published by UNESCO in 1979 (*An Integrative Ecological Approach to the Study of Human Settlements*) and in a book released by the Australian National University in 1981 (*The Ecology of a City and Its People: the Case of Hong Kong*).

The Hong Kong project inspired and helped shape a score of somewhat similar ecological studies of such cities as Georgetown (Guyana), Rome (Italy), Mexico City (Mexico) and Seoul (Republic of Korea). Stephen

Boyden has himself been invited to provide advice to a fair number of these projects and has been directly concerned in two specific follow-ups to the Hong Kong project, in Lae, Papua New Guinea and in Bangkok, Thailand. More recently, he has been a moving force of an innovative 'Fundamental Questions' programme at the Australian National University. Such activities have served as testing grounds and sounding boards for Stephen Boyden's thinking on the interplay between cultural and natural processes, which is described in the present book.

A substantive introduction provides background on the concept and dimensions of biohistory and the various phases in the history of humankind, as well as a rationale for including a major biohistorical input in the educational process. There follow twelve substantive chapters on the biosphere, biological evolution, patterns in nature, humans and the emergence of culture, the biosphere and human society, farming, technological developments and the metabolism of society, warfare and weaponry, changes in human society, biological impacts on human populations, human behaviour and the less tangible aspects of human experience, and the present and the future in a biohistorical perspective. An overall conclusion is that the environmental problems facing humanity are unlikely to be overcome unless there is a major shift in our cultural systems and in our programmes of formal and community education.

It is hoped that the book will be of interest to researchers, educationalists and students interested in the interactions between human society and bio-physical systems, especially as they relate to the role of culture and the sustainability of ecological systems.

MAN AND THE BIOSPHERE SERIES

CONTENTS

INTRODUCTION

The emergence in evolution of the human capacity for culture was a development of overwhelming biological importance – not only for the human species itself, but also, as it has turned out, for the rest of the living world. The product of this capacity – that is, culture itself – was a new force in the biosphere, and it eventually gave rise to changes that were quite different in kind from anything that had occurred in the previous four or five thousand million years of life on Earth.

From the beginning, the interplay between cultural and natural processes resulted in significant changes in both the biophysical environment and the life conditions of humans. Initially, these impacts were manifest only locally, and had little effect on the biosphere as a whole. However, with the increasing intensification of culture–nature interplay and the concomitant explosive growth of the human population, changes are now evident on a massive scale, affecting the quality of human life and the functioning of biological systems the world over.

Some of the culture-inspired changes in biological systems can be perceived as 'desirable' from the human point of view. These include the introduction of farming, which has allowed many more people to exist on Earth at any given time than would otherwise have been the case, and the various factors that have increased life expectancy in the developed regions of the world to around 76 years. On the other hand, culture has been responsible for an immeasurable amount of human suffering arising, for example, from human violence, epidemic disease, slavery and other forms of social discrimination. It has also been the cause of a great deal of damage to the ecosystems on which human populations have been dependent, resulting in land degradation and serious loss in bioproductivity. In very recent times, serious ecological disturbances resulting from culturally-induced human activities have been detected even at the level of the planet as a whole.

The second half of the present century has seen a growing concern among the scientific community about the negative impacts that human society is having on the ecosystems of the biosphere at all levels – that is, locally, regionally and globally. One of the most important manifestations of this concern is UNESCO's Man and the Biosphere Programme (MAB). This Programme was launched in 1971, and its general objective has been defined as:

> ... to develop within the natural and social sciences a basis for the rational use and conservation of the resources of the biosphere and for the improvement of the relationship between man and the environment; to predict the consequences of today's actions on tomorrow's world and thereby to increase man's ability to manage efficiently the natural resources of the biosphere.

In the words of the Secretary of the International Co-ordinating Council of MAB: 'The MAB Programme ... stressed the need for an integrated, interdisciplinary rather than multidisciplinary approach and brought the social sciences into ecological research as an equal partner with the natural sciences'.

The MAB Programme has involved a wide range of projects on different kinds of ecosystems (e.g. tropical and temperate forests, grazing lands, arid zones, mountain and island ecosystems) and on various important ecological themes (e.g. conservation of natural areas, pest management, environmental pollution). It has also included projects on ecological aspects of urban systems, with particular emphasis on energy utilization. The Programme is thus concerned with matters of overwhelming significance for humankind.

The present volume aims to present an overview of the interplay between cultural and natural processes throughout human history and up to the present day. It is based on a conceptual approach which found early expression in a MAB Pilot Project on the ecology of the city of Hong Kong and its hinterland and which we now refer to as *biohistory*.

Although initially applied in a research project on an urban ecosystem, the conceptual framework of biohistory is applicable at all levels of human organisation, from the individual and family, through the city or state to the global level. It could usefully be applied, for example, to all the theme areas covered by the MAB Programme. It ensures that, in the analysis of ecosystems, full consideration is taken not only of the impacts of human activities on the biophysical characteristics of the ecosystem, but also of the implications of these activities for human health and well-being and the quality of human life. It also ensures that the complex of cultural, social, historical, ethnic and biological influences are taken fully into account, both as they contribute to our understanding of human situations, and as they can help in planning changes for the future.

The remainder of this introductory chapter briefly outlines the conceptual approach of biohistory and states arguments for its acceptance as an essential theme in education and research.

Figure 1   Basic conceptual model of biohistory

Biohistory is defined as a coherent system of knowledge, or field of study, which reflects the broad sequence of happenings in the history of the biosphere and of civilization, from the beginning of life to the present day (Figure 1). Its starting point is the history of life on Earth, and the basic principles and facts of evolution, genetic inheritance, ecology and physiology. It is thus concerned at the outset with the sensitivities and diversity of living organisms and ecosystems, and with the interrelationships between different forms of life, and between them and the non-living components of the biosphere. Next, it turns to consider the evolutionary background, biology and innate sensitivities of the human species, and the emergence in evolution of the human aptitude for culture.

Biohistory then moves on to the study of the history of humankind, paying attention especially to the changing patterns of interplay between cultural and biophysical systems. Thus it considers culture–nature interplay in the long hunter–gatherer phase of human existence, and then in the early farming economies that emerged around 480 generations ago. One generation is taken as 25 years. Next, it deals with the highly significant biosocial changes which came about when urbanisation began some 200–250 generations ago and which involved, for example, the institutionalisation of violent combat between human populations and marked differentiation within societies with respect to human life conditions.

Finally, biohistory turns to the modern high-energy phase of human history. It considers the patterns of resource and energy use and of waste production in contemporary societies, the interrelationships between human populations and the ecosystems of the biosphere and the biosocial disparities and differentials that exist between different human populations and sub-populations in today's world.

Biohistory is concerned not only with unravelling and describing significant interrelationships in human ecosystems between cultural and biophysical variables, but also with the identification of fundamental principles that help us to understand the nature of the constraints imposed on human society by virtue of its dependence on biological systems and processes. Some of these principles come directly from the biophysical and social sciences, and these include principles relating to thermodynamics, biogeochemical cycles, soil ecology, natural selection, physiology, health and disease, alienation, anomie, and corporate behaviour. Others arise from biohistory itself and concern specifically the interplay between biophysical and cultural processes. These biohistorical principles, which will be discussed throughout this volume, are important for the understanding of human affairs at all levels of organisation.

Another important aspect of biohistory is the study of the *adaptive processes*, biological and cultural, that come into play when societal activities have impacts on biological systems which are disadvantageous, or which are perceived to be disadvantageous, for humankind. Attention is paid especially to the processes of *cultural adaptation* that may be brought into action in response to culturally-induced threats to human survival and well-being. Such cultural adaptive responses have played a major role in human history – sometimes successfully and sometimes not; and whether humankind survives the next century will depend on the extent to which they are successful in the near future.

It is clear, of course, that a good deal of information pertaining to aspects of biohistory is already presented in educational programmes in zoology, botany, chemistry, physics, biochemistry, meteorology, geology, geography, human biology, environmental science, human physiology, psychology, health studies, sociology, history, prehistory, archaeology and so forth. However, biohistory as an *integrated and coherent subject* in its own right, aimed at improving understanding of human situations in terms of the place of humankind in the natural world and of interactions between biological and cultural aspects of reality, does not feature in the learning experience of the great majority of people in all societies all over the world. It is true that there are some individuals in our midst who do have a biohistorical understanding of human situations, but when this happens it is not due to enlightened programmes of education, but is rather the result of fortuitous encounters with relevant pieces of knowledge – combined, perhaps, with a certain intuition.

The arguments for including a major biohistorical input into the educational process are simple and rather obvious. They follow from three inescapable and closely related aspects of reality:

(1) Human beings are totally dependent, for their sustenance, their health and well-being and their enjoyment of life, on the underlying set of biological systems and processes which operate in the biosphere, in its ecosystems and in their own bodies. Dependence on these underlying processes is very basic. All the products of culture – our institutions, ideas, knowledge, machines, computers, high technology, military strength, politics and economics – all these count for nothing if the societal system of which they are all a part does not satisfy the

biologically-determined health needs of the biosphere and of our own bodies.

(2) Every human situation, at the level of individuals, small groups or whole societies, involves continual interplay between biological and cultural elements, and the outcome of this interplay is often very important for human health and well-being or for the ecosystems on which we depend.

(3) Human culture has influenced, and now increasingly influences, the biological processes on which we depend and of which we are a part. From the anthropocentric point of view some of these influences may be seen as good and desirable, others as bad and undesirable; and some of them even threaten the survival of the human species.

In the light of these facts, it stands to reason that some understanding of human situations in biohistorical perspective, of fundamental ecological and biosocial principles, and of the potential and limitations of the various adaptive processes available to humankind, is a prerequisite for sensible behaviour, individual and collective, in the complex world of the late twentieth century.

General educational programmes in biohistory would not necessarily deal with particular issues in great detail, but would rather introduce students to the biohistorical perspective and to essential facts and principles relevant to the human situation in the biosphere. They would, however, offer ample scope for in-depth treatment of particular themes of local or topical interest. Thus, for example, such topics as health in cities, local conservation strategies, international co-operation and the greenhouse effect, war and peace, and the occupational structure of society all lend themselves to in-depth, integrative biohistorical analysis. Indeed there is a place for educational programmes in economics, politics, sociology, political economy and other social sciences in which these subjects are treated in terms of the conceptual framework of biohistory.

Apart from its role as an educational theme, biohistory also provides a rational framework for integrative research on human situations, all of which involve continual interplay between cultural and biophysical processes, and all of which are the product of such interplay in the past. There are, for example, important linkages between the cultural assumptions and value systems of a society, its economic arrangements and its patterns of use of resources and energy, and all of these have a powerful influence on the behaviour, time budgets, health and well-being of people, as well as on the characteristics of local, regional, and now even global, ecosystems. An improved understanding of these interrelationships is a precondition for wise policy formulation and decision-making at all levels of societal endeavour.

Biohistory cannot be classified as belonging to the natural sciences, social sciences or humanities. It is about the real world, in the sense that it is concerned with the patterns of interplay in human situations between the various aspects of the total system that are traditionally studied separately in these three different academic arenas.

Biohistory deals with the common heritage and common dependencies of all humankind. It is, perhaps, the one and only theme which ought to be incorporated in all educational programmes in all human communities in all parts of the planet. Moreover, apart from its value to society for the important reasons already discussed, it is also an extraordinarily interesting subject in its own right – and, as such, it has the potential to be a source of continuing enjoyment for students of human affairs of all ages the world over.

FURTHER READING

Boyden, S. (ed.). (1970). *The impact of civilisation on the biology of man.* ANU Press, Canberra.
Boyden, S. (1987). *Western civilization in biological perspective: patterns in biohistory.* Oxford University Press, Oxford.
Boyden, S., Millar, S., Newcombe, K. and O'Neill, B. (1981). *The ecology of a city and its people: the case of Hong Kong.* Australian National University Press, Canberra.
Boyden, S., Dovers, S. and Shirlow, M. (1990). *Our biosphere under threat: ecological realities and Australia's opportunities.* Oxford University Press, Melbourne.
Brabyn, H. and Hadley, M. (1988). *Man belongs to the Earth: international cooperation in environmental research.* UNESCO, Paris.
Carson, R.L. (1962). *Silent spring.* Boston, MA: Houghton Mifflin.
Crosby, A.W. (1986). *Ecological imperialism: the biological expansion of Europe 900–1900.* Cambridge University Press, Cambridge.
Ehrlich, P.R., Ehrlich, A.E. and Holdren, J.P. (1977). *Ecoscience: population, resources, environment.* 2nd edn. W.H. Freeman, San Francisco.
Goldsmith, E. and Hildyard, N. (eds) (1988). *The Earth report: monitoring the battle of our environment.* Mitchell Beazley, London.
Holdgate, M.W., Kassas, M. and White, G.F. (eds.) (1982). *The world environment 1972–1982: a report by the United Nations Environment Programme* (Natural Resources and the Environment Series) Vol.8. Tycooly International, Dublin.
Hughes, J.D. (1975). *Ecology in ancient civilizations.* University of New Mexico Press, Albuquerque.
Lovelock, J.E. (1987). *Gaia: the new look at life on earth.* Oxford University Press, Oxford.
World Commission on Environment and Development. (1987). *Our common future.* Oxford University Press, Oxford.

CHAPTER 1

THE BIOSPHERE

The Earth is an almost spherical planet which bulges a little at the equator and is slightly flattened at the poles. It rotates a full circle on its axis in about 24 hours, and it orbits around the sun once in every 365.25 days.

When the first living organisms appeared on this planet, probably around 4000 million years ago, it consisted, as it does today, of two fundamental divisions – the *core* and the *mantle* (Figure 1.1). The innermost part, the core represents about 16 per cent of the Earth's volume and it has a radius of about 3500 km. It is made up mainly of iron, which is in liquid form, except at the centre where it appears to be solid. The radius of this inner solid zone is about 1300 km. The high temperatures of around 2400 to 2500°C in the core are due to the radioactive decay of certain minerals. This radiogenic heat is responsible for the fact that the temperature of the earth increases about 3°C every 100 m down from the surface. The mantle, which makes up nearly 84 per cent of the Earth's volume, is about 2900 km thick and consists of rock in the solid state. Outside the mantle there is a comparatively very thin layer of less dense rock known as the *crust*, and the dividing line between the crust and the mantle is relatively sharp.

The average thickness of the crust below the continents is about 35 km, and below the ocean floors 5 or 6 km. Today the highest point on the Earth's crust is Mount Everest in the Himalayas, and this is nearly 19 km above the lowest point, which is in the Pacific Ocean off the coast of the Philippines.

Ninety-eight per cent of the solid matter of the Earth's crust is made up of eight elements. These are, in order of abundance: oxygen, silicon, aluminium, iron, calcium, sodium, potassium and magnesium. Oxygen accounts for about 94 per cent by volume, and 47 per cent by weight, of the crust, and silicon 1 per cent by volume and 28 per cent by weight. The basic homogeneous units which combine in different ways to form rocks are referred to as *minerals*. The silicate minerals are the most abundant

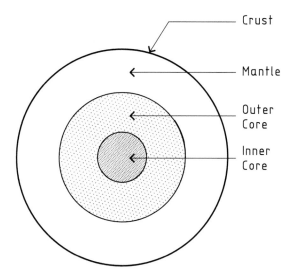

Figure 1.1 Basic structure of the planet Earth

kind in the crust, and they include the feldspars, pyroxenes, amphiboles, micas and quartz. In fact, about three quarters of the crust of the Earth is silicon dioxide.

As a result of weathering processes, both physical and chemical, the rocks of the crust become broken up on the surface, giving rise to a layer of particles of disintegrated rock of various sizes. This layer is known as *regolith*, and its depth varies from many metres to zero according to the terrain. The unbroken rock below regolith is called *bedrock*.

The rocks of the crust of the earth are, broadly speaking, of three kinds. First, there is the original *igneous rock* which is formed by the cooling and solidification of hot molten liquid. This hardening may occur within the crust, giving rise to *magma*, or on its surface, resulting in *lava*. Basalt, obsidian and granite are examples of igneous rock, the last of these being by far the most abundant. Second, there is *sedimentary rock* which is formed as the result of pressure, or of the action of some cementing material, on accumulations of fragments of mineral matter. Common types of sedimentary rock are: *conglomerates*, formed from gravel; *sandstone*, formed from sand; *shale*, formed from mud or clay; and *limestone*, formed mainly from the accumulation of fragments of shells and other calcium-containing organisms.

The third main category is *metamorphic rock*, the original structure of which has been altered by heat, pressure, or the action of solutions of various kinds of chemical compounds. *Gneiss*, for example, is a coarse-grained metamorphic rock, characterised by the segregation of the different minerals of which it consists and by their arrangement in roughly parallel bands. Others examples are schist and slate, which are much more finely grained and which have a tendency to break along closely-spaced parallel surfaces into flat slabs. Another metamorphic rock is *marble*, which is recrystallised limestone.

The weathering processes which result in the fragmentation of rock and the formation of regolith are of two kinds – mechanical and chemical. Mechanical breakdown, which includes the effects of gravity, movements in the Earth's crust and the roots of plants, is referred to as *disintegration*, and chemical breakdown, such as the effect of acid, as *decomposition*. Fragments of rock can also be moved by wind or by water from one place to another. This process is known as *erosion*.

The term *lithosphere* is sometimes used for the outer 50–100 km of the solid outer shell of the Earth, which is made up of the crust and the outer-most part of the mantle. Apart from the lithosphere, the matter at the surface includes two other phases, the *atmosphere* and the *hydrosphere*.

The atmosphere is the gaseous envelope which surrounds the planet, and it contains permanent gases (that is, gases which under natural conditions exist only in the gaseous state, such as nitrogen and carbon dioxide) and water vapour. The main gases in the atmosphere in today's world are nitrogen (78 per cent), oxygen (21 per cent), argon (0.93 per cent) and carbon dioxide (0.03 per cent). However, as we shall discuss later, the composition of the atmosphere when life first began on Earth was very different from this. Indeed, if we could be transported back in time to the world of four thousand million years ago, we would not survive very long. Apart from the fact that there would be nothing for us to eat and that we would be exposed to lethal levels of ultraviolet radiation from the sun, we would immediately suffocate because of the lack of oxygen in the air. Some scientists suggest, paradoxically, that the lack of oxygen and the intensity of ultraviolet radiation were among the prerequisites for the initial emergence of life on the primordial Earth.

The hydrosphere is the water that exists on the surface of the Earth. About 97 per cent of it is in the oceans, which have an average depth of 4 km. Approximately 2 per cent of the water is in the form of ice and snow in the polar regions; around 0.5 to 1.5 per cent is in the soil and in cracks between rocks; from 0.014 to 0.03 per cent is in streams, rivers and lakes; and only about 0.001 per cent is in the form of water vapour or droplets in the atmosphere.

Water is an unusual compound in a number of ways, and its unique physical and chemical properties account to some extent for its extraordinary biological importance. For example, while water becomes denser (and so shrinks) as it cools down to 4°C, it becomes less dense again and expands as its temperature drops further to 0°C, with the result that ice always forms on the top, rather than at the bottom of water masses. Also, compared with other liquids, it is particularly slow to warm up and to cool down.

Another outstandingly significant feature of the surface of the Earth, in both primordial and modern times, is the electromagnetic radiation that it receives from the sun, where it is generated through nuclear fusion. This input of energy ranges from the shorter wavelength ultraviolet rays (from around 300 nm) through visible light (from about 400 nm to nearly 800 nm) to infrared (from about 800 nm to 2000 nm). This radiation falls upon the Earth's surface unequally, according to latitude and season. Eventually it is all re-radiated into space, mainly in the form of heat.

This energy input from the sun is largely responsible for the two great thermally-powered circulatory systems on the Earth's surface – that of the atmosphere and that of the oceans. The flows in the atmosphere are caused by the unequal heating of large masses of air, and this results in air movements which then set in motion flows of water in the surface layers of the oceans. The patterns of flow in both the atmosphere and the oceans are further influenced by the rotational movement of the planet – the so-called Coriolis effect. The end result is that heat becomes more evenly distributed over the surface of the planet than would otherwise be the case.

Another important process driven by the energy from the sun is the water cycle. Heat from the sun causes water to evaporate from the surfaces of the oceans, lakes and waterways, and from the land itself, to form water vapour in the atmosphere. When this vapour cools, the water condenses and eventually gravity causes it to fall back to the Earth in the form of rain or snow. Gravity also plays another essential role in the cycle, causing much of the water which falls on land areas to travel down into the soil, and into streams and rivers, and ultimately back into the oceans.

The overall picture of the effects of solar energy on the Earth's crust (excluding effects on living organisms) are depicted in Figure 1.2.

THE BEGINNINGS OF LIFE

The actual mechanism by which life came into existence on the Earth has been the subject of a great deal of speculation. According to the prevailing view at the present time, ultraviolet radiation from the sun and (or) electric discharges from storms acted on mixtures of water vapour, carbon dioxide, ammonia and certain other gases in the atmosphere to produce various carbon-containing 'organic' molecules, such as amino acids, nucleic acids, sugars and lipids. Just which particular gases were the most important in this regard has been a matter of debate. Indeed, the actual composition of the atmosphere at that time is uncertain, although it is generally agreed that it must have contained little or no oxygen. In any case, it is thought

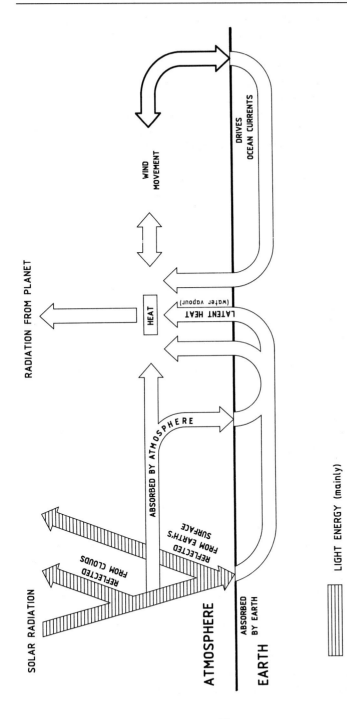

Figure 1.2 Overall flows of solar energy

11

that these simple carbon-containing molecules became dissolved in the water of the oceans and of lakes and freshwater ponds, progressively increasing in concentration over the millions of years, and reacting together, possibly in association with clay, to form more complex organic compounds. Eventually globule-like agglomerations of compounds came into existence, each possessing a membrane, genetic apparatus in the form of deoxyribonucleic acid (DNA), and the ability to reproduce. According to this interpretation of events, these early bacteria-like organisms, which may have been the only form of life on the planet for a thousand million years, fed on the organic molecules which had been accumulating in the aqueous environment as a result of ultraviolet radiation and electrical storms.

This explanation of the origin of life is not universally accepted among scientists, and a number of authors have proposed other mechanisms (see *Further Reading* list at the end of this chapter). But, whatever the precise mechanism, by 4000 million years ago there had emerged, out of the inorganic world, a new set of processes – the processes of life. These *biotic processes* differed in important ways from the physicochemical processes which gave rise to them. The growth of a living organism is very different from the growth of a crystal, and biotic evolution is very different from inorganic evolution. Nevertheless, the processes of life incorporate and involve inorganic processes, and they are totally dependent upon them for their continued existence.

One factor that contributed to the conditions which made the emergence and maintenance of life possible was the relative constancy of the Earth's temperature, so that there was always water in existence at temperatures favourable for living processes. This was apparently the case in spite of the fact that the intensity of the sun's luminosity is believed to have increased 30–40 per cent since the Earth was formed. The reasons for the relative stability of the global temperature are not understood.

PHOTOSYNTHESIS, FOOD CHAINS AND MULTICELLULAR ORGANISMS

The genesis of life, involving the rearranging of matter and the building up, growth and reproduction of organisms, required a flow of energy into and out of the total system. As mentioned above, it is generally considered that the most important sources of this energy in the early period were ultraviolet radiation from the sun and electrical discharges from storms. This electromagnetic energy was converted into potential energy in the form of complex chemical compounds, which not only gave rise to the first forms of life, but which were also used by them as their source of sustenance. However, this source of energy was clearly limited, and could not have sustained life on the scale at which it exists on Earth today. In fact, the living world as we know it is totally dependent on the process of *photosynthesis* – that is, the capture of energy from sunlight and its conversion into chemical form through the action of chlorophyll in the leaves of green plants.

In the first photosynthetic organisms, the conversion of light energy into chemical energy probably involved the reduction of carbon dioxide by hydrogen sulphide. Eventually a more complicated two-step process evolved in which hydrogen is provided by water rather than by hydrogen sulphide, and which results in the release of free oxygen. The fossil record indicates that single-celled organisms capable of this kind of photosynthesis were in existence by around 3500 million years ago – that is, around 1300 million years after the formation of the planet Earth.

The development of photosynthesis had far-reaching evolutionary consequences. To begin with, it resulted in the release and eventual accumulation of oxygen in the atmosphere. This change led to the evolution of organisms which, unlike earlier forms, were able to tolerate oxygen in their environment; and eventually cells evolved which actually made use of oxygen, and which were indeed dependent on it for their metabolic processes.

Also of great evolutionary significance is the fact that some of the oxygen in the air became converted to ozone, which accumulated in the upper layer of the atmosphere – the *stratosphere* – where it acted as a filter, absorbing some of the ultraviolet radiation from the sun. As a result, by the time that human beings appeared on Earth, and probably by two thousand million years before then, only about half of the total solar ultraviolet radiation, and a much smaller fraction of the short-wave ultraviolet radiation, penetrated through to the Earth's surface. Had it not been for this change in the intensity of ultraviolet radiation, life as it exists on land today would not have been possible. As we shall discuss in a later chapter, there is at present concern about the fact that the concentration of ozone in the stratosphere is beginning to decrease again as a result of certain human technological activities.

It is worth mentioning here that the ultraviolet rays which do still penetrate to the Earth's surface play a number of positive and useful roles in the biosphere, including the promotion of the synthesis in the human body, just beneath the skin, of vitamin D. Thus, too much or too little ultraviolet radiation can be detrimental to human health and well-being – an example of the optimum range principle which will be discussed later in this volume.

To recapitulate, the earliest reproducing organisms were, ecologically speaking, *consumers*, meaning that they derived their energy from the energy-rich organic molecules which were present in their environment. Later on the first *producers* evolved – organisms which manufactured their own energy-rich molecules through the process of photosynthesis. The consumers in the environment were in a position to exploit this new situation, deriving energy from local concentrations of energy-rich molecules resulting from the activities of the photosynthetic organisms. Accordingly, when a producer cell was damaged or died, microbial consumers, now playing the role of *decomposers*, were poised to break down and use its component parts.

By the time the first *eucaryotic* cells came into existence – that is, cells with nuclei and well-defined chromosomes – the Earth's atmosphere was already rich in oxygen. This occurred around 1500 million years ago, and it seems that at about that time a great diversification began to take place among living organisms, suggesting that a form of sexual reproduction was by then in existence. Previously all reproduction had been asexual, involving the simple division of one cell into two. In sexual reproduction a new individual comes into existence through the union of two cells, or *gametes*, each bringing from the parent organism its complement of chromosomes containing the genetic material (DNA) (see Chapter 3).

The first *multicellular organisms* are believed to have appeared on the scene around 1000 million years ago. The different forms of life of that time, like the organisms of today, can be classified as belonging to three Kingdoms, the Plant Kingdom, the Animal Kingdom and the Protista (which includes bacteria, protozoa and unicellular algae). The plants and some of the protists were capable of photosynthesis and so played the role of producers. The animals derived their energy by consuming other organisms. The role of the decomposers continued to be played by various forms of protists, especially bacteria and, later, a new group of organisms – the *fungi*.

The tissues of a multicellular animal clearly offered a rich nutritional environment for many sorts of single-celled organisms. However, the multiplication of large numbers of bacteria or other protists between the cells or within the various body cavities of a multicellular organism would obviously have interfered seriously with its ability to survive. The emergence in evolution of multicellular animals was therefore dependent on the concomitant development of a mechanism for discouraging such foreign organisms from colonising their tissues. This, in turn, depended on the evolution of a mechanism by which the tissues of animals could distinguish between 'foreign' organisms and their own cells. These mechanisms eventually evolved into the complex set of *immune processes* found in all the higher animals today.

As the processes of biotic evolution continued to operate over the aeons, more and more new and increasingly complex kinds of animals and plants came into existence. In the next chapter we will briefly discuss the history and mechanisms of the evolution of life on this planet.

FOOD, ENERGY AND ECOSYSTEMS

Energy flows

By a few hundred million years ago the biosphere had developed the fundamental ecological characteristics which form the basis of life on Earth as it exists today. The whole system depends on the constant input of energy from the sun. Of the total solar radiation falling on the atmosphere, about 35 per cent is reflected before reaching the surface of the Earth, and 17.5 per cent is absorbed by the atmosphere itself. Of the remaining radiation that penetrates through to the Earth's surface, about 30 per cent is reflected as heat, about 49 per cent is involved in the evaporation and condensation of water and about 21 per cent drives the winds. Estimates of the proportion of solar energy reaching the Earth's crust that is converted to chemical energy through photosynthesis range from 0.2 to 1.0 per cent. Half to two-thirds of this photosynthesis takes place on land, and the rest occurs in the upper layers of the oceans. More than half of the energy fixed by photosynthesis is used by the plants themselves in their respiratory processes. The rest is used by herbivores that consume the plants, by carnivores that consume the herbivores (or other carnivores), and by microbial decomposers and other protists (Figure 1.3).

Within this great global *ecosystem* – the biosphere as a whole – we can recognise countless smaller local ecosystems, ranging from islands and chains of mountains to village ponds and backyards. The boundaries of ecosystems are, of course, arbitrarily defined by humans, each ecosystem being seen as a relatively discrete functional unit made up of both biological and inorganic components and involving complex patterns of interplay and interdependence between different species, and consisting characteristically of producers (green plants), consumers (animals) and decomposers (e.g. bacteria and fungi). In all ecosystems there is an input and output of energy. Indeed, this one-way flow of energy through the system constitutes one of the most fundamental and essential characteristics of biotic ecosystems. In accordance with the First Law of Thermodynamics, the energy is not destroyed in the process, but at each stage in the food chain some of it is converted to heat, which then disperses into the environment.

Each individual species in an ecosystem is said to occupy its own particular *ecological niche*, a term which alludes not only to the physical space in which the population lives and to which it has become adapted through evolution, but also to its functional role in the ecosystem. Competition within species and between species for ecological niches is one of the most important determinants of evolutionary change (see Chapters 2 and 3).

An essential aspect of the whole ecological process is the *cycling*, within the system, of key chemical elements which are taken up from the

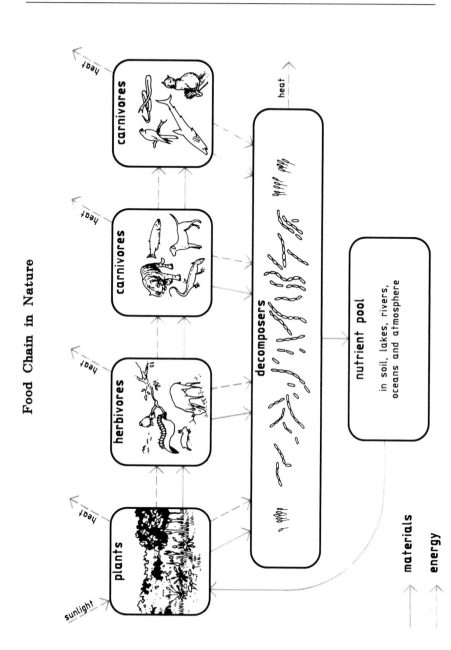

Figure 1.3   Food chains in a natural ecosystem

environment and built into the tissue of living organisms and eventually released again into the environment to become available once more for incorporation into new life. Before we discuss these cycles, however, something must be said about soil.

Soil

The kind and amount of vegetation that grows in a natural terrestrial ecosystem, and consequently many other properties of the system, including its animal populations, are largely a function of the properties of that part of the system which is known as *soil*. Soil may be defined as any part of the unconsolidated portion of the Earth's crust which supports plant growth. It is made up of debris resulting from the weathering of rocks (regolith) as well as organic matter. The fragments that constitute the rock debris may be *residual* – that is, of local origin – or *transported* from elsewhere by wind or by water. They range in size from largish lumps of rock, through sand, down to fine clay.[1] The inorganic component of soil can be regarded as a transient stage in the transportation of minerals and rock fragments from their source of origin to the oceans.

The organic content of soil consists of decomposing plant and animal matter, micro-organisms (involved in the processes of decomposition or, for example, in fixing nitrogen) and various animals, including millepedes, mites, insects, nematodes, earthworms and burrowing mammals.

The living organisms in the soil play an essential role in the biogeochemical cycles on which all terrestrial life depends. Although the organic component of soil usually represents less than 0.1 per cent of the total soil mass, it may still amount to several tonnes per hectare. In the case of grassland, for example, the weight of the organic component of soil in a given area is many times the weight of herbivores that can be supported in that area.

Some components of the decaying organic matter, like lignins, waxes, fats and some proteinaceous compounds are relatively resistant to decomposition, and together they form a colloidal substance known as *humus*. Humus has an important influence on the capacity of the soil to support plant life.

---

[1] Clay is defined as particles less than 0.002 mm diameter, silt as particles between 0.002 and 0.02 mm, and sand as particles between 0.02 and 2 mm. Loam is a mixture of particles of sand, silt and clay.

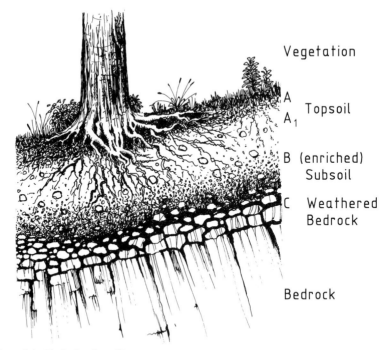

Vegetation

A

Topsoil

A₁

B (enriched)
Subsoil

C Weathered
Bedrock

Bedrock

Figure 1.4 Typical soil profile

In most soils it is possible to recognise three fairly distinct zones, usually known as the *A horizon*, the *B horizon*, and the *C horizon*[2]. (Figure 1.4). The A horizon, or *topsoil*, is the result of the weathering of the underlying parent material (i.e. bed rock or regolith) and it also contains organic matter. It is the habitat of most soil organisms and contains the greatest abundance of roots. It is often somewhat depleted of soluble compounds which have been leached out and deposited in the underlying subsoil or B horizon. The finest particles also tend to be moved downward, by percolating water, out of the A horizon. The B horizon or *subsoil* receives the minerals and fine particles from the A horizon as well as some upward migrating substances from the weathered parent material below. For this reason, the B horizon is sometimes known as the *zone of accumulation*. The C horizon is essentially a transitional zone between the soil above and the unweathered parent rock below.

---

[2] Two other zones are also recognised at the surface of soil. They are the Aoo horizon, which is made up of *litter*, which is fresh dead organic matter, and the Ao horizon, which consists of partially decomposed organic matter.

The clay particles in soil carry a negative charge at their surface, and so do humus particles. This is important to soil fertility, because the negatively charged particles adsorb anions like calcium, magnesium, potassium and sodium, and this results in the retention of these anions in the top layers of soil and their consequent availability for plant use. Excessive acidity of soil counteracts this effect.

The physical structure of soil also has a significant influence on its potential to support plant growth. An important variable is *pore space* – that is, the total space between the fragments of rock. This space is occupied by air and water in varying proportions, so that the soil acts like a massive sponge. On average, the pore space in soil represents about half the total volume. However, the total amount of pore space is less important than the size of the individual spaces. Clay soils have more total pore space than sandy soils, but because the pores are very small, air and water move through clay more slowly than through sand. Consequently, when clay soils become saturated with water very little air gets through to the roots of plants, and growth is impeded. On the other hand, soils with a very large pore size drain very quickly, so that lack of water becomes a limiting factor. Soil texture is also a function of its content of humus, which tends to make the soil crumbly and enhances its bioproductive potential.

Soils are thus highly complex systems, and there is much variability among them. Their properties are determined not only by the nature of the parent rock from which their inorganic components are derived and the size of the rock fragments, but also by the climate and the general topography and biological history of the region. These factors affect, for example, the degree of leaching that takes place (and hence the distribution of nutrients in the A and B horizons), the rate of bacterial decay, the rate of evaporation and the degree of drainage. All these variables influence the type of vegetation that is likely to grow in the soil, and this in turn has further consequences for soil quality.

As we shall discuss later, certain human activities which modify the nature of the cover of vegetation can have profound and long-lasting impact on the properties of soil, and hence on its potential for bioproduction.

Nutrient cycles

The viability of the biosphere as a life-supporting system depends on a series of cyclical processes which involve the incorporation of the various elements required for the growth and functioning of living tissue and their eventual return to the inorganic state, so that they are available again for the building up of new living tissue. While this principle applies to all the elements required for the processes of life, the most important, or at least the best understood, are the cycles of carbon, oxygen, nitrogen, phosphorus, sulphur and water.

The cycles of carbon and oxygen

The carbon and oxygen cycles are intimately connected, and it is sensible to consider them at the same time. Together they represent one of the most essential aspects of the life-producing processes of the biosphere, and indeed the intensity of life in any region is basically a function of these two cycles. For example, when land becomes degraded, the change is reflected first and foremost in the carbon and oxygen cycle. As we shall see later, the cycles have recently been modified to an important degree by culture-induced activities of human society.

The basic features of the carbon and oxygen cycles are relatively simple as compared, for example, with the nitrogen cycle, and they are depicted in Figure 1.5. There also exist some more complicated 'side cycles' or 'epicycles', but these will not be discussed here.

The cycles of carbon and oxygen can be taken as beginning with the process of photosynthesis which takes place, under the influence of sunlight, in the leaves of green plants on land and in algae and phytoplankton in water. In this process carbon dioxide is removed from the atmosphere (or from water) to be combined chemically with water to form energy-rich carbon-containing organic molecules; as a part of this process, oxygen is released into the environment.

About half of the energy converted into chemical form in this way is used in the metabolic processes of the photosynthesising plants themselves. It is made available through the process of *respiration*, which involves the uptake of oxygen and the release into the atmosphere, or into the surrounding water, of about half the carbon dioxide and water initially taken up in the photosynthetic process. The energy-rich material which remains in the plant may be eaten by herbivores (first order consumers), or it may fall to the ground and, through the action of micro-organisms, decay. In the latter instance, the decomposition process results in the release of carbon dioxide and water and the uptake of oxygen.

If the plant material is eaten by herbivores, some of the carbon in the energy-rich molecules becomes incorporated in the tissues of these animals. Some of it, however, is oxidised in respiration, resulting again in the uptake of oxygen and the release into the environment of carbon dioxide and water. As in the case of plants, herbivores may die and become subject to the activities of decomposers, which give off further carbon dioxide and water and take up more oxygen; alternatively, they may be eaten by other animals, carnivores, in which case the remaining carbon-containing molecules would be used partly to build up the tissues of the carnivores

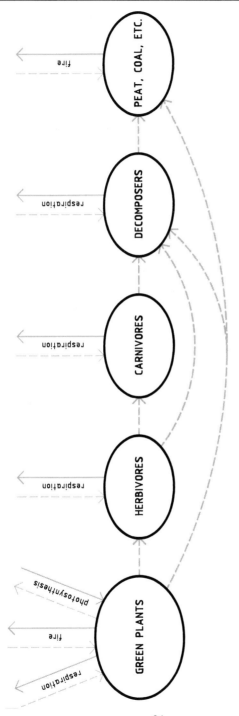

Figure 1.5 Carbon and oxygen cycles

21

and partly as a source of energy in their metabolism, involving once more the uptake of oxygen and the release of carbon dioxide and water. Finally, the carnivores die and undergo bacterial decomposition, with the consequent release of further carbon dioxide and water and uptake of oxygen.

The forests of the world are the main consumers of carbon dioxide on land, and they also constitute the biggest reservoir of biologically fixed carbon (with the exception of fossil fuels). They contain around 400,000 to 500,000 million tonnes of carbon (equivalent to about two-thirds as much carbon as exists in the atmosphere as carbon dioxide). About 15,000 million tonnes of carbon are transformed into wood each year.

While the essential role of the carbon and oxygen in the atmosphere is obvious, by far the greater part of these two elements in the Earth's crust is, in fact, incorporated in the lithosphere. As mentioned above, 97 per cent by volume of the rock of the Earth's crust consists of oxygen; and, with respect to carbon, only a few tenths of one per cent of the carbon at or near the surface of the Earth is in circulation in the biosphere. The overwhelming bulk of the carbon is present in organic deposits, chiefly as carbonates, and in the organic fossil deposits of coal, petroleum and oil shale.

It will be noted that water plays an essential role in the carbon and oxygen cycles. It is a key reactant in the process of photosynthesis itself, and some of the hydrogen molecules from water are incorporated in the energy-rich molecules which are formed (about half the water necessary for this reaction is liberated again as water at the end of the process). Water is also necessary for respiration in plants and animals, and in this case twice as much water is released at the end of the process as is used at the outset.

The nitrogen cycle

The main reservoir of nitrogen is the atmosphere, where it exists as a relatively inert gas; but animals and plants are not able to make use of it in this form. The nitrogen which is incorporated into the structure of plants (and which is thus indirectly the source of nitrogen-containing compounds in animals and decomposers) is taken into the plants in the form of nitrate from the soil or from water. Most of this nitrate is formed by the action of certain bacteria and algae which take nitrogen from the atmosphere and convert it into nitrate. This process is known as *nitrogen fixation*. These micro-organisms thus play an absolutely essential role in the whole life process. Broadly, they are made up of two groups. First, there are the *symbiotic* nitrogen-fixing bacteria which live in close association with the roots of certain plants. The best understood are the bacteria, belonging to the genus *Rhizobium*, which are found in the root nodules of legumes.

Nitrogen-fixing bacteria also exist in nodules of various other plants, including the acacias (or mimosas), the ginkgos (maiden-hair trees) and the relatively primitive cycads. The second group comprises the *non-symbiotic* or *free-living* nitrogen-fixing organisms. These include certain bacteria, which derive their energy from plants, and blue-green algae, which derive their energy directly from sunlight. Some nitrate, probably one-fifth to one-twentieth as much as is provided by micro-organisms, is formed by nitrogen fixation occuring as a result of electrochemical and photochemical reactions in the atmosphere.

The nitrogen incorporated into the organic molecules of plants is eventually passed on to animals and to decomposers. It is finally broken down in the soil and released as ammonia, part of which is liberated into the atmosphere while some is converted into nitrite by other bacteria. This nitrite in turn may be attacked by denitrifying bacteria which return nitrogen to the atmosphere in gaseous form, or by nitrate bacteria which convert it to nitrate, making it available again for plant growth.

Ecological balance

An ecosystem can be said to be in a state of balance when the interrelationships of the components of the system are such that the overall rate of bioproduction through photosynthesis is more or less equal to the rate of decay on the other, and such that the overall rates of bioproduction and of decay are more or less constant from year to year. In such a system the amount of energy fixed in photosynthesis in one year is about the same as that used up in the metabolic processes of the living components, including the micro-organisms, of the system. Such balance in natural ecosystems is the product of the evolution of the system and the living organisms within it.

In nature the balance of an ecosystem may be disturbed by a variety of factors, including unusual climatic events and eruptions of the Earth's crust. When the balance is disrupted in this way there is often a period in which the system can be described as 'seeking a new balance'. Initially, if there has been great destruction of life forms, there will be a period when the rate of decay greatly exceeds the rate of bioproduction. But this is likely to be followed by a period in which, as some species re-establish themselves in the environment, the rate of fixation of energy in photosynthesis exceeds the rate of decay, so that there comes about a progressive build-up of organic material, or *biomass*. A system with these characteristics is referred to as an *immature ecosystem*. Eventually, the system again reaches a state of balance, in which the annual rate of bioproduction and the rate of decay are about the same – that is, it becomes a *mature ecosystem*. Usually mature ecosystems are more diverse than immature ecosystems in terms of the number of species they contain. There is much variability among mature ecosystems with respect to rates of bioproduction. This variability is mainly the result of differences in the water and nutrient content and depth of the soil, and in environmental temperature.

In some cases the rate of bioproduction in ecosystems which have been disturbed, but which have achieved a new equilibrium, may, as a result of long-lasting changes in the systems, be substantially lower than it was in the original mature ecosystems before the disturbance. This may be the result, for example, of massive loss, through erosion, of top-soil that has taken thousands of years to build up.

Kinds of ecosystems

The Earth contains a great range of different kinds of bioproductive ecosystems, differing in rates of photosynthesis, in intensity of life and in diversity of living forms. At the most basic level, we can recognise two broad categories: aquatic ecosystems and terrestrial ecosystems. Aquatic ecosystems may be in salt water, in fresh water, or in brackish water and they vary enormously in temperature and in the degree of penetration of sunlight (and hence in their bioproductivity and other properties).

The characteristics of terrestrial ecosystems relate especially to latitude and altitude. In the case of both these factors, the main influences are temperature and rainfall. The quality and depth of the soil are also obviously important, these being determined not only by topography and by the kind of rock from which its inorganic components are derived, but also by the climate and the vegetation of the region. Thus, the soil and the vegetation develop together, each influencing the other and each being influenced by, and to some extent influencing, the climate. The main kinds of ecosystems of the world are conventionally classified as follows: desert; tropical grassland and savannah; tropical scrub forest; tropical rain forest; temperate grassland; temperate forest (deciduous, or eucalypt and acacia); the northern coniferous forests; tundra (a treeless zone lying between the ice cap and the timber line in the northern hemisphere and also found in the southern tip of South America).

The annual rate of photosynthesis varies greatly from one kind of ecosystem to another. For example, 1 square metre of tropical forest typically produces around 6700 grams of organic matter in one year (2000 grams of which is net production), while the same area of temperate forest produces about 4300 grams, and the same area of natural grassland about 500 grams. Taking the world as a whole, tropical forests fix more carbon than all other kinds of terrestrial ecosystems put together.

As regards *biomass*, the largest accumulation is in forest ecosystems, and it is greater towards the equator. For example, in northern taiga spruce forests in North America, the biomass accumulation per square metre is around 10,000 grams, whereas in the same kind of forest further south, the figure is 33,000 grams per square metre. In the case of deciduous forests, those further north contain about 37,000 grams of organic matter per square metre, and those to the south about 40,000 grams per square metre.

Under certain conditions, such as those which are likely to exist in swamps or bogs, dead plant material may accumulate faster than it can be broken down by bacterial activity. Decomposition may thus be incomplete, due to lack of oxygen in the stagnant water and to acidity resulting from organic acids released in the decay process. The soft fibrous material formed in this way is called peat. Downward pressure resulting from accumulating sediments above may eventually transform this peat, first into *lignite*, then into *soft* or *bituminous coal*, and finally into *hard coal* or *anthracite*. Petroleum and natural gas are also believed to be of organic origin, perhaps produced by the breakdown of vast quantities of microscopic plants in the oceans. Unlike coal, the liquid and gaseous hydrocarbons may migrate from their place of origin to become concentrated in distant reservoirs.

The formation of the deposits of these fossil hydrocarbon substances, coal, petroleum and natural gas, spanned several hundred million years. They are now being used by human society as sources of extrasomatic energy at a rate which is several million times greater than the rate at which they were formed.

Healthy and unhealthy ecosystems

In this book the concept of *health* is applied not only to individual plants and animals, and to animal and plant populations, but also to ecosystems. A *healthy ecosystem* is one in which the annual rate of bioproduction is more or less constant (or increasing), and an *unhealthy ecosystem* is one in which it is declining.

Apart from such naturally occurring events as changes in climate, volcanic action and fire, there are three main causes of ill-health in ecosystems. These are:-

(1) *Nutrient exhaustion.* Exhaustion or depletion of nutrients is unlikely to occur in mature ecosystems in which the total *biomass* remains more or less constant. However, it can become an important limiting factor in artificial ecosystems, such as agricultural systems, when the rate of net bioproduction is high and when the biomass is removed from the system, so that the rate of bioproduction exceeds the rate of decay within system.

(2) *Erosion.* The transport by water or by wind of the products of the weathering of rocks away from their site of origin is a natural process

Table 1.1 Basic health needs of the ecosystems of the biosphere

A rate of soil loss no greater than the rate of soil formation

Intact nutrient cycles maintaining the nutrient properties of the soil over long periods of time

The absence of polluting gases or particles in the atmosphere which interfere with living processes or significantly modify the climate

The maintenance of an intact ozone layer in the stratosphere protecting the Earth's surface from ultraviolet radiation from the sun

The absence, in the oceans, lakes, rivers and streams and in the soil, of concentrations of chemical compounds likely to be harmful to living organisms

The absence of levels of ionising radiation that can interfere with the normal processes of life and of bioproduction

The maintenance of biological diversity.

and was certainly taking place before the advent of terrestial life. When a cover of vegetation becomes established on the regolith, the process of erosion is slowed down, and further accumulation of debris, as well as of organic matter, occurs at the site. Thus, as an ecosystem becomes established, so does the soil become enriched and the whole system moves towards a state of ecological balance. While natural vegetation slows down the process of erosion, certain activities of humankind, particularly some farming practices, can increase its rate. As we shall discuss later, good fertile soil which has taken millennia to form may, as a result of such practices, be swept away by water or by wind within a few years.

(3) *Chemicalisation.* This term applies to the accumulation in soil of chemical compounds which interfere with bioproductivity. Salinisation (the accumulation especially of sodium chloride) and alkalinisation (the accumulation of sodium carbonate) are particularly important examples. Most cases of salinisation and alkalinisation are the consequence of human activities, such as irrigation and deforestation.

From the standpoint of human well-being, it is essential that the ecosystems on which we depend for our food remain healthy. This applies as much to local ecosystems providing food for nearby populations as it does to the total global ecosystem – the biosphere. The health needs of ecosystems are summarised in Table 1.1.

In later chapters we will give further consideration to the various ways in which the activities of human populations have affected, and are affecting, the health of ecosystems, locally and globally.

FURTHER READING

Delwiche, C.C. (1970). The nitrogen cycle. In *The biosphere*. pp.71–80. W.H. Freeman, San Francisco.

Eardley, A.J. (1972). *Science of the earth*. Harper and Row, New York.

Kormondy, E.J. (1969). *Concepts of ecology*. Prentice-Hall, Englewood Cliffs.

Odum, H.T. and Odum, E.C. (1976). *Energy basis for man and nature*. McGraw-Hill, New York.

Ordway, R.J. (1972). *Earth science*, 2nd edn. Van Nostrand Reinhold, New York.

Raiswell, R.W. Brimblecombe, P. Dent, D.L., Liss, P.S. (1980) *Environmental chemistry*. Edward Arnold, London.

Ricklefs, R.E. (1980). *Ecology*. 2nd edn. Nelson: London.

Strahler, A.N. (1972). *Planet earth: its physical systems through geologic time*. Harper and Row, New York.

Watts, D. (1974). Biogeochemical cycles and energy flows in environmental systems. In *Perspectives on environment*. (eds. I.R. Manners and M.W. Mikesell). Association of American Geographers, Washington D.C.

Wiens. J.A. (ed.) (1972). *Ecosystem structure and function*. Oregon State University Press. Portland.

CHAPTER 2

BIOLOGICAL EVOLUTION

In this chapter we will look more closely at the evolution of living organisms on Earth as reflected in the fossil record. We begin with a short summary of the history of life in the aquatic environment, bearing in mind that for nine-tenths of the time that life has existed on this planet, it occurred only in water (Figure 2.1).

LIFE IN WATER

As discussed in the last chapter, the majority of evolutionary scientists suspect that life on Earth originated in water – possibly in 'warm little pools' as Darwin suggested, or in the oceans, or at the water-clay interface in moist earth.

For some unknown reason, the fossil record of living organisms that existed before around 700 million years ago is extremely scanty. At the time of writing the oldest known (or suspected) fossils are probably those of globular bacteria-like organisms revealed by electronmicroscopy of sections of sedimentary rock believed to be about 3500 million years old. There is also clear fossil evidence of the existence, 3000 million years ago, of *stromatolites*, which are made up of alternating layers of inorganic and organic material – the latter consisting mainly of photosynthesising blue-green algae (cyanobacteria). These structures became very widespread between 2000 million and 600 million years ago. After that they almost disappeared, possibly as a result of being grazed by the newly-evolved molluscs. Some stromatolites, however, still survive today in parts of California, Mexico and Western Australia, mainly in areas where periodical dessication, hot water springs or high concentrations of sulphide discourage the various animal species that graze on them.

The earliest animal fossil so far described was found in sandstone in Sweden and is about 800 million years old. It has been called *Xenusion*,

29

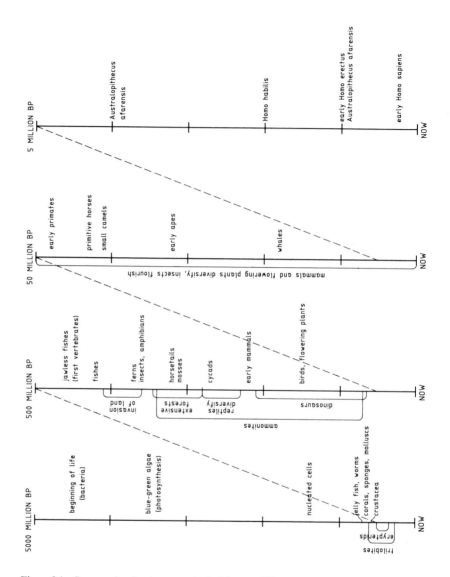

Figure 2.1   Some major developments in the history of life on Earth from 5000 million years before the present (BP) to the present day

and its body has 14 segments with paired stump-like limbs. It seems to represent a form intermediate between *worms* and the *arthropods* – the group of invertebrates with jointed limbs, segmented bodies and hard outer skeletons which includes the crustaceans, insects, spiders and centipedes. A relatively rich collection of fossils has been found in South Australia dated at between 700 and 800 million years ago. It includes the remains of jelly fish, sea urchins, sea pens and some worms, as well as traces of various other animals of uncertain nature.

Six hundred to 700 million years ago is the earliest period from which well-preserved fossils are found in large quantities. Fossil deposits from this time and from 500 million years ago provide clear evidence of seaweeds, protozoa, sponges, jellyfish, corals, worms, molluscs, sea urchins, starfish, lamp shells and trilobites (Figure 2.2).

The first chordates – that is animals with an internal supporting structure or backbone – made their appearance just over 400 million years ago. The earliest of these were the so-called jawless fishes (*Agnatha*), a group which today is represented by the lampreys. They differ from other backboned creatures in that they do not have a moveable lower jaw jointed to the skull. The next chordate group to make its appearance was the placoderms, which were bony-plated fishes with truly moveable jaws jointed to the skull and backbones made of true bone. They are now extinct. Next to evolve were the cartilaginous fishes (*Chonrichthyes*). These are characterised by the absence of true bone, the skeleton consisting only of cartilage. The sharks and rays are surviving representatives of this group.

The last group of fish to emerge was the 'true fishes' (*Osteichthyes*), and the great majority of fish species known to us today belong to this group. The true fishes have retained the bony skeleton, and the early forms possessed both lungs and gills. However, lungs are found in only a small number of the surviving members of this group, and in most of the others these organs are now represented by an air bladder which has no respiratory function.

By 400 million years ago all the main phyla of the animal kingdom were well established. The oceans were mainly dominated by arthropods, especially the trilobites. The main predators were arachnids (arthropods with four pairs of jointed legs and simple eyes), of which the sea-scorpions (erypterids), were especially important; some of them grew to be a metre long. Vertebrates existed in the form of various kinds of fish, and the 'true fishes' were just emerging. With respect to plants, there was much less diversity. Apart from the unicellular organisms, all plants were thallophytes – that is, they exhibited no real differentiation into stems, leaves and roots. This group included multicellular algae of various kinds, like stoneworts and brown seaweeds.

Figure 2.2 Representation of life in the oceans 500 million years ago

Although the main plants of the oceans have changed little since that period, important evolutionary changes took place among animals in the aquatic environment. The trilobites, for example, which dominated the scene for so long, had entirely disappeared by 200 million years ago. There was great diversification among the bony fishes, giving rise to the immense variety of these creatures found in the ponds, streams, rivers, lakes and oceans of the modern world. Another striking development was the appearance of a group of molluscs known as ammonites. At one time there were over 20 different families of these animals, and some of them had a diameter of at least 1 metre; but the group was extinct by 60 million years ago. Other important changes included the reinvasion of the water by various lines of land animals, giving rise, for example, to the sea-turtles and various fish-like reptiles (e.g. the ichthyosaurs) and, much later, to aquatic mammals, including dolphins and whales.

LIFE ON LAND

Land plants

The earliest plants to grow on land appeared just over 400 million years ago on the edge of the shallow water of estuaries. Unlike the thallophytes, which were the most developed plants in the oceans, the earliest land plants possessed a distinct stem. This stem, which was necessary to give them support in their new environment, was continuous with an underground stem, which at first was not differentiated into a true root, although it did carry absorbent root-hairs. In the part of the stem which was above ground there were many small holes, or stomata, to let in air, and the branches of the stem carried sacs full of spores. Some of these early land plants had rudimentary leaves. Fossilised remains have been found of two distinct groups of vascular plants from this time, related to the modern psilotums and club mosses. In time, plants appeared which showed more definite differentiation of tissues; they had distinct roots which took up water and nutrients from the soil, stems which allowed them to stand erect, and leaves which contained chlorophyll and in which most of the photosynthesis took place.

Eventually larger types of plant developed with further differentiation of the tissues into various vessels running up from true roots, through the stems and branches, to the leaves. The most important of these plants were the seed ferns (now extinct) and the horse-tails, and both groups formed extensive forests around 350 million years ago (Figure 2.3). These plants could grow only in moist areas, because, as in the case of the very earliest plants to invade the land, reproduction depended on the sperm being able to swim in a film of moisture in order to reach the ovum. This is still the

Figure 2.3 Plant life on land about 300 million years ago

case at the present day for the mosses, liverworts, psilotums, horse-tails, ferns and club mosses.

The colonisation of drier land by plants depended on the development of a mechanism of reproduction which did not require the spermatozoa to swim through a film of water. This was achieved by the eventual development of an arrangement by which the sperm passes through a *pollen tube* to reach the ovum, which is situated within a protective capsule called the ovule. The first group of plants with such a mechanism was the *gymnosperms*, which appeared around 300 million years ago. There were four main kinds of gymnosperms – the cordaites (which are now extinct), the cycads, the ginkos (the maidenhair trees) and the conifers.

The first true flowering plants, or *angiosperms*, appeared about 160 million years ago, and since that time they have undergone spectacular diversification. They are now the dominant division of plants, and comprise two main groups, the *monocotyledons* and the *dicotyledons*. In the former, which includes the grasses, lilies, irises and crocuses, the seedling has a single leaf and the stems do not thicken. The seedlings of dicotyledons have two leaves and the stems thicken as the plant grows.

In the angiosperms the ovule is protected by being completely enclosed in a chamber called the ovary. Projecting upwards from the ovary there is a thin pillar or style. In fertilization the pollen grain adheres to the end of the style, and a pollen tube grows down towards the ovum. Two male nuclei pass down this tube and one of them unites with the ovum to form the fertilized egg, or *zygote*. The other unites with another cell which then, through multiple cell division, gives rise to a mass of food-storing cells.

While many angiosperm flowers contain both male and female elements, various mechanisms exist that prevent individual flowers becoming pollinated by their own pollen. Although pollination may occasionally come about as the consequence of chance dissemination of pollen by wind, by far the most important pollinating agency is insects, which visit the flowers in search of food and, in doing so, incidentally transfer pollen from one flower to another. Some birds also play this role.

This relationship between insects and flowering plants has resulted in an extraordinary range of mutual evolutionary adaptations. On the side of the flowers, adaptations have included the display of bright colours to signal their presence and the production of nectar as a food source for insects. In some plants, notably the orchids, the structure of the flower is specifically adapted to the visits of certain insect species, especially bees and wasps, with a platform of fixed petals for the insects to alight on, and with the nectar located so that the insects have to penetrate deep into the flower to reach it, ensuring that their bodies come in contact with the pollen. Among insects numerous adaptations have evolved arising from the use of flowers as a source of food, one of the most interesting being the elaborate dance routines by which honey bees communicate to each other about the location of important sources of nectar.

Land animals

It was also a little over 400 million years ago that the first animals ventured onto land. Except in the case of worms, in which little major adaptation was necessary, this move involved some important structural modifications enabling the animals to breath atmospheric oxygen, resist drying out, and move around from one place to another. The first two of these requirements were met by the formation of a resistant outer skin, and of cavities in the body into which air could pass and from which oxygen could be transported to the various tissues. The needs of locomotion in the arthropods, such as crustacea, centipedes, spiders and, later, insects were met by modifications of limbs already existing in aquatic forms. The five-toed limbs of the vertebrates evolved directly from the fins of fishes.

The adoption of the terrestrial lifestyle also involved important adaptations in the reproductive process. In all groups except the amphibians, which still had to return to water for spawning and fertilization of the eggs, mechanisms were developed so that the eggs could be fertilized inside the female body. This adaptation is seen in snails, insects, reptiles, birds and mammals. In birds, most reptiles and the great majority of invertebrates, the female later lays the fertilized eggs and the embryos develop in the eggs outside the mother's body. In all mammals, in some reptiles and even in some invertebrate species the embryos develop in the uterus of the female.

Eventually, four classes of vertebrates evolved on land – the amphibians, the reptiles, the birds and the mammals. The last two groups developed directly from reptiles, which in turn had evolved from amphibians. The heyday of the amphibians was around 300 million years ago, when very many diverse forms existed; but by 200 million years ago they had declined drastically, and their place had been taken by reptiles. It was about this time that the first dinosaurs appeared.

The reptiles showed extraordinary diversification, with different groups becoming adapted to a wide range of different kinds of habitat (Figure 2.4). Several different aquatic groups evolved, some of them looking very much like fish, although they did not possess gills but breathed air through a respiratory tract. There were also various forms of flying reptiles, with wings consisting of a leathery membrane supported and extended by a very elongated finger. Some of the larger of these flying reptiles had a wing span of 7.5 metres.

Around 60 to 70 million years ago a great crisis occurred in reptilian history, and many forms, including all the dinosaurs and flying reptiles and most of the large marine reptiles became extinct. However, some groups

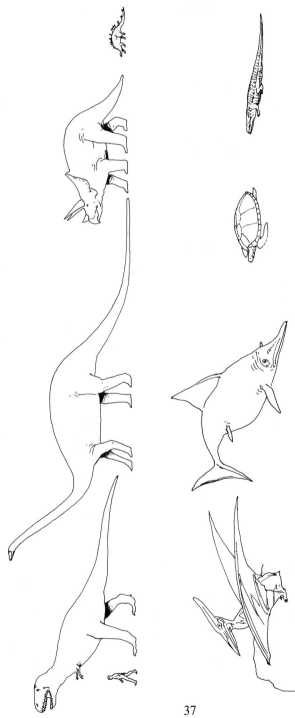

Figure 2.4 Some reptiles in existence between 150 and 200 million years ago (Note: The human figure is included only to illustrate the size of these animals. In fact, of course, no human has ever seen a living dinosaur, nor vice versa.)

survived and have continued to exist into recent times; they are the snakes and lizards (*Squamata*), the crocodiles and the turtles. The tuatura or sphenodon, a lizard-like creature which lives on a few islands near New Zealand is the sole survivor of another group known as *Rhynchocephala*. Many other kinds of organism disappeared during this period of reptile extinction, including various microscopic foraminifera, and many gastropods, cephalopods (including all the ammonites), and bivalves in the oceans, and many marsupials on the land. Whatever the cause of this wave of extinction it appears that placental mammals, birds, turtles, crocodiles, fishes and plants were relatively unaffected.

The earliest mammals had come into being by 200 million years ago, but they remained a relatively insignificant group during the period of reptile dominance. The transition from reptiles to mammals involved three especially important changes. First, except in the case of the platypus and the echidna which both lay eggs, a mechanism evolved by which the embryo, developed from the fertilized egg within the mother's body, attached to maternal tissue by a special organ, the *placenta*, through which oxygen, carbon dioxide, nutrients and waste products pass to and from the embryo. A somewhat similar arrangement is found in a few reptiles, such as the blue-tongue skink that occurs over wide areas of Australia. Second, in all mammals, including the monotremes, the newborn young are cared for by the mother and nourished by milk from mammary glands. Third, a mechanism exists in mammals by which the temperature of the body is maintained at a more or less constant level, relatively independently of muscular activity and environmental temperature.

After about 60 million years ago a spectacular evolutionary diversification occurred among birds and mammals. The range of mammals in existence after this diversification include: hedgehogs and shrews; marsupials; armadillos; primates, sloths and anteaters; carnivores (dogs, cats, racoons, bears, civets, hyenas); ruminants (deer, giraffe, cattle, sheep, buffalo); pigs, hippopotami and camels; rabbits and hares; scaly anteaters; coneys and hyraxes; rhinoceroses, tapirs and horses; sea cows; and various other less well-known types. Apart from these, one group of mammals returned to live permanently in the water – the whales and dolphins. Another group, the bats, took to the air.

Of particular interest to us are the *primates*. This group of mammals emerged during the last part of the dinosaur era, around 65 million years ago, and among them were the ancestors of humankind. Today four main groups of primates are recognised. The first, the *Prosimians*, is the most ancient group, and it includes lemurs, aye-ayes, lorises and tarsiers. The three other groups apparently developed from Prosimians. The second group is the *Ceboids* – the monkeys of South America. These animals have tails by which they can hang from branches of trees, and the group includes marmosets, howling monkeys and spider monkeys. The third group is the *Ceropithecoids* – the monkeys of Africa and southern Asia – and it includes baboons, mandrills, langurs, and macaques. They also have tails, but they are unable to hang by them. The fourth group, the *Hominoids*, do not possess tails. The group includes humans, gibbons, orangutans, chimpanzees and gorillas.

THE EVOLUTIONARY PROCESS

The term evolutionary adaptation is used to describe the set of processes by which different species of animals and plants and other organisms have come into existence and by which changes take place over the generations in the genetic characteristics of populations.

According to the Darwinian explanation, evolutionary change comes about through *natural selection**. This process depends on the fact that at any given time the individuals in a population of living organisms are not genetically identical. This genetic variability is due partly to changes or mutations that occur spontaneously from time to time in the deoxyribonucleic acid (DNA) of the genes, and is partly the consequence of the fact that genes occur in different combinations in different individuals. Because the individuals in a population are not all the same genetically, some of them are likely to be somewhat better suited in their genetic characteristics than others to the prevailing conditions. These better-suited individuals will tend to be more successful than the less well-suited ones in surviving and reproducing, and they are therefore likely to contribute a greater number of individuals to the next generation. And the progeny of these better-suited individuals will carry the genes that rendered their parents at an advantage; and so through this process a population may, generation by generation, become increasingly well-suited in its genetic characteristics to the environment in which it lives.

---

* Simpson 1950; de Beer 1975. However, classical neo-Darwinism (i.e. Darwinism explained in terms of Mendelian genetics) is not universally accepted by biologists. For example, M.W. Ho and P.T. Saunders have argued that it should be replaced by an 'emerging alternative framework', which has variously been referred to as the epigenetic approach, the process view and the dynamic unity of 'nature from within'. This hypothesis emphasizes the connectedness between the organism and its environment and suggests that, through 'action' organisms can actually 'participate in shaping their evolutionary future' ... 'the organism and environment engage in continual mutual transformation and structuration through the activities of the organism' (see Ho, 1990).

The arguments developed in the present chapter about the implications of the evolutionary background of a species for its health and well-being apply whichever of the two interpretations of evolution we accept. In either case, evolution results in species becoming increasingly well suited to their environments, and consequently they are likely to be less well-suited to environments which differ from the evolutionary one in significant ways.

Similarly, when a significant and lasting change occurs in the environment of a population, some individuals, because of the genetic variability in the population, are likely to be better suited in their genetic characteristics to the new conditions than are others. These individuals are more likely to survive and successfully reproduce, and so pass on their genes to subsequent generations. Not all populations adapt successfully in this way to environmental change; indeed, the majority of species that have existed in evolutionary history have failed to adapt to new environmental conditions and have become extinct, leaving no descendants. This fact draws attention to an interesting evolutionary paradox: for all species evolutionary adaptation is important because it has given rise to them in the first place; but for most of them it will not be sufficiently effective to permit them to survive the environmental changes that lie ahead. Just as they are the product of natural selection, so will they eventually be eliminated by it.

The rate at which evolutionary adaptation occurs in a population following environmental change depends on a number of different factors. Especially important among these are the frequency in the initial population of 'favourable' genes associated with resistance to the threats inherent in the new situation, and the extent to which such genes confer an advantage on the genotypes which carry them (i.e. their *selective advantage*).

The mutation rate for individual genes is estimated to be around one mutation per 100,000 spermatozoa or ova, and most mutations are harmful rather than beneficial. The chances of a suitable or helpful mutation arising by this means in an appropriate gene in a small population suddenly exposed to a new detrimental environmental condition are therefore negligible. In the long run, however, at least according to neo-Darwinian theory, all major evolutionary change depends on the introduction of new genetic characteristics through random mutation.

It is necessary to emphasize certain characteristics of evolutionary adaptation that distinguishes it in an important way from the other classes of adaptive process. First, evolutionary adaptation, although the result of the differential reproduction of individuals (because of genetic differences between them), is a process which takes place in populations, not in individuals, and the adaptive changes in populations undergoing evolutionary adaptation are evident only in subsequent generations. Evolutionary adaptation does not involve a *response* to environmental threats, in that no new processes are brought into play as a result of these threats. It is simply a consequence of the differential elimination of less resistant genetic types from a population, through differential mortality and differential reproduction. Consequently, none of the individuals in a population which is first exposed to a new detrimental influence benefit in any way from the process of evolutionary adaptation.

One reason why most species have become extinct is the fact that, while natural selection has the effect of promoting what is immediately useful, it involves no mechanism for ensuring that the genetic changes which it brings about will be of value under entirely new conditions not yet experienced by the species. For example, after a sufficient number of generations a population may, as a result of evolutionary adaptation, be better able to cope in its particular ecological niche than its ancestral populations. On the other hand, it may well possess *less adaptive potential* than these populations, should the conditions change in the future. Thus, while the processes of natural selection ensure that animals do not develop structures or genetically-determined behaviours which are harmful to them in the environment in which they are evolving, there is no guarantee that the new structures or behaviours will not be disadvantageous to them under novel environmental conditions that the species may encounter at a later date. In this book the term dead-end adaptation is used for adaptive changes which, while increasing the fitness of a population in a given set of conditions, render it at a disadvantage when the environment changes again later. Two often-quoted examples of apparent dead-end adaptation are the Irish elk and the sabre-tooth tiger. In the case of the former the males developed, through natural selection, extraordinarily large and complex antlers. We can only speculate about the nature of the selective advantage of this characteristic in the period during which it was evolving. However, it has been suggested that eventually, under changed conditions, these huge structures were a biological disadvantage and contributed to the ultimate extinction of the species. The very large canine teeth of the sabre-tooth are similarly believed to have been maladaptive when environmental conditions deviated from those which prevailed in the environment in which they were evolving. Nevertheless, we can be sure that they had been of biological advantage in that environment.

The converse situation, open road adaptation, occurs when genetic changes resulting from selection pressures operating in one set of environmental conditions by chance render organisms better able, at a later date, to cope with, or further adapt to, new conditions. For example, some of the characteristics which evolved in primates as a consequence of the selection pressures operating in the arboreal environment, such as the development of the hands as grasping organs, later proved an advantage in the very different ecological niche of the early hominids.

One of the great challenges facing the human species is to ensure that the human biological characteristic, the *aptitude for culture*, does not prove to be a prime example of dead-end adaptation.

Two ways can be envisaged by which new species come into existence through natural selection. One is known as phyletic or linear evolution (or anagenesis). This term refers to the process by which gradual evolutionary change occurs in a population through the process of natural selection, either as its adaptedness to a relatively stable environment improves or as it adapts to environmental changes. Eventually the degree of genetic change in such a species may be so extensive that it would not be sensible to regard the later populations as belonging to the same species, or even to the same genus as this original population. The other kind of evolutionary change is known as branching evolution (or cladogenesis). This occurs when populations of a species become separated so that they are no longer an interbreeding (or 'Mendelian') population. The separate populations may be exposed to different selection pressures, so that eventually their genetic constitutions become significantly different. Ultimately, the separated sections of the original population may become so different that even if they were to come together again interbreeding would not be possible; and at this stage the two populations would be regarded as two separate species. The diversity of species in the plant and animal kingdoms today is clearly mainly the consequence of such branching in the past.

Another phenomenon which has played an important role in evolution is *genetic drift*. Groups within populations sometimes become split geographically as a result, for example, of migration. Although the distribution of genotypes between the two such separating groups may be random, if the groups are small one of them may well, by chance, contain a higher proportion of particular genes than the other. Then if both populations increase in size and at the same rate, there will ultimately be two large populations, each with its own distinctive pattern of gene distribution. Alternatively, at the time of separation of the two small groups one of them may contain a higher proportion of individuals carrying a gene which favours the survival of the group as a whole. This group will thus tend to increase in numbers, whereas groups containing a lower proportion of such genes are less likely to do well and may decline in numbers or die out. Thus, although separated and not in direct competition with each other, some groups may do better in the Darwinian sense than others. A mechanism such as this could be partly responsible, for example, for any genetically inherited tendency that may exist in the human species towards altruistic behaviour.

It appears from the fossil record that the evolution of life on Earth has not been an entirely gradual process. For example, there have been periods when the rate of extinction of species has been much higher than others. One of these waves of extinctions occurred around 65 million years ago when the dinosaurs, of which there were many different kinds, all disappeared, as well as many other kinds of animals. According to one school of thought, there has been a surge in extinctions about every 26 million years.

The cause of these waves of extinctions is not fully known, although a number of theories have been put forward. It has been suggested, for example, that they have been the indirect consequence of the collision of the Earth with a comet or massive meteorite (or, according to one theory, with a shower of comets over a period of several thousand years). Such an event would result in the expulsion into the atmosphere of enormous quantities of dust and/or smoke resulting from forest fires, and this would block the light and heat rays from the sun and cause a major decline in plant growth.

After a wave of extinctions many ecological niches are left vacant, and this fact encourages relatively rapid evolutionary change and diversification among surviving populations. This is what happened after the disappearance of the dinosaurs. Before many million years had passed, the niches vacated by the dinosaurs and many other reptiles were occupied by new kinds of mammals.

Phyletic or linear evolution also tends to proceed in an irregular manner. A single line of animals may remain unchanged for a long period of time, the forces of natural selection selecting for maintenance of the existing type, and then, quite suddenly, a surge of evolutionary change may occur, resulting in major changes in a relatively short time.

It is significant that the rate of extinction at the present time is exceptionally high, due to the activities of the human species. According to one estimate, species are becoming extinct at rate about 1000 times greater than was the case in the late Pleistocene epoch, a period when the extinction rate was well above average for geological time as a whole.

Comment

As we shall discuss in a later chapter, the processes of evolution through natural selection resulted in the emergence, by 2 million years ago, of an upright-walking and tool-making primate which was more like a human being than any other animal in existence up to that time, although it was a good deal smaller than present-day humans. From this tool-making animal there eventually evolved the human species as we know it today – with its special innate aptitude for *culture*. We shall discuss this special aptitude and its far-reaching consequences for the biosphere later in this book. Here let us simply note that this particular product of the evolutionary process represented an extraordinarily significant new evolutionary force in the biosphere, giving rise to widespread extinctions on the one hand and to the development of genetically novel forms of life on the other. Indeed the human aptitude for culture in the modern world may well be introducing changes into the system at least as powerful as those which brought the dinosaurs to an end 65 million years ago.

FURTHER READING

Dodson, E. and Dodson, P. (1976). *Evolution: process and products.* D. van Nostrand, New York.

CHAPTER 3

PATTERNS IN NATURE

DIVERSITY AND UNIFORMITY

We have only to look around us anywhere in the natural environment to be struck by the fantastic diversity that exists among living organisms – diversity in size, shape and colour; and among animals, diversity in means of locomotion, patterns of behaviour and intelligence. Animal species also differ widely from each other in their food sources and in their resistance to heat, cold, dryness and wetness; and some are at home on the land, some in the water, some in the soil, and some in the air. It is impossible to be definite about the number of different kinds of forms of life, but a rough estimate suggests that there are about 300,000 species of plant in existence, and nearly 1,300,000 species of animal, about 850,000 of which are insects.

Underlying all this diversity, however, there are some remarkable and essential uniformities, especially at the molecular level. Before discussing further the diversity in the living world, let us briefly consider some of the uniformities.

UNIFORMITIES

One of the fundamental universals among living organisms is the mechanism of heredity – that is, the means by which information is passed from parent organisms to their progeny, providing the instructions which result in the new organisms developing and functioning as members of the species of the parents. The essential agent in this process is the genetic material – deoxyribonucleic acid (DNA). This substance is itself, when situated within a living cell, capable of self-replication; and it apparently contains, in coded form, the information necessary for the creation of a new individual. Chemically it consists of a long *sugar–phosphate* chain, along which are attached, to each sugar molecule in the chain, one of four *nucleotide bases*

45

(cytosine, thymine, adenine and guanine). The inheritable characteristics of an organism are determined by the arrangement of these four nucleotides in the *genes* – which are discrete areas or regions on the DNA chains and which are collectively responsible for the specific characteristics of the organism.

In plants and animals the DNA chains containing the genes are located in the nucleus of the cell and are, at the time of cell division, included in the chromosomes, which become visible at that time under the light microscope. In ordinary cell division each strand of DNA reproduces itself – a process known as mitosis – one of each of the strands then going to one of the two new cells, which thus contain identical genetic material.

Also almost universal among plants and animals is the involvement of the sexual process at some stage in the reproductive cycle. This consists of the fusion of two separate cells (*gametes*) which, in the case of multicellular organisms, usually come from two different individuals (or, in some species, from different parts of the same individual). In some very simple organisms, the two gametes seem to be identical; but in all the higher species of plants and animals they are clearly different. One, the male gamete or *sperm* is motile; the other, the female gamete or *egg* (or *ovum*) is larger and sessile. The fusion of the two cells results in the new cell or *zygote* (fertilized egg) containing in its nucleus, twice the amount of DNA contained in each of the gametes. So that the amount of genetic material does not double continually at each new sexual generation, there exists a mechanism, known as *meiosis*, by which the amount of genetic material in the cell is halved at a specific stage before the gamete is formed.

The fertilized egg thus contains genetic material from two different sources. Since it is very unlikely that the material from each parent will be identical, it follows that the offspring will be different, even if sometimes only slightly, from either parent.

As a result of this sexual process, the genetic material in the population is being constantly reshuffled. From the evolutionary point of view the importance of the emergence of sexual reproduction lies in the fact that, unlike the situation in asexual reproduction, the precise genetic make-up of the new individual is different from that of either parent. This fact tends to maximise the number of genetic combinations in the gene pool of the population, thus enhancing the potential of the population to adapt to environmental change through natural selection.

While the mechanism of sexual reproduction explains the continual rearranging, in different combinations, of the genetic material in populations, it does not explain how *new* genetically determined characteristics come into existence. There is, in fact, only one mechanism by which this can happen – the mechanism known as *mutation*. A mutation is a chemical change in a gene which is perpetuated when the gene replicates in cell division. The change thus affects the particular characteristic of the organism for which the gene is responsible. Mutations are normally very rare events, but their frequency can be increased by certain physicochemical agents, such as ultraviolet light, radioactive radiation and mustard gas. The great majority of mutations are deleterious, and the cells which carry them do not survive. Occasionally, however, a mutation arises which results in a change that renders the organism better able to survive and reproduce in the habitat in which it lives.

Another basic characteristic of nearly all forms of life is the fact that they depend on a continual supply of energy which is trapped initially from sunlight by green plants and stored in the form of large organic molecules. And there is also a basic similarity in the complex chemical processes by which this energy is used in living cells, be they animal, plant or protist. For example, a common denominator at the molecular level is the relatively simple molecule, *adenosine triphosphate* (ATP). This compound plays an essential role in all kinds of organism in the series of chemical reactions involved in the storage and release of energy used – as, for instance, in the synthesis of complex molecules and the contraction of muscles. Another similarity is the fact that all animals and plants and most protists require a constant supply of free oxygen for their metabolic or respiratory processes, which is then released again into the environment combined with carbon in the form of carbon dioxide.

All living organisms contain water (70–90 per cent by weight), and there is a basic similarity in the nature of the complex organic molecules of which they are made up. These molecules fall into four main classes: carbohydrates, proteins, lipids (fats) and nucleic acids.

Carbohydrates are compounds containing carbon, hydrogen and oxygen atoms in the ratio, approximately, of 1 carbon : 2 hydrogen : 1 oxygen. The simplest carbohydrates are the single sugars, like glucose and fructose. The largest carbohydrate molecules, or polysaccharides, are the starches and celluloses, which are made up of single sugars joined together either as a single long chain or as a branched chain.

Proteins are very large and complex molecules containing carbon, hydrogen, oxygen and nitrogen, and usually sulphur and phosphorus, and sometimes other elements such as iron and magnesium. Proteins are made up of simpler nitrogen-containing compounds, amino acids, and it is the sequence of these amino acids as well as the three-dimensional arrangement of the molecule that determine the molecule's specific biological characteristics and functions. All enzymes, certain hormones and many of the important structural components of cells are proteins.

Lipids are, like carbohydrates, composed of carbon, oxygen and hydrogen, but proportionately they contain much less oxygen. They are greasy or oily substances, and do not dissolve in water. Some, such as beef fat, are solid

47

at ordinary temperatures, while others, like cod liver oil and olive oil, are liquid. Lipids are important structural components of cells, and in animals they also play an important role as an energy store. A range of organic compounds exists which contain, are similar to, or are in some way related to lipids, but which also contain other components such as phosphorus, sugars or long-chain alcohols. These include the phospholipids, beeswax, lanolin, the cerobrosides and carotene.

A group of compounds known as steroids are usually grouped with the lipids because they are also insoluble in water. However, they do not resemble the lipids in chemical structure, each being made up basically of four interlocking carbon rings (three rings with six carbon atoms, and one with five), with various molecular attachments. Cholesterol is a steroid, and it is found particularly in cell membranes. For example, about 25 per cent (by dry weight) of the membranes of red blood cells is cholesterol. Vitamin D, the sex hormones and the hormones of the adrenal cortex are also steroids.

Nucleic acids are complex molecules, larger even than most proteins. They contain carbon, hydrogen, oxygen, nitrogen and phosphorus. There are two sorts of nucleic acids – ribonucleic acid (RNA) and deoxyribonucleic acid (DNA). Both are made up of units, called nucleotides, each of which contains a five-carbon sugar (ribose in the case of RNA, and deoxyribose in the case of DNA), phosphoric acid and a nitrogenous base. RNA contains the nitrogenous bases adenine, guanine, cytosine and uracil; and DNA contains adenine, guanine, cytosine and thymine. It is the sequence of these four kinds of nucleotides that determine the specific properties of nucleic acids. The role of DNA in the genetic process has already been mentioned. Ribonucleic acid plays an essential role in the synthesis of proteins.

Within these four main classes of organic molecules, however, there is immense diversity. In the case of proteins, for example, any single species of animal or plant has many different proteins with different functions (e.g. as enzymes, hormones, or playing specific structural roles), and proteins from each species are distinguishable from those of all other species. Indeed, subtle differences in protein structure exist between individual members of the same species. This is the reason why skin cannot be successfully grafted from one human being to another (except in the case of identical twins): the immune mechanism of the recipient recognises the donor's skin as 'foreign' and sets up an inflammatory response which ultimately destroys it. As mentioned above, the specific biological properties of proteins are determined by the particular amino acids of which they are made up and by the way they are arranged in the molecule. And yet, while the number of different proteins in existence is astronomical, only about 20 different amino acids are used in their construction. A single protein molecule may contain anything from 100 to 3000 amino acids. A single cell in a multicellular organism may contain several hundred different proteins, some of which are specific to that type of cell.

Turning now to the means by which nutrients and water become incorporated into multicellular organisms and distributed to their cells, and by which waste products are eliminated, it is clear that big differences exist between plants and animals. Nevertheless, among plants, as among animals, there is remarkable uniformity in this regard at a basic level, both structurally and functionally. The great majority of vascular plants consist, in essence, of a stem and green leaves above the soil, and roots in the soil. Water, containing traces of elements like nitrogen, phosphorus and sulphur needed for plant growth and metabolism, is taken up by the roots and transported upwards in the plant through a special part of the vascular system known as *xylem*. The leaves, and in some plants, the stem, are the site of photosynthesis. The carbon dioxide necessary for this process reaches the cells by diffusing directly from the atmosphere through small pores or *stomata* in the leaf surface into air spaces in the tissue of the leaf, and the oxygen given off escapes by the same route. Water vapour also reaches the atmosphere through the stomata. The sugars formed by photosynthesis are transported in veins in the leaves to a part of the vascular tissue in the stem known as *phloem* (running up and down the stem outside the xylem), which carries them to all the living cells of the plant, and especially to regions of growth in the root system and at the top of the plant.

All multicellular animals derive their energy from large energy-containing organic molecules which they obtain from plants or from other animals and which are taken into the body, as is water, through a single opening or mouth. This food then passes (except in the very simple organisms like hydra and in some internal parasites, like tapeworms) into a stomach where it is mixed with various digestive juices. It then moves into an *intestine* where further digestion takes place and where most of the nutrients pass through the gut wall into a circulatory system, which transports them to cells throughout the body. The undigested contents of the intestine are discharged into the environment through a single opening – the *anus* or *cloaca*.

All animals also have mechanisms for eliminating nitrogen-containing waste products which, if they were not removed, would be toxic for cells. These waste products are derived from excess amino acids. In vertebrates the kidneys and urinary system achieve this function, while in earthworms, for instance, these wastes are excreted directly to the outside through small openings in the skin (two per segment). In insects the nitrogenous wastes are discharged into the intestines. Plants do not need such a mechanism because they possess a biochemical means of storing and later reutilizing the nitrogen contained in excess amino acids.

49

Also common to all animals is the need for a constant supply of oxygen for cell respiration and a means of eliminating carbon dioxide. There is, however, considerable variation in the means by which this oxygen is acquired.

DIVERSITY

Despite the fundamental uniformities mentioned above, the evolutionary processes by which different species become adapted to the enormous range of different ecological niches have given rise to an amazing variety of structural forms, physiological mechanisms and ways of life. It is not our purpose here to attempt even a summary of all the kinds of adaptations to different habitats found in the plant and animal kingdoms. This would be impossible. The intention is rather, by introducing a few examples, to give some idea of the extent of diversity that exists, and at the same time to illustrate some important biological principles. We will consider diversity with respect particularly to two main characteristics of life – the *procuring and digestion of food* and *reproduction*. But first, a few further comments are called for on the term *ecological niche*.

The concept of the ecological niche

The existence on Earth of so many different kinds of living organisms is the outcome of two interdependant factors. The first is the evolutionary process itself, by which, over long periods of time, modifications have taken place in the characteristics of populations of animals and plants, resulting in their progressive adaptation to prevailing conditions. The second factor is the vast range of different kinds of environment and of food sources in existence in the natural world, each providing a potential livelihood for living organisms of one kind or another.

The physical components of the biosphere alone present a wide range of different kinds of conditions – varying, for example, in environmental temperature (and range of temperatures), in degree of seasonal change, in the chemical and physical properties of the soil, in wetness as opposed to dryness, and in sunniness as opposed to cloudiness. But as soon as forms of life came to occupy some of these niches, they created new niches, which in turn became occupied by new forms of life, and these again resulted in further new ecological niches. An oak forest in northwestern Europe or a rain forest in north-eastern Australia are prime examples of ecological communities providing countless niches for a wide range of species of plants and animals – each of them occupying a niche resulting from the presence of other members of the community, and each of them contributing to ecological niches occupied by other species. Each species is nicely adapted, morphologically, physiologically and behaviourally, to its own particular ecological niche, and each has its characteristic set of biologically-determined needs for health, survival and reproduction, needs which are satisfied by the conditions normally prevailing in its ecological niche.

The procurement and digestion of food

The range of ecological niches exploited by plants is vast, and is reflected in the wonderful array of different forms of vegetation that can be found, for instance, in the deciduous and the coniferous forests of the northern hemisphere, the dense evergreen forests of the tropical and subtropical zones, the eucalypt and acacia forests of Australia, mountainous terrains and savannah country in Africa, Australia, and South America, and in low-lying marshlands, deserts, heathlands, and sand-dunes, as well as in the meadows and downs of old, established agricultural systems in temperate regions of the world.

Each plant form is adapted through evolution to certain conditions of temperature, humidity, soil quality, soil wetness, light and wind. With respect, for example, to photosynthesis, some plants fix carbon from the atmosphere more effectively in the relatively shady places. Examples include various herbaceous plants common in beech forests in Europe, like wood-sorrel and dog's mercury; but if the trees of these forests are felled, so that more light falls on the ground, these shade-adapted plants are soon displaced by plants that need, and can make full use of, the increased supply of sunlight – plants which are not adapted to shady conditions. In some trees, like the European beech, the lower leaves are relatively thin, and undergo photosynthesis at lower light-intensities than the thicker leaves at the treetops.

While some water is essential for the survival and growth of all plants, enormous variation exists with respect to the amount of water required by different plants. Some forms, such as most reeds and bulrushes, cannot survive in soil which does not have a high water content, while others are adapted to extraordinarily dry conditions. Plants found in dry habitats often have small, leathery leaves. An extreme example is provided by the desert cacti in which the leaves are hard, spiny structures which do not support photosynthesis. In these plants the photosynthetic process takes place in the fleshy stems, which are also organs for storing water. Their water content may account for up to 98 per cent of their weight.

There are many other kinds of adaptation in plants to dry conditions. One of these takes the form of very short life cycles. Parts of the Australian desert may receive a reasonable rainfall only once in every few years. When this occurs, the previously parched and apparently lifeless ground quickly becomes an amazing mass of small flowering plants, and in a very short time seeds are produced. If there is no further rain, the soil returns to its state of dessication, containing the drought-resistant seeds which lie dormant until next time it rains.

In most leafy plants the size of the pores, or *stomata*, on the leaves can be varied in response to changes in the moisture content of the soil and the humidity of the atmosphere, thus controlling the rate of water loss by evaporation. In some plants that live naturally in dry regions, the stomata are permanently sunken into the surface of the leaf, minimising evaporation, while in others the leaves are covered with hairs which have the same effect. In many plants the leaves fold up when conditions become dry, and in some forms the leaves fold regularly after dark and sometimes in the late afternoon. In most plants only about 1 or 2 per cent of the water taken up by the roots is used in photosynthesis: the rest is released through the stomata into the atmosphere – a process known as *transpiration*.

Variability also exists among plants in their requirements with respect to other chemical and physical properties of soil. If a heather, adapted to acid, sandy soil is moved to a clay soil rich in nutrients, it will soon die; and, conversely, many plants growing naturally on a clay soil could not survive in a sandy habitat. Many plants are capable of growing in a fairly wide range of different soil types, but in fact are usually found only in quite specific situations. This is because, although they would be able to survive and grow in other places if they were on their own, they are unable to compete with the other plants that are better adapted to these areas.

A particularly interesting adaptation to nutrient deficiency in soils is seen in the carnivorous plants, of which there are at least 350 different species. They are usually found in swamps, bogs and peat marshes where acids have leached the soil of nutrients; and their prey may consist of insects and other invertebrates and sometimes even small birds and amphibians. The sundews, for example, are very small plants, usually not more than 5 cm across, and they have tentacles on the upper side of the leaf which secrete a clear sticky fluid that attracts insects. As soon as an insect is caught by one tentacle, the others bend inwards towards it, so that the animal is thoroughly trapped. The tentacles also secrete enzymes which digest the insect tissues, the nutrients being absorbed by the leaf surface. Other carnivorous plants include pitcher plants and the Venus flytrap, which occurs naturally only on the coastal plain of North and South Carolina, in North America. Unlike carnivorous animals, the carnivorous plants do not use their prey as a source of energy, but rather as a supplementary source of certain nutrient elements, especially nitrogen and phosphorus.

A much more common way of acquiring nitrogen is that which operates in the legumes, such as the clovers, vetches, lucernes, peas and beans, as well as in some other plants, and which involves a symbiotic relationship between the plant and certain nitrogen-fixing bacteria. When the plants are seedlings their root hairs are invaded by the bacteria (*Rhizobia*), and eventually these give rise to small nodules in which the bacteria live and multiply. These micro-organisms fix free nitrogen and release it in the form of ammonia, which combines with carbon compounds in the plant cells to produce amino acids. In agricultural systems the beneficial effects of growing legumes has been appreciated for at least 200 years. Some of the fixed nitrogen is released into the soil around the legumes and so becomes available to other plants. If the leguminous plants are ploughed back into the soil, much of the nitrogen incorporated in the tissue of the legumes becomes available for other crops. A crop of lucerne ploughed back into a field may add as much as 350 kilograms of nitrogen to the soil per hectare.

Turning to the procurement and assimilation of food in animals, the basic arrangement of the digestive tract (a single mouth, a stomach and intestines containing digestive juices, and a single anus) is, as discussed above, common to all multicellular animals above the sponges, coelenterates and flatworms – from mosquitos to elephants. However, the extent of structural and physiological variation on this common theme is enormous. To begin with, the great variation in food sources characteristic of different ecological niches has resulted in wide variation in the structure of the mouth region. The following examples serve to illustrate this point:- the grinding molars of herbivores (e.g. ox, horse); the sharp cutting teeth of carnivores (e.g. dog, tiger); the beaks of the sparrow and the pelican; the sucking mouthparts of leeches; the powerful biting and chewing jaws of the preying mantis; the proboscis of the mosquito; the fly-catching tongue of the chameleon; and the simple oral cavity of the earthworm.

Similarly, there is great diversity in the various organs concerned in the digestive process, and in the biochemical properties of the digestive juices. Because of the specificity of these adaptations, if animals are forced to feed on a diet significantly different from that to which they are adapted through evolution, it is likely that they will show signs of maladjustment. Tigers will not last long on a diet of honey, and bee larvae cannot survive on a diet of meat.

A few examples will suffice to illustrate the range of these adaptations in the internal digestive organs. Consider, for example, the case of the termite, an animal whose diet consists almost entirely of dead wood. Like other animals, the termite does not produce in its digestive juices any enzymes capable of breaking down cellulose, the chief component of its diet, and it is entirely dependent for its nutrition and survival on certain protozoa which it harbours in its stomach. These micro-organisms produce an enzyme that splits the cellulose into soluble carbohydrate molecules which can be utilized by the termite.

Among birds, there is wide variation in the morphology and physiology of the gastro-intestinal tract, depending on the kind of diet that each species has become adapted to through evolution. In most birds the lower end of the oesophagus swells into a large storage chamber, the crop, where the food remains, sometimes for as long as 2 days, until the stomach can accommodate it. In pigeons the crop takes the form of a large double sac that not only stores grain, but also secretes 'pigeon's milk' for feeding the young birds. Crops are generally prominent in grain-eating birds, allowing them to swallow a relatively large column of food in a hurry, so shortening their time of exposure to predators.

The actual stomach of birds consists of two parts, the anterior glandular stomach, which secretes digestive juices, and the posterior muscular stomach, or *gizzard*. The gizzard is especially well developed in grain-eating birds, and it is lined with horny plates or ridges that serve as millstones for grinding the food. This process is often furthered by the abrasive action of small pieces of grit that the birds have swallowed. The gizzard of the domestic goose may hold 30 grams of grit. In carnivorous birds the gizzard usually has much thinner walls and has a completely different function. In owls, gulls, swifts, grouse and some hawks, for example, it operates as a trap that stops sharp bits of bone and other non-digestible fragments from passing on through the alimentary canal. This material is rolled up into elongated 'pellets' which are regurgitated through the mouth.

A further example of an alimentary adaptation to a specific kind of diet is provided by the four 'stomachs' of cattle, giraffes and other ruminants. These animals tear the leaves off the plant they are eating with their incisors and swallow them almost immediately, without making any attempt to chew them up. The food bypasses the 'first stomach', or *rumen*, and goes directly to the smaller 'second stomach' or *reticulum*, where it is compacted into balls. At a later time, when the animal has stopped feeding, these balls – referred to as the *cud* – are regurgitated to the mouth. The cud is then properly chewed by the grinding action of the animal's molars, before being swallowed a second time, this time to be retained in the rumen. This organ is very large, and represents about 80 per cent of the total volume of the four stomachs. It is colonised by bacteria and protozoa which not only break down cellulose, as in termites, but also synthesise proteins, using urea and ammonia as nitrogen sources. Some of these micro-organisms pass on down the alimentary canal and are digested, thus contributing to the animal's intake of protein. Some of the products of the fermentation are absorbed directly by the lining of the rumen. The rest of the food passes into the *omasum*, or third stomach, which basically functions as a strainer, and then on to the *abomasum*. This is the true stomach, where peptic enzymes are secreted. Anatomically, the other chambers are expansions of the oesophagus. Interestingly, the stomach of kangaroos is also complex and very similar to that of ruminants. It also contains micro-organisms that play a major role in the digestion of cellulose and, as in the case of ruminants, the stomach, when full, accounts for about 15 per cent of the animal's weight.

Recently concern has been expressed about the possibility that ruminants, which now exist in much larger numbers than in the past as a consequence of human intervention, may be making a significant contribution to global climatic change due to the so-called greenhouse effect (see page 169). This is because they release into the environment considerable quantities of methane, which is produced as a product of bacterial fermentation in the rumen, and which is a potent greenhouse gas.

Mention must also be made of the great variety of ways by which different animals, in their respective ecological niches, find and procure their food, and the physiological, and the behavioural adaptations which have evolved to that end. Again, a few examples are selected to illustrate the extraordinary range of different kinds of adaptation.

A large number of animals locate their food simply by going around looking for it, in much the same way as we would ourselves, using especially the senses of sight, smell and hearing. Clearly there is a broad distinction between the techniques of herbivores and carnivores, in that the latter (except in the case of scavengers) have not only to locate their food source, but also to catch it. However, some groups of animals have evolved very specialised modes of food location and procurement. Bats provide a fascinating example. This group of animals has exploited a series of otherwise empty ecological niches in which their source of nutriment is insects flying in the night sky. Bats have evolved a special mechanism, known as *echolocation*, for detecting their prey, involving the emission of sounds at very high frequencies, and the detection, by means of highly evolved listening devices, of echos coming from objects in the environment. When the returning signal indicates that the object detected is of an appropriate size and is moving in the air, the bat flies rapidly and unerringly towards it, and catches it. The bat is able to discern from the signal whether the object is flying towards or away from it. Different species of bat are adapted, in various ways, to a range of slightly different ecological niches – some operating effectively, for instance, among shrubs, others among tall trees, and others high up above the tree cover. A similar mechanism has evolved independently in dolphins which also emit ultrasonic pulses, and the pattern of returning echoes provides them with a picture of the world around them. The dolphin's lower jaw seems to play a key role in the reception of the returning sound.

In some animals that feed in water, natural selection has resulted in the development of receptors that detect very small electric impulses generated by the muscular movements of their prey. The platypus, for example, which is effectively blind under water, detects the small crustaceans and worms

55

that form its diet in this manner. Frog tadpoles and some fish have evolved a similar mechanism.

Another important factor in the food quest in some species is the existence of mechanisms by which animals communicate with other members of their own kind about the location of important food sources. Such mechanisms are especially well developed among the social insects. Ants, for example, returning from a food source leave a trail of a specific chemical compound which is secreted from a special gland situated in the final segment of the body. Other ants can discern from this trail the direction the maker of the trail was travelling and the richness of the food source. And bees, on returning to the hive from successful foraging expeditions, perform special dances, from which other bees can deduce the direction, and to some extent the distance, of the source of food. To find the food, the bees that have witnessed the dance must make use of their sensitivity to the polarisation of light from the sun. Without this capacity, the message communicated in the dance would be useless.

We cannot leave the subject of food acquisition in animals without reference to the farming practices of a certain species of ant that live in tropical and subtropical regions in the New World. Some of these species collect pieces of leaves or flowers from living plants and carry them back to the nest, where they cut them up into smaller pieces and mix them with saliva and faeces. The ants spread out the resulting compost in an underground garden, and then place pieces of mycelium from a certain kind of fungus on top of it. The fungus, digesting and deriving nourishment and energy from the cellulose in the leaves or flowers, grows profusely. As the mycelium grows, the ants continually make cuts in it, and at the site of each cut the fungus develops a nodular proliferation. These nodular proliferations are harvested by the ants as a major food source. Other more primitive ants in the region make use of the same principle, but use insect faeces or dead insects as a substrate for the fungal mycelium instead of plant material.

Reproduction

The ability to reproduce and so perpetuate the species is, of course, an outstanding and essential feature of the phenomenon of life. Reproduction ranges from the simple division of one-celled organisms through to the very complicated structural, physiological and behavioural processes that occur in higher plants and animals.

Despite the underlying uniformities at the molecular level mentioned at the beginning of this chapter, the details of the actual processes of reproduction at the level of whole organisms vary enormously. First, let us note the all-important distinction between sexual and asexual reproduction.

In asexual reproduction there is only one parent, which splits, buds or fragments to give rise to two or more new individuals, all of which have hereditary characteristics identical with those of the parent. Asexual reproduction is common among simpler forms of life, such as bacteria, algae, fungi, mosses, protozoa, coelenterates and flatworms. In the case of the last group, if the animal becomes fragmented into several pieces, each may develop into a new whole animal. If starfish are cut in two, each part will regenerate tissue to form a complete new starfish.

Among plants, even the higher seed plants (angiosperms) are capable of reproducing asexually by one of several means. Some species, such as English elms and Lombardy poplars, may propagate by putting out 'suckers', so that new trees grow up from the distal roots of the parent trees. Reproduction by *rhizomes* (actually stems growing laterally underground) and by *tubers* is also common, as horticulturalists have appreciated for many thousands of years. Propagation of plants by means of *cuttings* is another example of asexual reproduction. Indeed, asexual reproduction also occurs in higher animals, including humans, when a newly fertilized egg divides in the uterus to give rise to two or more genetically identical eggs, each of which develops as an independent organism.

Turning to sexual reproduction, we have already referred to the basic differences in this regard between the simpler, more ancient plants, such as mosses and ferns, and the more recent conifers and flowering plants. Here let us consider a few of the adaptations that have evolved in this last group since the first of their kind came into existence around 250 million years ago. There are now about 235,000 species of flowering plants, each with its own characteristic size, shape, kind of leaf and flower and life cycle, and each beautifully adapted to its own particular ecological niche.

The most striking feature of the reproductive processes of the flowering plants is the fact that, while the wind sometimes plays a part in transporting pollen from flower to flower, the great majority of species rely entirely on insects, or in some cases on small birds, to bring about pollination. For this to work, the insects have first to be attracted to the flowers, so that they pick up pollen and later drop it off when they visit other flowers of the same species, where it can bring about fertilization. The basic attractant for insects in the great majority of plants is food, in the form of nectar, which is produced at the base of the flower solely for this purpose. Another feature of the adaptation of the flowering plant is the development of petals, which are often conspicuously displayed and in bright colours, signalling to insects the presence of nectar.

While this basic pattern is very common, there are numerous interesting and sometimes bizarre variations on the general theme. The orchids, as Darwin noted in his remarkable book on these plants, are especially interesting from this point of view, and the evolutionary process has resulted in some extraordinarily specific relationships between some orchids and certain insect species. In one species of orchid, for example, the shape and colour of the flower bears a strong resemblance to the female of a certain species of wasp, complete with eyes, antennae and wings. It even gives off an odour which is the same as that emitted by a female wasp that is ready to mate. Male wasps, deceived by this arrangement, attempt to copulate with the flower. In doing so, they pick up pollen, which they inadvertently deposit on the next flower with which they try the same thing.

Another interesting example is provided by a plant known as the dung lily, which is related, and is similar in appearance, to the more common cuckoo pint (or 'lords and ladies') of north-western Europe. The dung lily gives off an odour which resembles that of herbivore dung, and the male floral parts are warmed to a temperature of 38°C. When a dung beetle happens to fly overhead, it responds to these dung-like stimuli by dropping head first into the funnel-shaped flower. Because the inside of the flower is lined by small hairs pointing downwards, the beetle is unable to climb out, and if it happens to be carrying pollen from a previous encounter with a dung lily, some of this will come off and fertilize the ova. By morning, the flower tips over, and the one-way hairs no longer prevent the beetle from escaping – which it does, picking up some pollen on its way out (this pollen had not been available when it entered).

In multicellular animals, two main mechanisms exist for achieving union of egg with sperm – one operating only in the case of animals living, or at least mating, in water. This mechanism involves the male liberating spermatozoa into the water in the region of recently laid, but unfertilized, eggs of the female. Usually certain courtship behaviours come into play which ensure that the male is at the right place at the right time. This method operates in most marine animals, from molluscs to true fishes, as well as amphibia, which return to the water to mate. In frogs, for instance, the male arranges himself on the back of the egg-laden female, keeping firmly in place by means of special clasping pads on the front of his forelimbs. He remains in this position until the female begins to lay her eggs, at which time he ejects spermatozoa into the water, a small porportion of which find, and unite with, ova. The pattern in newts and salamanders is somewhat different. In the common newt of north-western Europe, *Triturus vulgaris*, for example, the male courts the female with a dance display involving a rapid waving movement of the end of his tail, which is turned back on itself, so pointing forward. When the female is appropriately aroused, apparently as a result of a hormone discharged into the water from the male cloaca, the male newt deposits a mucilagenous bundle of spermatozoa, which the female picks up with her hind limbs and inserts into her cloaca, so that fertilization actually takes place internally.

The main mechanism for bringing sperms and eggs in contact in land animals involves the insertion of a male copulatory organ into the genital tract of the female, and the ejection from the male organ of spermatozoa, which then swim their way to the ova. This mechanism exists in most insects, and in all reptiles, birds and mammals. Different procedures operate, however, in worms and some of the arthropods. The reproductive pattern of the earthworm, for instance, is a particularly complex adaptation to terrestrial existence. Earthworms are hermaphrodite, and during mating the two worms, heading in opposite directions, lie with their ventral surfaces in opposition and are held together by a sticky secretion. Each worm donates spermatozoa to the other, which temporarily stores them in a seminal receptacle. After the worms have separated, a ring of thickened epidermis called the clitellum secretes a membranous cocoon. As the worm frees itself from this cocoon, it discharges into it both ova produced in its own body and the spermatozoa contributed by the other worm and temporarily held in the seminal receptacles. As the cocoon slips off the worm, its two openings constrict and the eggs develop within the cocoon into new worms.

Another interesting mechanism has been observed in certain species of *peripatus*, which are curious caterpillar-like animals that live in moist forests in Africa, Asia, Australia and South America. They have many pairs of legs, and they share characteristics both of the annelid worms and of arthropods. They carry two antenna-like protrusions on the head, with which they are able to shoot a slimy fluid, with great accuracy, at prey or enemies up to 20 cm away. The slime thickens on contact with air. In certain Australian species of peripatus, males have a special protuberance on their head which is used to carry around a drop of semen, as the animal searches for a female. When the female is found, the male deposits the semen somewhere on the surface of the female's body, and a cellular reaction immediately begins to take place inside the body of the female, as a result of which certain cells transport the sperms to the ova in the uterus.

Reproduction in spiders involves a mechanism somewhat similar to the first part of this peripatus procedure. The male spider produces a ball of sperm-containing material which he picks up with one of his *pedipalps*. These are limb-like structures placed just in front of the foremost of the four sets of legs, one on each side of the body. He then sets out in search of a female which, in most cases, he must approach with considerable caution, identifying himself by certain species-specific signals in order to avoid being attacked and eaten. On reaching the female, the male inserts the spermatozoa, by means of his pedipalp, into the female genital tract. In most cases, he then quickly makes his get-away, although in some species it is usual for the female to consume the male as soon as mating is completed.

A great variety of procedures exist in different species for ensuring that males and females find each other for mating purposes. In many instances the female gives off a specific odour which attracts males. In some moths, the males are exquisitely sensitive to such odours – responding when there are only about 100 molecules of the specific agent per millilitre of air. It has been estimated that in some species of moth the male can detect a female over 4000 metres away, if a gentle breeze is blowing from her in his direction.

In other animal species, the male attracts the female to a particular place or territory that he has selected, often by emitting a distinctive call. This pattern is common among birds and frogs. In one group of birds, the bower birds, the male attracts the female by decorating his 'bower' with all sorts of colourful objects; and many birds, the peacock and Australian lyre bird being notable examples, achieve the same objective by extending and displaying their tail feathers.

In the great majority of mammals, females undergo a hormonally controlled cycle, and are attractive or receptive to males only at the certain periods that coincide with ovulation. This mechanism operates throughout the mammals, from rats, mice and shrews, to dogs, zebras, elephants and monkeys. Biologically, its important consequence is that mating takes place only at times when ova exist in the female genital tract to be fertilized. An outstanding exception to this generalisation is *Homo sapiens*, in which species females are attractive to males at all times and in which female receptivity is not restricted to a single period in the hormonal cycle.

A feature relevant to reproduction and common to all species of mammal is the production of milk in the *mammary glands* of females, which is the only source of nutrients for newborn offspring. Only one species of mammal is known in which the newborn young animals can survive without milk, consuming a solid diet immediately after birth, and this is the guinea-pig. Nevertheless young guinea-pigs do drink milk from their mothers when it is available. At the other extreme is the young grey kangaroo, which weighs less than a gram when it is born and which, although it makes its own way from the urogenital opening of the mother to the pouch, is otherwise completely helpless. Once in the pouch it immediately becomes attached to one of the nipples, and it does not leave the pouch, even for short periods, for 9 months.

Comment

The examples given above only touch the surface of the vast range of different life forms that exist on Earth. Indeed, the shelves of science libraries hold countless volumes providing detailed information on the structural, physiological and behavioural diversity encountered among living organisms with regard not only to reproduction and the procurement and digestion of food, but also to all other aspects of the processes of life. Moreover, apart from all that has already been described in the literature, much has yet to be discovered.

This diversity (as well as the uniformity) among plants and animals is the outcome of the natural processes of evolution. During relatively recent times human cultural processes have also contributed, mainly through selective breeding of animals and cultivation of plants, to biological diversity in certain groups of organisms. The latest development in this area are the scientifically sophisticated techniques of genetic engineering.

A NOTE ON ANIMAL BEHAVIOUR

Every species of animal has its characteristic patterns of behaviour, patterns which are appropriate and advantageous in its natural habitat. Some aspects of behaviour are aimed at procuring food, avoiding predators and building shelters or nests. Others are social, involving interaction with other members of the same species, as in sexual interaction, parental behaviour, status-determining behaviour, mutual grooming and simply staying together in a group.

Many animals, herbivorous and carnivorous, are fiercely territorial, at least at certain times of year: that is, they will vigorously defend their living space against intruders, especially intruders of the same species and sex. In poplar aphids, for example, two females may be locked in a kicking and shoving contest for hours, even days, as one of them attempts to take over a potential gall site selected by the other at the base of a leaf. Territorial behaviour is common among birds, and in many species the male selects a territory in which he and his mate will build a nest and raise their young. Occasionally, birds attack not only members of their own kind, but any intruders, regardless of the species to which they belong. Australian magpies are notorious for their attacks on humans, and people who enter a bird's territory in spring-time without due caution can receive nasty wounds on their ears or heads. Territorial behaviour is also seen in many kinds of fish, reptiles and mammals. On the other hand, there are also numerous species that show no signs of territoriality at all, permitting other members of the same species to come and go around them without interference. There is also tremendous variation in other aspects of social behaviour. Some animals spend most of their lives as part of a social group (e.g. a flock or a herd), while others live continually with just one partner of the opposite sex, and others spend most of their lives in a state of solitude.

Reference must be made to the distinction between innate and learned behaviour. The former is basically automatic, and is programmed by the genetic information that the animal inherits from its parents. Learned behaviour is the consequence of previous experience and of learning ways of achieving pleasurable sensations or experiences, and of avoiding unpleasant ones. This topic has generated much lively debate among biological scientists, some of whom have even denied the usefulness of making the distinction between innate and learned behaviour, and there has been a great deal of argument about the use and meaning of such terms as 'instinct', 'drive' and 'displacement behaviour'. We do not have to concern ourselves here with the finer points of these controversies. For the purposes of this volume, the distinction between innate and learned behaviour is both valid and useful, so long as we appreciate that many actions are mixtures of both. Even in the case of lower animals, such as insects, we must be careful in jumping too readily to conclusions about the innateness of their behaviour patterns. There can be little doubt that the dances that the honey bee performs when it returns to the hive from a food source are phylogenetically programmed, just as the interpretation of these dances by the spectator bees must be innate rather than learned. However, an interesting experiment has shown that innate factors are not the sole determinants of the response of the spectator bees to the dance. In this experiment an attractive food source was placed on a boat in the middle of a lake not far from the hive, and some bees were taken to this food source by the experimenters. These bees eventually returned to the hive and performed the appropriate dance, correctly indicating the location of the food. However, the bees watching the dance were not convinced, and instead of setting off for the middle of the lake, they turned away to watch, and eventually respond to, other dancing bees which were communicating more reasonable messages.

The contribution of learning to behaviour patterns becomes increasingly important in animals higher in the evolutionary scale, and in humans it clearly plays a bigger role than in any other species. However, there are still, even in the human species, phylogenetically determined tendencies to behave in certain ways in certain situations. Apart from such obvious innate behaviours as sucking behaviour in newborn infants and the tendencies to eat when hungry and to drink when thirsty, it is highly probable that phylogenetic behavioural propensities lie behind much social behaviour. For example, there is a strong case for the view that the tendency for people to identify with an in-group, to seek the approval of the members of this group and to avoid their disapproval is innate. But environmental factors, especially cultural forces, largely determine the *criteria* of approval and disapproval, and consequently affect the specific behaviour performed in seeking approval and avoiding disapproval.

As a consequence of the processes of natural selection, animals tend to enjoy forms of behaviour that are of selective advantage to them in their natural environment. For example, they enjoy eating, sexual activity and, in some species, building nests.[1] On the other hand, they do not continue to enjoy any single form of behaviour indefinitely. After a while they tire of it, and find some other behaviour more enjoyable – some other behaviour, that is, that is also necessary for, or that contributes to, survival and successful reproduction.

Conversely, evolutionary processes have determined, at a basic level, sources of distress in animals, so that they seek to avoid pain, harmful temperatures, abnormal population densities and other circumstances likely to interfere with their biological success.

Another important aspect of animal behaviour is the fine balance that exists in higher animals, including humans, between an apparently innate attraction towards novelty, or *neophilia*, and the opposite – that is, an innate fear or dislike of anything new, or *neophobia*. Basically, animals tend to be interested in and to explore novelty up to a certain level or intensity; but if the novelty is extreme, they are repelled by it. Linked with this phenomenon is the fact that animals become accustomed to the environment in which they live, and develop a preference for this environment over others, even if these have some apparent biological advantages. H. Hediger reported that on one occasion a gate to an enclosure at Zurich Zoo was mistakenly left open, with the result that the herd of roe deer that had been kept in the enclosure escaped to freedom. They disappeared into a nearby forest where other members of the same species lived and thrived – in other words, into a biologically favourable environment. It was not long, however, before the animals returned to the enclosure of their own free will.

COMMENTS ON ENVIRONMENTAL CHANGE

Every single species of plant and animal is adapted to a specific ecological niche; that is, it is adapted to a certain habitat and to a certain way of life within that habitat. Its inherited characteristics – structural, physiological and behavioural – are the products of natural selection and their combined effect is to increase the likelihood that individual specimens will perform optimally in that habitat, that they will successfully overcome the hazards inherent in it, that they will live in a state of health, and that they will survive long enough to successfully reproduce.

One consequence of this principle is the fact that, if an animal is removed from its natural environment or if the environment changes in some

---

[1] No apologies are offered for introducing the notion of enjoyment in a discussion about animals. Although obviously a subjective phenomenon, there is no reason to suppose that animals do not experience pleasure – and hence enjoyment – on the one hand, and distress on the other. Indeed, there is every reason to suppose that they do.

significant way, the likelihood is that it will be less well adapted to the new conditions and some signs of physiological or behavioural maladjustment can be expected. In this volume this fundamental concept is referred to as the *principle of evodeviation*, and the adjective *evodeviant* is used for life conditions which are different from those characteristic of an organism's natural habitat. Physiological or behavioural disturbances that result from evodeviations are referred to as examples of *phylogenetic maladjustment*, because they are due to the fact that the phylogenetic (inherited) characteristics of that species are not suited to the different, evodeviant conditions.

It is not to be inferred from this principle that every conceivable evodeviation in the conditions of life of a species will necessarily give rise to signs of phylogenetic maladjustment; but it is reasonable to regard any definite deviation from an organism's natural habitat and lifestyle as a potential cause of maladjustment until proven otherwise.

Another way in which animals may be disadvantaged by exposure to conditions which deviate from those of their natural habitat relates to their innate behavioural characteristics. These characteristics, being the product of natural selection, result in behaviours which are of selective advantage under the conditions prevailing in the animal's evolutionary environment. However, if the animal is exposed to new conditions which differ significantly from those of its natural habitat the same behavioural characteristics may lead to behaviours which are not advantageous, or which are even frankly disadvantageous. This has been referred to as the *flaming moth principle*. It is a common observation that at night-time moths often fly directly into exposed flames, thereby incinerating themselves. This behaviour, which is apparently an expression of an innate behavioural characteristic of these insects, is clearly not, under the artificial or unnatural circumstances, of biological advantage to the moth. Nevertheless, the instinct which underlies this behaviour is the product of natural selection, and consequently can be assumed to be of selective advantage in the environment in which moths normally live and in which naked flames are a rare occurrence. In the changed or evodeviant situation, however, the instinct represents a distinct survival disadvantage to individual moths, and to moth populations.

Many forms of traps for different kinds of animals are based on the flaming moth principle. For example, we noted above that bats, through echolocation, detect insects in flight at night, and fly swiftly and with extraordinary accuracy to capture them. Some human students of bats, who wish to catch specimens for their research, have discovered that if they swing a fish hook around in the night sky at the end of a line attached to a fishing rod, bats home in on the hook as if it were an insect. Thus, under the changed conditions, this innate tendency leads to behaviour which is definitely to the bat's disadvantage.

In the final chapter of this volume, we will raise the question whether some of the innate behavioural characteristics of the human species might, in habitats very different from those in which the species evolved, lead to specific activities which are against the survival interests of humankind.

SYMBIOSIS, PARASITISM AND INFECTIOUS DISEASE

Many organisms live in intimate association with other organisms belonging to different species. In some cases these associations are of mutual benefit to both organisms, as, for instance in the case of lichens. Each lichen consists of an organised network of hyphae of a fungus in which are entangled the cells of green algae (or, more rarely, cells of blue-green algae). The algae carry out photosynthesis and so contribute large energy-containing food molecules to the complex, while the fungus provides support and absorbs water and soluble nutrients. The algae of the lichens can grow independently, but the fungus cannot.

The word *symbiosis* is used to describe mutually beneficial associations of this kind. Such associations, which are a product of the evolutionary process and which may involve animals or plants, are sometimes obligatory, sometimes optional, sometimes permanent and sometimes transient. They are always of some benefit to one of the partners, and sometimes they benefit both of them.

Parasitism is a type of association between two organisms in which one of them, the *parasite*, is dependent on, and lives at the expense of the other, the *host*. The host thus provides the habitat in which the parasite lives and provides it with nourishment. This habitat may be within the hosts body or tissues, in which case the parasite is referred to as an internal parasite. Examples are the parasitic worms that live in the guts of animals, and various bacteria that live and multiply in internal organs. External parasites are those which, like the fleas of mammals and the mistletoes of plants, live on the outside surface of the host, but which still derive their nourishment from it.

Parasitism is extremely common, and there would not be a single species of animal or plant (except for extremely small forms) that does not normally harbour parasites of one kind or another. The parasites of mammals include not only numerous kinds of parasitic (or pathogenic) bacteria, but also various kinds of protozoa (e.g. trypanosomes, malarial sporozoa), roundworms, tapeworms, hookworms, liver flukes, mange mites, ticks, fleas and many others. All parasites feed on nutrients supplied by their hosts, but the damage they cause is very variable. Under typical natural conditions animals are not seriously disadvantaged by the parasites they carry. This fact is in part the result of natural selection, for in most cases, it is clearly not in the biological interests of the parasite for the host to die. Consequently, there is selective advantage for parasites which, while gaining nutrients and protection from their hosts, do not bring about their early death. However, unnatural crowding and ill health from other causes often result in an unusually high rate of parasitic infestation. Many animal parasites (i.e. parasites which are animals) are highly host specific, and are unable to establish themselves in or on species other than that species to which they have become adapted through evolution. The human tapeworm, *Taenia saginata*, is an example. As far as is known this parasite cannot infect individuals of any other species. However, some parasites are much less host-specific and can live in a wide range of hosts. For instance, the adult form of *Trichinella spiralis*, the cause of trichinellosis in humans can live in the mucosa of the small intestine of humans, pigs, walruses, rats, beavers, racoons, skunks, seals, bears, polar bears, wolves, lynxes and many other mammals, as well as birds.

Some animal parasites have complicated life cycles involving two or even three different species of hosts. An example is provided by a small tapeworm, *Echinococcus granulosus*, which lives in the intestines of members of the dog family. The tapeworm periodically sheds its final segment, which contains fertilized eggs, and these are excreted into the environment with the dog's faeces. If they are then taken up and swallowed by certain species of herbivore (eg. sheep or cattle), they will hatch in the animal's intestines, giving rise to very small 'hooked' embryos. These burrow through the walls of the intestine into the bloodstream, and eventually they become lodged in the lungs or the liver, or occasionally in some other organ, where each embryo develops into a round, fluid-containing sac, called a *hydatid cyst*. In each of these cysts large numbers of minute 'tapeworm heads' grow from the cyst lining; several million may be produced in a single cyst. The cysts remain in this form until the animal dies or is killed. Then, if the affected organ is eaten by a dog, the cyst is broken, and the tapeworm heads can become attached to the wall of the dog's intestine, to grow into adult tapeworms, so completing the life cycle. Hydatid cysts sometimes develop in humans who have swallowed the eggs of this tapeworm – picked up, for example, from the hair of an infected dog – and may cause severe illness.

While the vast majority of single-celled micro-organisms – bacteria, protozoa and fungi – are free-living and incapable of multiplying in the tissues of living animals and plants, some have become adapted through evolution to a parasitic way of life. Needless to say, in order to do so, they must possess a certain resistance, at least for a while, to the natural defense mechanisms by which the tissues of the host normally detect and eliminate alien cells. Infection with parasitic micro-organisms often causes signs of overt disease: well-known examples include potato blight (due to a fungus), wheat rust (also due to a fungus), malaria and dysentery (due to protozoa), and tuberculosis and cholera (due to bacteria). Parasitic micro-organisms which cause disease in their hosts are called pathogens. The mechanisms by which they cause damage to the host's tissues are variable. In some infectious diseases the injury is due to toxic proteins produced by the invading organism, as, for instance, in the case of diphtheria. In some others the inflammatory response of the host's tissues aimed at eliminating the intruding organism is the main cause of the trouble as in tuberculosis, plague, and pneumonia.

When the tissues of a mammal or a bird are invaded by a micro-organism of a kind that the animal has not experienced previously, there usually occurs an immediate inflammatory response in which mobile phagocytic cells attempt to ingest and digest the intruding cells. If the microbes are able to withstand these mechanisms, a second phase of the defence process comes into play – the *immune response*. As a consequence of this response, after about a week or 10 days the host tissues become very much more sensitive to this particular micro-organism and its products. This increased sensitivity is associated with the appearance in the blood and other body fluids of *antibodies*, which are protein molecules that have the property of combining specifically with the macromolecules which are produced by, or which form part of the organism. As a result of the presence of the antibodies and of some other specific changes in the host's tissues, the cellular reaction to the micro-organisms is greatly enhanced and generally more effective. In the case of cholera, for example, if infected humans are able to survive long enough for this immune response to develop properly, they are likely to survive and overcome the infection. The specific immunity produced in this way is usually long-lasting, so that if the host becomes infected with the same pathogenic organisms at some future date, the initial response of the tissues is likely to be vigorous and effective. All immunisation procedures (vaccinations) are based on this principle: that is, they are aimed at bringing about, by artificial means, an immune response in the host against given pathogenic organisms or their products, thereby conferring protection against subsequent infection.

Most pathogenic bacteria, protozoa and fungi are obligatory parasites; that is, they are incapable of multiplying outside the bodies of their hosts. However, there are a few normally free-living micro-organisms that can, under certain circumstances, multiply in animal tissues and cause disease. An example is the bacterium *Clostridiums tetani*, whose natural habitat is the soil. If this organism gains access to the body of an animal through a wound and becomes surrounded by dead tissue, resulting in a relatively oxygen-free environment, it may be able to multiply. As it does so, it releases a protein compound that happens to be extremely toxic for most mammals, causing the symptoms of tetanus.

Some of the more severe infectious diseases of both plants and animals are caused not by bacteria, protozoa or fungi, but by viruses. These organisms are much smaller than bacteria, and most of them are not visible under the light microscope. They range in size from the virus of foot and mouth disease which has a diameter of only 21 nm, to cowpox virus, which measures about 210 nm by 260 nm (most bacteria measure 1000–2000 nm). Viruses are relatively simple structures, with a central core of nucleic acid, which is usually surrounded by a layer of protein. They are capable of multiplying only within living cells.

The presence of a virus in the cells of a host does not necessarily cause any serious harm, and viruses can sometimes lie latent in the tissues for long periods without giving rise to any symptoms. Some plant viruses, for example, may cause a mottling effect on the leaves or on the petals of the flowers, without apparently interfering significantly with the viability of the plant. On the other hand, some viruses cause very severe disease. In humans, infectious diseases due to viruses range from such relatively mild conditions as the common cold and 'gastric flu', to herpes, influenza, measles, mumps, poliomyelitis and smallpox. In the majority of virus diseases the immune response of the host is effective in bringing the infection to an end. However, in the more severe diseases, such as poliomyelitis or smallpox, serious and lasting damage and even death may come about before the immune response comes into play.

However, despite the potential threats inherent in the existence of parasites and pathogens, under natural conditions animal and plant populations live, for most of the time, in a healthy state and free from serious disease.

FURTHER READING

Barnett, S.A. (1981). *Modern ethology; the science of animal behavior.* Oxford University Press, New York.

Krebs, J.R. and Davies, N.B. (eds.) (1978). *Evolutionary ecology: an evolutionary approach.* Blackwell, Oxford.

Noble, E.R. and Noble, G.A. (1982). *Parasitology: the biology of animal parasites.* 5th edn. Lea and Febiger, Philadelphia.

Rogers, W.P. (1962). *The nature of parasitism: the relationship of some metazoan parasites to their hosts.* Academic Press, New York.

Wilson, E.O. and Peter, F.M. (eds.) (1988). *Biodiversity.* National Academy Press, Washington D.C.

CHAPTER 4

HUMANS

EVOLUTIONARY BACKGROUND

About 65 million years ago, during the last part of the dinosaur era, there existed on Earth a small group of mammals which we classify as primates. They were small, shrew-like creatures and they lived in trees, where most primates have remained to the present day, and among them were the ancestors of humankind.

The arboreal environment had important consequences for primate evolution and left its mark on the later forms which, like *Homo sapiens*, seldom climb trees. These consequences included the development of the limbs as grasping organs, the replacement of claws by flattened nails, the development of the fore-limb as exploratory organs, the development of herbivorous digestive systems, a reduction in the olfactory sense and a compensatory development of great visual acuity and, eventually, stereoscopic vision. The evolution of the primate brain involved a progressive development of the parts of the cerebral cortex concerned with sensory representation, and because the precarious arboreal habitat demanded fine coordination of movement and balance, the cortical areas of motor control and the cerebellum became elaborated. The end result was the development of a relatively large brain. Changes in the skull included a downward movement of the foramen magnum, reduction in the size of the snout and enlargement of the eyes, which migrated to the front of the face.

Some time before 5 million years ago, and probably by about 15 million years ago, the group of primates which was destined to include the ancestors of human species had come down from the trees and was living mainly in open savannah country.

From palaentological work carried out over the last two or three decades we know that by 4 or 5 million years ago there were terrestrial primates walking upright in the African savannah. One fossil that has aroused special interest is that of a young female hominid found at Hadar in Ethiopia and dated about 3 million BP. She is known informally as Lucy, and the species to which she belonged has been called *Australopithecus afarensis*. This remarkably complete specimen (40 per cent) had a skull and brain case very like that of a chimpanzee, but she walked upright. Remains of about 34 other individuals have been found at the same site, but there is some uncertainty and disagreement about whether they were all members of the same species. More recently a jawbone similar to Lucy's has been found and dated about 5 million BP.

By two million years ago there was a hominid in East Africa that has been ascribed by some workers to the genus *Homo*, and named *Homo habilis*. One skull of a member of this group, found at Koobi Fora near Lake Turkana in northern Kenya, had contained a brain with a volume of $800 \, cm^3$ – that is, about $300 \, cm^3$ bigger than that of the average chimpanzee. Members of this species may have been only 3 or 4 feet (90–120 cm) tall, and their arms were proportionally considerably longer than those of later forms of humanity. *Homo habilis* was an omnivorous animal, consuming both plant and animal food.

It seems that there were at least two other species of hominid also living in Africa at this time. They have been ascribed to the genus *Australopithecus* and differ from *Homo habilis* in having smaller brains, and their faces were bigger and more protruding. Some specimens of the larger of these two species, called *Australopithecus robustus*, were about 5 feet (152 cm) tall and had a brain size of $550 \, cm^3$. The skull had a distinct central crest, and the teeth differed from those of all other hominids in that the molars and premolars were enormous and the incisors and canines quite small. This has been interpreted as indicating that this animal was almost entirely herbivorous, while the other hominids were omnivorous. The smaller and more 'gracile' form that co-existed with *Homo habilis* in Africa has been named *Australopithecus africanus*. It stood about 4 foot tall and had a cranial capacity of around $450 \, cm^3$.

By about 1.6 million years ago there were creatures in Africa that looked much more like modern human beings. Their general physique was similar, although they were of a somewhat stockier build. They were about 5 feet (152 cm) tall and their skulls were characterised by strongly developed brow ridges extending as uninterrupted bars of bone above the orbits of the eyes (Figure 4.1). They are classified as early examples of *Homo erectus*, a species which is considered to have persisted until around 300,000 years ago. The brain size ranged from about $900 \, cm^3$ in early forms to $1200 \, cm^3$ in later specimens. In its early days *Homo erectus* shared the African savannah with the two australopithecine species mentioned above, but these eventually died out about a million years ago.

The oldest stone tools found in East Africa consist of choppers, scrapers and flakes. These date back at least 2.5 million years and are generally

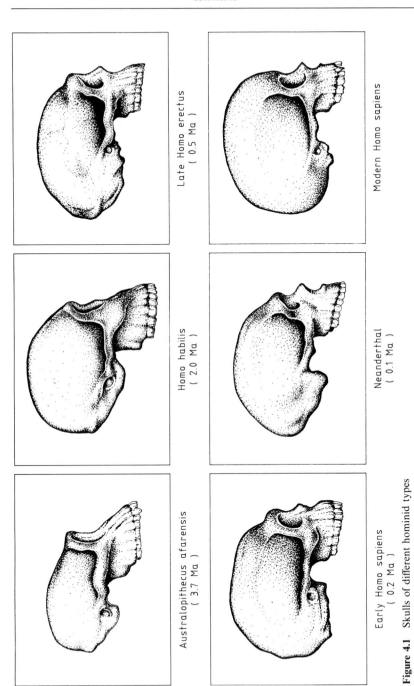

Figure 4.1 Skulls of different hominid types

considered to have been made and used by members of the species *Homo habilis*. Recently it has been reported that bone tools have been found in China associated with hominid remains dating back 4 million years. Gradually, over hundreds of thousands of years, the hominid tool-kit became more varied and complex. About 1.5 million years ago a new stone industry appeared, known as Acheulian, which was characterised by its 'hand axes'. These are pear-shaped implements, some of them of a size that can be comfortably held in the palm of a hand, but others are much larger. They were presumably made by members of the species *Homo erectus*. These hand axes were also made in Europe where they were used until about 200,000 years ago.

The very few human remains that have been found dating back to between 200,000 to 300,000 years ago suggest that at this time evolutionary change in the hominid line was proceeding more rapidly. The people of this period, as represented by the remains of skulls found at Steinheim in Germany and at Swanscombe in Britain, were sufficiently like ourselves for some authorities to classify them as members of our own species, *Homo sapiens*. They have variously been described as *Homo sapiens presapiens* and as *Homo sapiens steinheimensis*. Their brow ridges were less pronounced than those of *Homo erectus*, and their brain size was $1200–1300\,\text{cm}^3$. Recent work in China shows that similar *Homo sapiens* types were also in existence in the Far East around 280,000 years ago – apparently at the same time as populations with the distinctive characteristics of *Homo erectus*.

It is likely that the people of this period who were living in Europe took to wearing clothes for the purpose of keeping warm, a practice which would have stood them in good stead for the approaching Third or Riss glaciation. They also developed a new sophistication in tool manufacture, involving striking a stone core with a softer material such as wood – a method known as the Levallois technique. They were also using fire, as had their *Homo erectus* predecessors some two or three hundred thousand years before them. Indeed, it has recently been suggested that hominids were using fire as long ago as 1.5 million years, although this view is not universally accepted.

From the ecological standpoint, the use of fire by early humans represents a development of great significance. It was the first example of the regular and deliberate use by human beings of *extrasomatic energy* – that is, energy distinct from the *somatic energy* which is consumed in food and which flows through the human organism. It thus added a new dimension to the metabolism of human populations which we refer to in this volume as *technometabolism*. This is defined as the inputs and outputs of human populations of materials and energy which are due to technological processes. Technometabolism contrasts with biometabolism, which is the material inputs and outputs, and the throughputs of energy, of human organisms themselves.

The course of human evolution over the following 200,000 years or so is far from clear. It has recently been suggested on the basis of pollen analysis that human beings using fire arrived in Australia about 150,000 years ago, but this suggestion must be treated with caution at present. But it is known that by about a hundred thousand years ago, and during most of the first part of the fourth or Würm glaciation (70,000–40,000 BP), western Europe was occupied by a distinctive form of humanity which has been classified as *Homo sapiens neanderthalensis*. The 'classic Neanderthals' were short people of a generally stocky build, the men being on average a little over 5 feet tall and the women a little less. The skull was rather flattish on top and noticeably rounded at the back, and a characteristic feature was a pronounced brow ridge reminiscent of *Homo erectus*. The jaws were massive. The size of the adult brain ranged from 1450 to 1650 cm^3, and the average brain size seems to have exceeded that of modern humankind. These people well acquainted with the use of fire, hunted big game and dressed themselves in animal skins. Some of them buried their dead and they made use of paints for decorating their bodies.

By around 40,000 years ago, between the 1st and 2nd phases of the Fourth or Würm glaciation, another type of human being had appeared in Europe. If it were possible to bring some of these people back to life and dress them in 20th century costumes and set them loose on a city street, they would be indistinguishable from the better physical specimens of modern humanity. They were tall, had rounded skulls and steep foreheads, and had an average cranial capacity of about 1400 cm^3. Their brow ridges were only moderately developed and were not continuous from one side to the other, and they had well developed chins. They are classified as *Homo sapiens sapiens*, the same species and subspecies as ourselves.

It is now clear that people of this kind, much more like ourselves than the classic Neanderthals, were in existence in Africa, and probably elsewhere, around 60–100 thousand years ago, when the Neanderthals were still occupying Europe. Some of them were living in Australia 40,000 years ago, and possibly long before that date.

People of this kind eventually became the dominant human type in Europe. Their implements were distinctly superior to those of the Neanderthals and over the 20,000 years following their arrival they were responsible for a marked diversification and sophistication of culture, as reflected in the tangible evidence that they left behind in the form of many kinds of artefacts, including scraping tools, knives, burins, awls, needles, spatulas, various kinds of weapons, pendants, necklaces, arm bands, musical instruments, statuettes and paintings.

The emergence of human culture

As the anatomical changes were taking place in our ancestors over the several million years before the appearance of modern humankind, something else was happening of tremendous significance. This was the evolutionary emergence of the *human aptitude for culture*, and hence the emergence of culture itself.

At some time in the distant past, some of our ancestors must have experimented with making new sounds, distinct from the various innate expressions of emotion, and the idea must have occurred to them of using these new sounds to convey certain meanings. We see in this step the first inkling of one of the most essential features of culture – the invention, learning and use of symbols for purposes of communication. Eventually, some of these early humans developed the capacity to use several symbolic sounds, or *words*, in combination to communicate more complex thoughts or observations, leading ultimately to the development of language as it exists today.

At what particular stage in hominid evolution our ancestors developed this ability to commmunicate through the spoken word is a matter for speculation. Although it has been suggested that it did not happen until after the Neanderthal era, a more common view is that the capacity for speech, if less developed than in modern humankind, existed in *Homo erectus*. It may well go back further than this, since it is reasonable to suspect that this emerging capacity for inventing and using language played a decisive role in the relatively rapid increase (on the biological time scale) in the size of the brain in the hominid line, and this enlargement of the brain was already well underway before *Homo erectus* appeared on the scene.

In this volume the expression *aptitude for culture* is taken to embrace the following characteristics of the human species:

The ability to invent symbols. Initially, this ability, together with the ability to make a wide range of different sounds from the mouth, resulted in the development of language. Although all human beings have the ability to invent symbols, most of them invent very few. Language is an accumulative phenomenon, the consequence of very small contributions made by a very large number of people over a very long time. Thus this particular human capacity can be regarded as a relatively small 'step forward' as compared with other primates.

The ability to learn the meaning of symbols. This capacity is well developed in human beings, but it is also found in many other animals, and especially in mammals. Dogs and chimpanzees are good at it (but less so than human beings).

The ability to communicate with learned symbols. This is very well developed in the human species, and only weakly so in other primates.

The tendency to be sensitive to, to accept and absorb the messages transmitted (largely by means of symbols) from the cultural environment. As a consequence of this general propensity, the cultural environment becomes the main determinant of an individual's knowledge, beliefs, general understanding of the world, aspirations, opinions, attitudes and assumptions.

Another aspect of human behaviour usually considered as an expression of culture is the ability to learn new skills and techniques and to pass on this technological know-how from one individual to another or from generation to generation. Some other primates share this ability to some degree. An incident among Japanese macaque monkeys is often cited in this connection. A young female was observed to devise a novel means of washing sand from sweet potatoes, and 9 years later more than 80 per cent of the group washed sweet potatoes in this way. In another place, monkeys worked out a technique for separating wheat from sand by plunging it into water – the wheat floats and the sand sinks. And several other learned differences in behaviour patterns have been observed in macaque monkeys living in different regions of Japan.

In the human species this technological aptitude is greatly assisted by the use of symbols, as in spoken or written words or mathematical formulae.

It makes no sense to try to determine precisely at what point in our evolutionary history culture actually began. We know that it has been in existence for many tens of thousands of years, and that it was presumably not in existence 5 million years ago. One sometimes comes across discussions on whether or not the australopithecines or *Homo habilis* possessed culture. While such debates are intellectually fascinating, they contribute little to our understanding of hominid evolution. Apart from the difficulty in deciding what is culture and what is it not, there is also the problem that, while we know that members of the species *Homo habilis* made tools, we will never know whether they communicated through the use of learned symbols.

The capacity to invent and use symbols for purposes of communication gave rise over time to the evolution not only of the countless different spoken languages and dialects which exist on Earth today, but also to many which are now extinct, as well as to the arts of writing, reading, mathematics and computer science. It has also found expression in the design of clothes to indicate the profession and status of the wearer, and in the use of political and religious symbols which stand for a particular set of views or beliefs.

Although culture developed essentially as an attribute of only a single species of animal, the interplay between it and the processes of nature was eventually to become, as this species increased in numbers and as culture itself became more complex, a major feature of the biosphere. In recent decades, the power of human culture has increased dramatically, and the ecological consequences have already been far-reaching. Indeed, the processes of nature have now become very vulnerable to culture, and in a way dependent upon it, in that the direction which culture takes in the future can determine whether or not the biosphere survives as a system capable of supporting humankind. On the other hand, of course, despite its immense potential and apparent autonomy, culture has definite constraints imposed upon it by the biophysical properties of natural systems. Human culture cannot, for all its influence as a force on Earth, dissociate itself from these underlying processes of nature from which it arose and on which it depends, any more than life itself can become independent of the inorganic processes out of which it grew and on which it is based.

Geographical distribution and genetic variation

By 40,000 years ago, perhaps much earlier, humans had penetrated to all habitable continents of the world, with the possible exception of North and South America, where they may not have arrived before around 30–35,000 years ago. The spread of humankind was associated with some genetic divergence, leading to observable differences between people living in different parts of the world – differences, for example, in stature, colour of skin, hair and eyes, distribution and type of hair and facial features. Other genetic differences, like variability in the distribution of blood-group antigens between populations from different regions, are detectable only by scientific procedures. Presumably all these differences were brought about partly by genetic drift (see page 42), but also to some extent by natural selection. It has been suggested, for example, that a light skin is of selective advantage in areas of the world where sunlight is relatively weak, because it allows the formation of Vitamin D below the skin, whereas in tropical areas a dark skin would prevent the synthesis of excessive amounts of the vitamin, which would be harmful. There is some evidence that dark skinned people living in northern latitudes are more likely to suffer from rickets due to Vitamin D deficiency than are people with light skin. Conversely, it is possible that certain pathological changes that sometimes occur in the skin of white people in the tropics, especially children, might be the basis of a negative selection for white skin.

The main observably different genetic divisions or races of humankind have conventionally been classified as Negroids, Caucasoids, Mongoloids and Australoids. Some authors have gone further and divided the human species into a larger number of racial groups than this, and one of them has even recognised 32 different races. However, partly because of the frequency of 'hybridisation', but also for other reasons, attempts to classify the different human groups in this way are of dubious value.

HOMO SAPIENS IN THE EVOLUTIONARY HABITAT

The human species with its combination of big brain, manual dexterity, and aptitude for culture on the one hand, but unimpressive physical strength, inability to move really fast, and feeble biting capacity on the other, proved to be biologically very successful. Its members, following the hunter–gatherer lifestyle, spread to all corners of the world, from the icy plateaus of northern Asia to the tropical forests of equatorial Africa and South America and the arid deserts of central Australia.

Just how long people lived on the Earth before some of them adopted the farming way of life depends on the point on the continuum between the australopithecines and *Homo sapiens sapiens* that we choose to regard our ancestors as being 'people'. If we take *Homo sapiens presapiens* (Swanscombe or Steinheim people), whose brains were almost the same size as those of modern humankind and who used fire, made tools and occasional buildings, and who are likely to have worn clothes, as representing an arbitrary threshold, then we can say that 200–300 thousand years passed before farming began. If, on the other hand, we decide the first 'true people' were represented by the *Homo sapiens sapiens* type which was in existence by 100 thousand years ago, then we can say that humans existed for around 90 thousand years (or 3600 generations) before any of them decided to take up farming.

For several reasons, some understanding of the conditions of life of humans who follow the pre-farming, or primeval, lifestyle is relevant to the study of humankind in the modern world. In the first place, the primeval situation provides a rational starting point from which to begin consideration of the implications, for the biosphere and for humans themselves, of the culturally-inspired changes in human society that have occurred over recent millennia. Moreover, some appreciation of the nature of this long early phase of human existence encourages a certain sense of perspective. In an era of ever-accelerating environmental change and sophisticated technological innovation, it is sobering to recall that the primeval conditions, hazardous as they were, satisfied the survival, health and reproductive needs of our ancestors for many thousands of generations (otherwise, we would not be here).

Another reason for interest in the conditions of life of people following the primeval lifestyle is the fact that all the innate characteristics of the human species were established long before farming came into existence, and were the product of evolutionary processes operating on the populations of the hunter–gatherer ancestors of modern humankind. This applies not only to structural characteristics, like general shape and size, and physiological traits, but also to the various innate health and survival needs of humans as well as the innate behavioural propensities of the species.

As discussed in an earlier chapter, if an animal is exposed to conditions that differ significantly from those to which the species had become adapted through natural selection, the likelihood is that it will be less well suited in its biological characteristics to the new conditions than to those prevailing in the evolutionary environment (see page 64), and as a result, it is likely to show signs of maladjustment. People tend to take this fundamental biological principle, referred to here as the *principle of evodeviation*, for granted in the case of animal species other than our own. If a wild creature is captured and put in a zoo and then begins to show some signs of maladjustment, the first question that the zoo authorities ask is 'what are we doing wrong?' and they look to the life conditions of the animal in its natural environment for clues – to check whether, for instance, they may be feeding it the wrong food, or whether perhaps it needs water to wallow in, or branches to climb. This principle applies as much to humans as it does to any other species.

If we consider in particular the conditions of life experienced by humans in modern urban society, there are several reasons why we can rule out the possibility of any major evolutionary adaptation in human populations to the new conditions. First, the earliest cities came into existence only about two hundred generations ago, and in any case until quite recently only a very small minority of the human population actually lived in an urban environment. Furthermore, many of the significant evodeviations associated with life in today's high-energy societies have been introduced only within the last one or two generations. Even over the longer period, significant change in the genetic constitution of urban populations in response to new environmental conditions would be expected only in cases in which the selective advantage of a given genetic variant was particularly strong. It has been suggested, however, that certain infectious diseases associated with crowding in cities, such as tuberculosis, have exerted selection pressures sufficiently powerful to render later populations somewhat more genetically resistant to them.

Despite these new causes of mortality, the human population has not declined since the time of the domestic transition: indeed it has increased about a thousand-fold. There are two reasons for this. First, the people in villages and cities who are unwell are at less of a survival disadvantage than they would be in the more hazardous primeval situation. They are not required to be nomadic, they have their food and water brought to them, they are protected from unfavourable weather conditions by permanent shelter, and they are unlikely to be attacked by predators. They are consequently more likely to be kept alive long enough to recover; and even if they do not fully recover they may continue to live and they may still be able to reproduce. The second reason, which applies especially to the last few decades, lies in the processes of cultural adaptation, which have taken the form of specific measures such as vaccination and the use of drugs aimed at countering undesirable forms of maladjustment, measures which render people better able to cope with the new conditions.

We can safely conclude, then, that modern cities are not inhabited by a new breed of the human species whose members are better adapted in their genetic characteristics than their Stone Age ancestors to the prevailing urban conditions.

The principle of evodeviation certainly applies to a wide range of material aspects of life conditions in humans. It is also clear that it applies to certain aspects of behaviour. Marked deviations from the natural sleeping patterns are well known to be a cause of maladjustment, and evidence is accumulating that health is likely to be impaired if levels and patterns of physical exercise deviate markedly from those of humans in their natural habitat. Moreover, it is reasonable to suspect that the principle of evodeviation similarly applies to other less obvious behavioural, social and psychosocial aspects of human experience. The life conditions of hunter–gatherers are usually associated with the existence of an effective emotional support network, a certain amount of creative behaviour, and situations which are conducive to a sense of personal involvement. It is suggested here that intangible factors like these which were characteristic of the life conditions of our species in its natural habitat are likely to promote human health and well-being also in other settings.

Clearly there has been a great deal of variability throughout the millennia and from place to place in the conditions of life of hunter–gatherers. However, the following brief account of the ecology and life conditions of primeval people, based on evidence from the palaentological, archaeological and anthropological literature, concerns mainly those features which are likely to have been universal, or at least most usual, among hunter–gatherers.

Ecology

Hunter–gatherers have existed in many different habitats, ranging from dense tropical rain forest, tropical and semi-tropical savannah and desert, through temperate forest and grassland, to the snow- and ice-covered plateaus in northern parts of the northern hemisphere. Most of them, however, have spent their lives in mild to warm, relatively fertile areas with moderate rainfall.

Hunter–gatherers are usually nomadic, and the length of time they spend at a single camp is very variable. Sometimes they construct simple shelters, and when caves are available they often use them as dwellings. The earliest known buildings, made of timber, are dated at about 300,000 years ago. Indeed there is suggestive evidence that *Homo habilis* built simple shelters around two million years ago.

Ecologically, primeval people fit into their habitats in much the same way as other omnivorous species. There is one important exception to this generalisation, and this is the use of fire by humans – a behaviour which, in some circumstances, has had major ecological impact on the local environment. As mentioned above, in using fire hunter–gatherers are exploiting an additional source of energy, distinct from the *somatic energy* which is acquired in their food, involved in their metabolism and necessary for muscular work. The uses to which the *extrasomatic energy* of fire is put depends largely on the local environmental conditions: it may be used, for example, to provide warmth, to clear forests or to drive game; and it is universally used for cooking. It has been estimated that the per capita use of extrasomatic energy in the form of fire in hunter–gatherer societies is roughly the same as that flowing through human organisms themselves as somatic energy – that is, 1 Human Energy Equivalent (HEE) (i.e. about 3.5×10^3 MJ per year), bringing the total per capita energy flow to about 2 HEE (i.e. about 7×10^3 MJ per year)[1].

In the food chain, hunter–gatherers, like other omnivores, play the roles of first-order consumers (deriving energy from plant materials), second-order consumers (deriving energy from the tissue of herbivorous animals), and to a lesser extent, third-order consumers (deriving energy from the tissue of meat-eating animals) (Figure 4.2). In the ecosystems in which hunter–gatherers live, probably only about 1/10,000th to 1/100,000th of the energy fixed by photosynthesis actually eventually flows through human beings. The population densities of hunter–gatherers range from 1 person per 5000 hectares to 1 person per 500 hectares (that is, 0.02–0.2 persons per km^2).

Social organisation

Humans are social animals, and in hunter–gatherer societies each individual belongs to a group or band, and nearly all social interactions are between

---

[1] 1 Human Energy Equivalent is defined as 10 MJ per day – that is, about the amount of somatic energy used by an average physically active adult human.

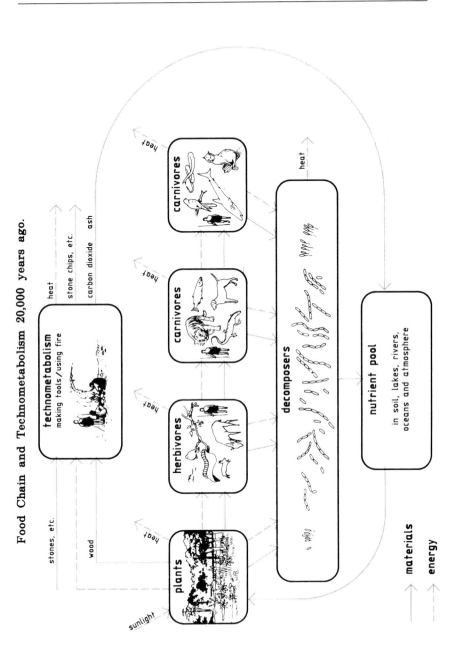

Figure 4.2   Food chains and technometabolism for hunter–gatherer populations

individuals who know each other well. The size of these bands is variable and is to a large extent determined by prevailing ecological conditions. There is considerable coming and going between neighbouring bands. Groups sometimes split into two or more parts as a result, for example, either of ecological pressures or personality clashes.

Leadership in hunter–gatherer societies is usually determined spontaneously, and it is based mainly on prowess and personality. It is often transient, and in any case usually relates only to a particular kind of activity. One individual may appear as leader, for example, of a hunt, another as leader in a honey-collecting expedition, another as leader in music-making or dancing and another as leader in religious rituals. There is usually no rigid hierarchical structure.

Decision-making in most primeval communities is a relatively democratic process, although in some groups, such as the Australian Aborigines, old age is associated with higher status and power. The relative influence of men and women at any particular time is likely to depend on the nature of immediate activities or circumstances, but in general the two sexes usually have equal status in the community.

With the exception of an age- and gender-based division of labour, there is no occupational specialism of the kind found in later societies. All the women take part in collecting plant foods (sometimes assisted by men) and all the men participate in hunting and making weapons.

Serious physical violence and other antisocial behaviour within bands is not common, at least under reasonably favourable ecological conditions. Important factors in the control of social behaviour are a strong desire for companionship and approval, a general dislike of being ridiculed or ostracised, and a real fear of being expelled from the group. All these tend to encourage individuals to conform to the norms of society. This does not mean that there are never any serious disputes, or that tempers do not flare on occasion; but when this happens, it is common for one or more of the individuals involved to move away temporarily to join another family group for a while – to return to the original group only when tensions have died down. This *reaction of mutual avoidance* works well as a mechanism for maintaining relative peace within groups not only in hunter–gatherer communities, but also in other human societies where the extended family provides a social framework for its operation.

Judging from evidence from recent hunter–gatherer groups, primeval society is not characterised by violent hostilities between neighbouring bands. Indeed, such behaviour would not be expected on evolutionary grounds, and it is not a dominant feature of the behaviour patterns of other mammalian species in their natural environment. On the other hand, it would be equally unreasonable to imagine that violent interaction, sometimes resulting in death, never occurs in hunter–gatherer societies. Humans are certainly capable of killing other humans, and in all likelihood they did so on occasion in the primeval setting. But homicide, whether within or between bands, is not likely to have been common in the pre-agricultural history of humankind. It is noteworthy, however, that while overt hostility towards out-groups is not inevitable, a tendency to be suspicious of strangers does seem to be universal.

The concept of personal ownership is weakly developed in hunter-gatherer societies, and it is usually restricted to those few objects that individuals can carry with them from camp to camp. Moreover, frequent exchange and sharing of utensils, weapons and ornaments seems to be commonplace. Indeed, for obvious reasons the material culture of primeval societies is very simple compared with that of all other kinds of human society. It consists mainly of weapons, knives, axes, ornaments, simple clothing and a range of tools used for preparing food, for sewing or for making nets.

Life conditions

Primeval society differs from that of most later societies in that, except for differences attributable to age or gender, the different members of a population all share very similar life conditions.

Diet and the collecting of food

There is a common misconception that before the advent of agriculture human beings were always on the verge of starvation. This is very unlikely. As in the case of other species in their natural environments, most of the time most of the people had a plentiful supply of food and were well nourished. Observations on recent hunter–gatherer societies fully support this notion.

The typical diet of humans in the evolutionary setting consists of a wide range of different foods of plant origin (berries and other fruits, nuts, roots, grain and leaves) and a certain amount (usually 20–30 per cent of the diet by weight) of cooked lean meat. This meat has a low fat content, and the ratio of polyunsaturated to saturated fat is considerably higher than that in the meat available in modern society. Clearly, there have been considerable variations from time to time and from place to place. The Eskimos, for instance, consume a higher proportion of meat than, say, hunter–gatherers living in certain parts of the African savannah where, at some times of year, the diet contains only a small amount of animal protein. However, it is very unlikely that any groups of primeval people have ever been entirely vegetarian. The diet of infants in primeval communities is, without exception, human milk.

In recent hunter–gatherer societies cannabalism is rare or non-existent. It may have been practised occasionally in the past in some groups under conditions of extreme famine.

Most of the food collected on hunting and gathering expeditions is taken back to the camp where it is shared among all members of the group.

It is worth noting that humans in the primeval habitat appear to enjoy both hunting and gathering. From the biological view-point this is to be anticipated because, as discussed in Chapter 3, in nature all animals enjoy behaviours which are necessary for their survival and successful reproduction. Of course, survival and success in reproduction among hunter–gatherers and other mammalian species demands a range of different activities. For example, excessive hunting beyond that necessary to satisfy nutritional requirements would have a number of disadvantages, ranging from the overkill of game to interference with other survival activities. Consequently, however enjoyable hunting, gathering or any other behaviour might be for humans in the short run, no such single behaviour would be enjoyable all the time. In the evolutionary habitat people tire of a particular behaviour after a while and turn naturally to alternatives which, for a time, are more enjoyable. The hunter–gatherer lifestyle involves considerable variety in daily experience.

Another essential form of behaviour associated with the search for food in humans in the primeval habitat is the manufacture of weapons for hunting and of tools for cutting up meat and scraping animal skins. In general, stone spearheads, axes and most other weapons and implements are made by men, whereas ornaments are made by both men and women.

Before leaving the subject of food something more must be said about energetics. The amount of food energy required by the human organism depends both on the size of the individual and on his or her pattern of behaviour. An adult male leading a somewhat sedentary life may use, each day, about 10 MJ (just over half of which is used in basic metabolic processes and the rest in voluntary muscular activity): the same individual leading a moderately active life would use about 12 MJ a day, but he could use as much as 30 MJ if he was performing exceptionally heavy work in a cold climate. Some idea of the relationship between food energy and physical work can be gleaned from the following facts: one teaspoonful of sugar (about 0.1 MJ) is sufficient fuel for an adult male to run for 5 minutes; and it takes 7 hours of non-stop cycling to 'burn off' 0.5 kg of body fat (one of the forms of energy storage in the body).

Rest and sleep

In primeval society, patterns of rest and sleep vary according to circum-stances. In general, people tend to sleep or to rest when they feel like it, and when there is nothing better to do. Most sleep is taken during the hours of darkness, but short naps are also common during the daytime.

Sexual activity and reproduction

In all primeval societies, positive sexual attraction between males and females of reproductive age results in cohabitation, pregnancy and birth of offspring. Once a baby is born, most of these unions are permanent. However, they are not always successful, and in all hunter–gatherer societies permanent separation of couples sometimes occurs. The majority of marriages are monogamous, but polygamy is permitted in all groups. Permanent homosexual relationships between two males or two females have not been reported.

Attitudes to extra-marital sexual relationships are variable. In some groups such behaviour is considered to be a very serious offence (even punishable by death), while in others it is not regarded as important unless it becomes a habit. Premarital sexual intercourse seems to be more or less the rule (except, for example, in parts of the Kalahari Desert, where girls become married before they reach sexual maturity).

Two characteristics of the human species relating to the reproductive process warrant special mention. First, unlike other mammals, the female human does not exhibit an oestrus cycle. An important consequence of this is the fact that mating may take place at any time in the reproductive cycle, and not only at or around the time of ovulation. Second, the period of maturation and of dependence of young individuals on parents or other adults for sustenance and protection is very long.

'Modesty', as expressed in terms of covering the genitalia, is variable among hunter–gatherers, and in some cases is non-existent. Clearly, attitudes toward the exposure of the body are not innate characteristics of the species, but are largely determined by culture.

The act of giving birth is usually a relatively easy process compared with the situation in modern Western society. The mortality rates for both infants and mothers are likely to have been higher in hunter–gatherer societies than in the modern high-energy populations. However, these mortality rates would almost certainly be much higher in the high-energy societies than in the hunter–gatherer societies if the former were denied the sophisticated medical facilities of the modern world.

Reliable figures are not available on fertility rates in hunter–gatherer populations. However, the most common picture is for couples to have three or four children, two or three of which can be expected to reach adulthood and to become parents themselves.

Children

The life conditions of children in primeval societies reflect the spontaneous nature and the relatively uncomplicated societal organisation of the communities. Babies are kept close to their mothers for the first year or so of life, but after this they may be left at the camp to be minded by relatives or friends when their mothers go gathering. For the first few years children are indulged by their parents and other members of the band and they are seldom severely reprimanded or punished for transgression of norms; but customs differ from one hunter–gatherer society to another with regard to the control of behaviour in children over the age of around five or six. In most of the societies studied, the laissez-faire attitude persists, but in a few of them older children are severely punished for misdemeanours.

The learning experience of children does not involve any formal programme of teaching. The process appears to be entirely spontaneous, and is based on such common behavioural characteristics as the tendencies to imitate and to seek approval or praise through doing things considered by the group to be good. Much learning in childhood takes the form of listening to, observing and copying slightly older children, who are in turn learning from their older siblings or peers. The playing of games based on mimicry of adult behaviour is universal among hunter–gatherer children. Aggressive behaviour is not uncommon in children, although it seldom involves injury.

Health and disease

The general impression is that most hunter–gatherers are in a good state of health. Undernutrition, malnutrition and obesity are rare in normal circumstances; and before contact with people from urban societies, hunter–gatherers were free from such infectious diseases of civilization as cholera, typhoid, typhus, measles, smallpox, influenza and the common cold. In periods of unusual drought, however, the condition of people is likely to deteriorate markedly, with signs of malnutrition becoming apparent.

Organic disorders, such as appendicitis, duodenal ulcer, diverticular disease of the colon, cardiovascular disease and cancer appear to be uncommon among hunter–gatherers, although there is little definitive information available. It is known, however, that blood pressure tends to remain more or less constant in adults after the age of about 20 years. Dental caries is virtually non-existent, and periodontal disease is uncommon, although it has been reported.

The average age in primeval populations is usually low as compared with high-energy societies. There are basically two reasons for this. First, the primeval lifestyle is characterised by certain built-in hazards which are more or less absent from modern society. For instance, there is a considerable risk of serious injury acquired during hunting or other pursuits in the natural environment, and the likelihood of a severe wound becoming infected and of gangrene or septicaemia setting in is relatively high. Second, incapacitation is of much greater survival disadvantage in the hunter–gatherer setting than under the protective conditions of modern civilization. Moreover, primeval people do not have the benefit of the artificial antidotal measures, like antibiotics, chemotherapeutic agents and surgery, that have been brought into use to counter ill health in the high-energy societies.

Psychosocial experience

Hunter–gatherers are usually members of close-knit communities, in which there is free and constant exchange of information on matters of mutual interest. They are very aware of their responsibilities in these communities, as determined by the prevailing social norms. While there is usually little or no daily contact with members of other human bands, there is considerable interaction with members of other animal species. The life style of hunter–gatherers is characterised by short goal-achievement cycles, in that the tasks which people set themselves are likely to be completed, successfully or unsuccessfully, within a few hours, or at most a few days.

Some other psychosocial characteristics of the primeval life style may be summarised as follows: considerable variety in daily experience; a high level of interest in the immediate environment and in the changes taking place within it; daily creative behaviour; considerable spontaneity in behaviour (tempered to some extent by cultural norms); and aspirations of a kind likely to be fulfilled.

Turning to the question of feelings, in particular those feelings which relate to health and well-being, it is reasonable to suppose that the following are especially characteristic of hunter–gatherer society: a sense of personal involvement; a sense of purpose; a sense of belonging (to a place and to an in-group and community); a sense of responsibility; a sense of interest; a sense of excitement; a sense of challenge; a sense of satisfaction; a sense of comradeship and love; and a sense of confidence. It would not be sensible to imagine that people in primeval communities experience all these positive feelings all the time. Indeed, such a state of mind would hardly be desirable in terms of well-being. The principle of optimum range operates with respect to most, if not all of these item (page 90). Thus, if a sense of satisfaction were never relieved by periods of dissatisfaction and occasional frustration, the individual might well lose interest in life. By and large, however, negative feelings, such as sense of alienation, sense of anomie, sense of loneliness, sense of boredom and sense of chronic resentment do not appear to be common among primeval people living under natural conditions.

Arts and crafts

Appropriately, prehistorians have put much emphasis on the capacity of humans and of our hominid ancestors to make and use tools. However, some other species of animals also use tools on occasion. Otters use stones to break open molluscs, and chimpanzees not only use sticks of wood for a variety of purposes but also sometimes actually manufacture simple implements. Humans, however, are more adept at inventing, manufacturing and using tools than any other species. As pointed out above, the ability to communicate by means of a learned language plays an important part in this aspect of human behaviour.

There is another highly significant aspect of manual dexterity and the capacity to make and shape things by hand, and this is the human tendency to rearrange matter simply for the purpose of achieving an aesthetically pleasing form or pattern. Even in the case of simple implements of the late Palaeolithic period, it is clear that much more work was often put into shaping them than was necessary to render them functional. And, apart from the manufacture of these utilitarian objects, Palaeolithic people spent part of their time making pendants, necklaces, arm bands, statuettes and paintings. Some authors see evidence for aesthetic sensibility in the work of tool-makers in the so-called Lower Palaeolithic period of a quarter of a million years ago. In fact, non-utilitarian creative behaviour in primeval people extends far beyond the manufacture of material objects, and includes such activities as making music, dancing and telling stories.

A great deal has been written about human creativity, but most of this literature has been concerned with the activities only of quite exceptional specimens of humanity, such as Leonardo di Vinci, Michelangelo, Picasso, Mozart and Beethoven. Less attention has been paid to creative behaviour as a feature of the everyday life experience of ordinary people. As mentioned above, in primeval society every individual spent part of every day making something by hand or creating new patterns in some other way. This kind of behaviour was inherent in the life experience of the human species in its evolutionary habitat. It is apparent that, to a considerable extent, civilization has removed the incentives and opportunities for creative behaviour for a high proportion of the population – depriving people of an important source of enjoyment and self-fulfilment.

BEHAVIOUR IN HUMANS

In the last chapter we noted the distinction between innate and learned behaviour in animals. The latter, although occurring throughout the animal kingdom, becomes increasingly important in species higher up in the evolutionary scale. In fact, most activities in vertebrates (and in some lower orders) are the consequence of both innate behavioural forces or 'drives' and learning. The relative contributions of learning on the one hand and innate or biological factors on the other in humankind continues to be the subject of unending controversy.

Certainly, culture has an enormous effect on what people actually *do* and this influence, of course, can only be exerted through the learning process. Everyday life in the modern world is full of examples – the wearing of clothes, driving motor vehicles, watching television, and participation in committee meetings, religious rituals and military parades. Nevertheless, it is reasonable to suppose that underlying these *specific* behaviours there exist some more *basic* behavioural tendencies which may well be inherited as innate characteristics of the human species. There is, in other words, something that we can call *human nature*. It is obvious to anyone observing the activities in a discotheque or an exclusive restaurant that some rather basic biologically-determined urges are contributing to what goes on, although the specific manifestations of these urges may be largely culturally-determined.

In this book, these basic behaviours are referred to as *common behavioural tendencies*. They range from some rather obvious behaviours linked closely with physiological functions to others, more difficult to define, of a psycho-social nature. The former include, for example, the tendencies to eat when hungry, to drink when thirsty, to copulate when appropriately stimulated, and to move from less comfortable to more comfortable positions. The more psycho-socially oriented tendencies include such basic behaviours as the tendencies to identify with an in-group, to seek the approval and to avoid the disapproval of members of the in-group, to show loyalty to members of the in-group, and to seek to maintain or improve status. It is clear that the actual outcomes of some of these behavioural tendencies vary enormously from one cultural or subcultural setting to another. For example, culture is the main determinant of both the criteria of approval or disapproval and the kind of behaviour which is likely to improve status.

A subject that has received a great deal of attention and that is still the cause of strong disagreements is *human aggression*. Some authors have argued that there is an innate aggressiveness in humankind towards other humans, especially in the case of males. According to one school of thought, this aggressive force tends to build up in the individual until it eventually finds some sort of behavioural outlet. Others have argued strongly that it is culture that determines whether humans behave aggressively towards one another. The view taken here is that, while humans are not 'innately aggressive', there is nevertheless an innate tendency for them to behave aggressively in response to a stimulus which is perceived as a threat to themselves or to members of their in-groups. Cultural factors, of course, have an important influence on what is, and what is not regarded as a threat. Aggressive behaviour may also be a direct consequence of cultural forces in those societies and groups in which aggression and violence are, in their own right, regarded as criteria for praise and approval.

Another related topic of continuing debate is the question whether or not genetic differences between individuals account for differences in their behaviour. Attention has been paid especially to criminal behaviour in this connection. On the whole, it seems likely that some genetic differences in this regard between people do exist, although it is also clear that environmental factors are the main determinants of the levels of criminal activity in different communities. There may well be genetically determined differences in the way in which, or intensity with which, different individuals respond to various aversive conditions of life.

HUMAN HEALTH NEEDS

According to the *principle of evodeviation* (page 64), when animals are exposed to conditions of life that deviate significantly from those to which their species is genetically adapted through evolution (that is, the conditions prevailing in the animal's natural habitat), signs of maladaptation (physiological or behavioural) are likely to be manifest. The fact that this principle applies as much to *Homo sapiens* as it does to any other species can be used as a basis for postulating the universal health needs of humankind – that is, the health needs that are characteristic of the human species as a whole.

With this principle in mind, we can put together a list of postulated life conditions likely to be conducive to health in *Homo sapiens*, this list being, in fact, a summary of the conditions likely to have prevailed in the natural habitat of the species. Such a list is presented in Table 4.1. and will be used as a basis for discussion about the impacts of culture on human health in later chapters.

It should be noted that, with respect to many items on the list the *principle of optimum range* applies; that is, significantly too little, but also too much of the given condition can be detrimental to health.

ADAPATION IN HUMANS

Adaptation can be defined as the process by which an individual organism or a population of organisms changes so that it is better able to cope under existing conditions or, more usually, under new conditions. Broadly, we can recognise three broad categories of adaptation in animals. First, there is *evolutionary adaptation*. This is a transgenerational phenomenon, and was discussed in Chapters 2 and 3. The phylogenetic or species characteristics of modern humankind are the outcome of the processes of evolutionary

Table 4.1 Universal health needs of humans

Clean air (not contaminated with hydrocarbons, sulphur oxides, lead, etc.).

A natural diet (that is: calorie intake neither less than nor in excess of metabolic requirements; food stuffs providing the full range of the nutritional requirements of the human organism, as provided, for example, by a diverse range of different foodstuffs of plant origin and a little cooked lean meat; a diet which is balanced in the sense that it does not contain an excess of any particular kind of chemical constituent or class of foodstuff; foodstuffs with a physical consistency of that of natural foods and containing fibre; foodstuffs devoid of potentially noxious containants or additives).

Clean water (free of contamination with chemicals or pathogenic micro-organisms).

Absence of harmful levels of electromagnetic radiation (e.g. alpha, beta, gamma, ultraviolet and X-rays).

Minimal contact with microbial or metazoal parasites and pathogens.

Dwellings that provide adequate protection from extremes of climate.

An emotional support network, providing a framework for care-giving and care-receiving behaviour, and for exchange of information on matters of mutal interest and concern.

Opportunities and incentives for co-operative small-group interaction.

Levels of sensory stimulation which are neither much lower, nor much higher than those of the natural habitat.

A pattern or physical exercise which involves some short periods of vigorous muscular work, and longer periods of medium (and varied) muscular work – but also frequent periods of rest.

Opportunities and incentives for creative behaviour.

Opportunities and incentives for learning and practising manual skills.

Opportunities and incentives for active involvement in recreational activities.

An environment which has interest value and in which changes of interest to the individual are taking place (but at a rate that can easily be handled by the human psyche).

Opportunities for spontaneity in human behaviour.

Variety in daily experience.

Satisfactory outlets for common behavioural tendencies.

Short goal-achievement cycles and aspirations of a kind likely to be fulfilled.

An environment and lifestyle conducive to: a sense of personal involvement, or purpose, of belonging, of responsibility, of challenge, of comradeship and love.

An environment and lifestyle which do not promote: a sense of alienation, of anomie, of being deprived, of boredom, of loneliness, of frustration.

(Note: with respect to many of the above postulated health-promoting aspects of life conditions, including the intangible aspects, the *principle of the optimum range* is applicable. That is to say, too little or too much of a given condition may be detrimental to health.)

adaptation acting on populations of our ancestors over many hundreds of millions of years.

The term *innate adaptation* is used here for all those forms of adaptation, physiological or behavioural, which occur in individual animals and which are automatic and genetically-determined. The human organism is provided with a battery of innate adaptive capabilities very similar to those of other mammals. These range from the adaptive responses of single cells to those of organs and tissues, and eventually to those which are evident at the level of the whole organism.

There are two kinds of innate adaptive response which are especially relevant to the responses or reactions of humans to the changing conditions of life resulting from the cultural developments. One of these is the set of processes involved in the reaction of the tissues of the body to threat of invasion by micro-organisms, and are basically the same as those that exist in other mammalian species (see page 67). Programmes of artificial immunisation, which have had so marked an effect on the incidence of certain diseases and which have resulted in the total elimination of one of the most severe of these diseases, smallpox, are based on our understanding of these processes.

The second especially important aspect of innate adaptation in humans is the complex set of psychological and physiological responses which come into play when individuals perceive a sudden threat and which prepare them to cope with this threat biologically. These responses involve not only parts of the central nervous system, especially the cerebral cortex and the hypothalamus, but also the so-called autonomic nervous system, as well as various endocrine organs, particularly the pituitary gland and the adrenal glands. When an acute threat is perceived, physiological changes occur almost at once, and they include an increase in the strength and rate of the heart beat, some contraction of the spleen, the release into the blood of glucose stored as glycogen in the liver, the redirection of the blood supply from the viscera and the skin to the muscles and the brain, a deepening of respiration, dilation of the pupils and an enhancement of the clotting potential of the blood. All these changes can be regarded as rendering the body better equipped, physically and mentally, to cope with the perceived danger.

When this set of adaptive responses comes into play in the natural habitat of the human species the perceived threat does not usually persist: the individual either escapes or overcomes the threat, or is destroyed by it. But if perceived threats do persist for long periods of time, or are repeated with great frequency, the adaptive response may result in pathological changes of one sort or another. Chronic stress of this kind is thought to play a role in the induction of heart disease, duodenal ulcers, possibly even cancer, as well as much neurosis.

The third category of adaptation in animals is adaptation through learning. An individual animal may learn from experience that certain

92

components of its environment are dangerous, and so modify its behaviour to avoid them. Adaptation through learning is especially important in animals high on the evolutionary scale, including humans.

The outstanding difference between adaptability in the human species and in other vertebrates lies in the human capacity for *cultural adaptation*, which is basically a culturally-dependent form of adaptation through learning. Anthropologists use the term 'cultural adaptation' for a wide range of patterns of behaviour that contribute to the survival and well-being of human groups in different environmental settings. These include techniques for extracting food from the environment, for minimising social conflict and for providing protection against inclement weather. In this book, however, the emphasis is on cultural adaptive processes that are brought into play in response to harmful and undesirable effects of culturally-induced changes in biological systems. A simple example of cultural adaptation of this kind is provided by the sequence of events that followed the introduction of refined carbohydrates into the diets of human populations. This change was culturally induced, in that it was the outcome of certain technological developments and economic forces. Biologically, it represents a significant deviation from the evolutionary conditions of life of the human species, and it has been blamed by different authorities for a range of different forms of phylogenetic maladjustment. For example, it is widely accepted that the high incidence of dental caries in some Western populations is a consequence of this change in diet. The cultural adaptive response of society to this culturally-induced maladjustment has involved the establishment of a profession of men and women trained in the art of filling cavities in the teeth. Other cultural adaptive responses to dental caries include the addition of sodium fluoride to drinking water, the daily cleaning of the teeth with special brushes and chemical cleansing agents and, occasionally, returning to a diet free of refined carbohydrate.

Examples of different forms of cultural adaptation will be encountered in subsequent chapters. Let us note here, however, one particularly important distinction between two classes of cultural adaptation: corrective and antidotal adaptation. Corrective adaptation occurs when the response results in correcting or eliminating the underlying cause of maladjustment or disharmony. Examples are the restoration of ascorbic acid to the diet of a population suffering from scurvy, and the reversion to a diet free of refined carbohydrates in the case of dental caries. In antidotal adaptation no attempt is made to modify the unsatisfactory conditions which are the fundamental cause of disturbance, and the adaptive response is aimed instead at alleviating the symptoms of the maladjustment or at an intermediate factor. Most of the work of the medical profession in present-day Western society is antidotal in nature.

Comment

This chapter has been mainly concerned with the evolutionary background of *Homo sapiens* and the fundamental biological characteristics of the species, as manifest in the natural habitat in which it evolved and in which it has spent by far the greater part of its time on Earth. The rest of this volume focuses on humans in the biologically novel environments which have been created by culture, from the advent of farming to the present day, and on the significant changes that have come about during this period in the interrelationships between humankind and the ecosystems of the biosphere.

FURTHER READING

Barash, D.P. (1977). *Sociobiology and behavior*. Elsevier, New York.

Brues, A. (1977). *People and races*. Macmillan, New York.

Cavalli-Sforza, L.L. and Bodmer, W.F. (1971). *The genetics of human populations*. W.H. Freeman, San Francisco.

Chalmers, N. (1979). *Social behaviour in primates*. Edward Arnold, London.

Clark, J.G.D. (1961). *World prehistory: an outline*. Cambridge University Press, Cambridge.

Dahlberg, F. (ed.) (1981). *Woman the gatherer*. Yale University Press, New Haven, CT.

Dawkins, R. (1976). *The selfish gene*. Oxford University Press, Oxford.

Dobzhansky, T. (1962). *Mankind evolving: the evolution of the human species*. Yale University Press, New Haven, CT.

Foley, R. (ed.) (1984). *Hominid evolution and community ecology: prehistoric human adaptation in biological perspective*. Academic Press, London.

Harrison, G.A., Weiner, J.S., Tanner, J.M., Barnicot, N.A. and Reynolds, V. (1987). *Human biology: an introduction to human evolution, variation, growth, and ecology*. 3rd edn. Oxford University Press, London.

Johanson, D.C. and Edey, M.A. (1981). *Lucy: the beginning of humankind*. Granada, London.

Leakey, R.E. (1981). *The making of mankind*. Michael Joseph, London.

Lee, R.B. and DeVore, I. (eds.) (1968). *Man the hunter*. Aldine, Chicago.

Martin, P.S. and Wright, H.E. (eds.) *Pleistocene extinctions: the search for a cause*. Yale University Press, New Haven.

Reynolds, V. (1980). *The biology of human action* 2nd edn. W.H. Freeman, Oxford.

Sahlins, M. (1972). *Stone age economics*. Aldine Publishing Co, Chicago, IL.

Service, E.R. (1962). *Primitive social organisation: an evolutionary perspective*. 2nd edn. Random House, New York.

Spuhler, J.N. (1959). *The evolution of man's capacity for culture*. Wayne State University Press, Detroit.

Turnbull, C. (1965). *Wayward servants: the two worlds of the African pygmies*. Natural History Press, Garden City.

Young, J.Z. (1971). *An introduction to the study of man*. Clarendon Press, Oxford.

CHAPTER 5

THE BIOSPHERE AND HUMAN SOCIETY

From its very beginning, the human aptitude for culture resulted in developments which, in a wide variety of ways, changed the relationships between human populations and the other living components of the ecosystems of which they were a part; and culture also affected the biological and psychosocial conditions of life of human beings themselves.

Among the early ecological consequences of human culture, that which had the greatest impact on ecosystems was probably the deliberate use of fire for driving game and clearing forest. In some regions this activity produced major modification in patterns of vegetation and distribution of fauna. The invention and use of spears, bows and arrows, harpoons and nets must also have affected the interrelationships between human beings and populations of other animal species as, indeed, must have the development of language and its use for communicating observations about the environment. Nevertheless, with the exception of the use of fire in some situations, the ecological impacts of these changes were not great and, in general, human populations fitted into their ecosystems in much the same way as other large omnivorous species.

The effects of culture on humans themselves in the hunter–gatherer phase included impacts on techniques of food-gathering, and especially of hunting; and the use of fire resulted not only in the introduction of cooked foods into the diet, but also in burns becoming an important new form of injury. Culture also brought about significant changes in various non-subsistence activities and in sources of enjoyment, such as dancing, music-making and story-telling. And, perhaps to a lesser extent, it may have given rise to new sources of distress, including the use of unkind words and occasional injury or death from sophisticated weapons like the bow and arrow.

Around 12,000 years ago, some people in south-western Asia, and others in south-eastern Asia, started cultivating plants and keeping animals for food production, and this development marked the beginning of an entirely

95

new era in the interplay between human society and biological systems. As a consequence, human populations no longer fitted into their ecosystems in much the same way as other large omnivorous species. With this *domestic transition*, humans set about, deliberately and systematically, to manipulate biological systems for their own perceived advantage. Moreover, it was not long before people were developing new techniques for transforming various material components of the environment, such as clay and various metals, for the purpose of manufacturing both ornamental and useful objects. Eventually, over the millennia cultural processes gave rise to a spectacular series of new technological devices, ranging from ploughs and pulleys through to clocks, guns, steam engines, internal combustion engines, radios, television sets, computers, nuclear weapons and artificial satellites. All this was made possible by the cumulative nature of the cultural process. Each new invention was a relatively small step forward, based on knowledge and experience that had been accumulating and expanding over hundreds or thousands of years.

An important development which contributed greatly to this accumulative process, as well as to the general elaboration of culture, was the introduction of the art of writing, which is the extension of the symbol-inventing and the symbol-using aspect of the human aptitude for culture to visual signs scratched or otherwise marked on a flat surface. Before this development took place, no more information could be transmitted from one generation to another than could be stored in a few human brains. After the invention and development of writing there came to be no limit to the quantity of information, true or false, which could be stored and subsequently communicated to people living in far away places or to later generations.

The rest of this book (Chapters 6–12) is about the patterns of interplay between human society and biological systems from the time of the introduction of farming some twelve thousand years ago to the present day. However, before proceeding to consider the dynamic interrelationships between human societies and biological systems since the domestic transition, something more must be said about the conceptual framework on which our discussion will be based. The following chapters, like Chapters 1 to 4, are based on the conceptual framework of biohistory which, as discussed in the introduction, reflects what actually happened in the history of life and of civilization on Earth.

Thus, in previous chapters we considered first the *biosphere* – its history, components and processes, and then *humans* as biological beings – and their evolutionary history, biological characteristics and capacity for culture. Now we turn to consider, from the domestic transition onwards, the patterns of interplay between human cultural processes and biological systems, especially the ecosystems of the biosphere and human beings themselves. There are two broad themes reflected in the pages which follow:

(1) interrelationships between the biosphere and society; (2) interrelationships between humans and society.

INTERRELATIONSHIPS BETWEEN THE BIOSPHERE AND SOCIETY

This theme takes the ecosystems of the biosphere as its starting point, and focuses on the interrelationships between these ecosystems and human populations.

Figure 5.1 depicts the basic conceptual framework on which our discussion will be based. It is the extension of the simpler model depicted in Figure 1 of the Introduction (page 3), and it draws attention to some additional features of the biohistorical approach. Thus, it includes a set of variables referred to as *cultural arrangements*, which are an aspect of abstract culture. These include, for example, social hierarchies, institutions and other aspects of social organisation as well as economic arrangements and legislation. The human component of the model has also been divided into two parts: *humans* themselves, as biological organisms, and *human activities*, which include all the things that people actually do. In the context of this volume, we are especially concerned with such human activities as farming, manufacturing, transportation, mining and waging war.

Especially important among the consequences of *human activities*, from the standpoint both of the ecosystems of the biosphere and of human experience, are various human artefacts which include, for example, all tools, ornaments, machines, works of art, buildings and roads.

Also of great significance ecologically is the fact that the human aptitude for culture introduced a new dimension to the metabolism of human populations. Thus, in addition to *biometabolism*, which is the sum total of the inputs and outputs of organic material and energy that flow through humans themselves, human society is characterised by *techno-metabolism*, that is the inputs and outputs of materials and energy that result from technological processes. This includes, for example, the inputs of minerals and fuels and the outputs, not only of the intended products of human activities, but also of technological waste substances.

It is necessary to draw attention to the important distinction in this model between *biophysical actualities* and *cultural abstractions*. Cultural abstractions are those abstract aspects of human situations comprising *culture* itself, including beliefs, assumptions, attitudes, and values, and *cultural arrangements*, such as the economic system, political organisation, and institutional structures. Biophysical actualities embrace all other aspects of the system, including the ecosystems and organisms of the biosphere, human artefacts and humans themselves (e.g. demographic variables, geographic distribution, health and disease etc.) and their activities. Con-

97

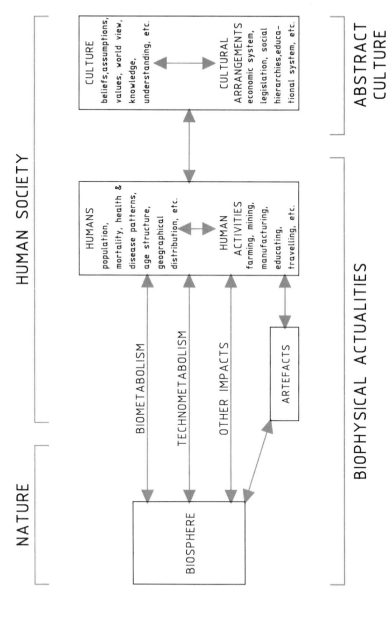

Figure 5.1 Conceptual model of culture – nature interplay. (Note: The term 'biosphere' in this diagram refers to all aspects of the biosphere other than those incorporated under the general heading 'human society'. In reality, of course, humans and their artefacts are all part of the biosphere.)

ventionally biophysical actualities are studied by various kinds of natural scientists, and cultural abstractions by students of the humanities and social sciences.

Clearly, there are very important links between cultural abstractions and biophysical actualities. For example, the value system of a society has important connections with its economic and political arrangements, and these in turn influence human activities which then have impacts on the biosphere. Appreciation of the distinction between these two aspects of human situations, the biophysical and the abstract, is an important aspect of the conceptual approach of biohistory, and it is helpful in our efforts to understand the dynamic interrelationships between natural and cultural processes.

Interrelationships between humans and society

This theme focuses attention on the effects of culturally-induced changes on individual humans, or groups of humans, as biological systems, and on the part played by individual humans, as biological organisms, in the societal process.

In considering this dimension of human situations it is useful to recognise three groups of variables which have to do with the immediate life experience and characteristics of human individuals or groups. These are referred to as: (1) the *biopsychic state*, (2) *personal* (or *immediate*) environment, and (3) the *behaviour pattern*. The last two sets of variables are, for some purposes, considered together under the single heading, *life conditions*.

The *biopsychic state* is the actual state of body and mind of an individual at any given time. It incorporates all aspects of the human organism that comprise health and well-being, and it includes both tangible or measurable variables (e.g. blood pressure, state of teeth, body weight, nutritional state) and intangible variables (e.g. sense of personal involvement, sense of being deprived, knowledge, understanding, values and aspirations).

The immediate (or personal) environment is that part of the total environment which impinges directly on an individual and which he or she experiences directly. It includes both material variables (e.g. air quality, noise levels) and psychosocial and intangible variables (e.g. family support, messages from the media).

The *behaviour pattern* is what an individual actually does and how he or she spends his or her time (e.g. physical work, sleeping and resting pattern, social interaction, creative behaviour, passive recreation).

Some components of the *life conditions* (i.e. personal environment and behaviour pattern), such as the quality of the air in the immediate environment or an individual's level of physical activity, are important influences on the biopsychic state. Another important influence in some

99

situations is an individual's *perception* of the components of his or her life conditions. For example, certain kinds of music may be a source of pleasure for some people, and a source of distress for others.

An individual's life conditions, and hence indirectly his or her biopsychic state, are greatly influenced by the properties of the *total environment* – that is the properties of society and of the surrounding biophysical environment. Individuals can be regarded as being separated from the total environment by a series of *filters* which determine what aspects of the total environment impinge directly on them and become part of their immediate environments. These filters may be cultural (e.g. food taboos) or economic (e.g. income).

The biopsychic state of humans is affected not only by their current life conditions, but also, of course, by their previous life conditions, as well as by their genetic constitution (Figure 5.2).

Arrangement of remaining chapters

In the present chapter, after introducing the four ecological phases of human existence, we will briefly summarise, mainly at a global level, the *demographic* aspects of the human condition since the domestic transition. The next three chapters are concerned with the interrelationships between human society and the biosphere and deal with three classes of societal activities in this context as follows: Chapter 6 – *Farming*; Chapter 7 – *Industrial activities*; and Chapter 8 – *Warfare*. Chapter 9 is concerned mainly with the societal organisation of human populations since the domestic transition. The next two chapters discuss the relationships in history between individual humans, as biological beings, and the societies in which they live. Thus Chapter 10 deals with some of the more material or tangible aspects of these relationships, while Chapter 11 focuses on psychosocial, behavioural and intangible dimensions. In the final chapter we will attempt an overall synthesis and raise some fundamental questions about the future of humankind.

THE FOUR ECOLOGICAL PHASES OF HUMAN EXISTENCE

The history of humankind, seen in biohistorical perspective, falls naturally into four different phases: *the primeval* (or *hunter–gatherer*) phase; the *early farming phase*; the *early urban phase*; and the *modern high-energy phase*. The classification of societies in terms of these phases is based on differences in the interrelationships between the biosphere and society, and in the interrelationships between humans and society. Although the distinctions between the phases are not always sharp, and occasional societies do not

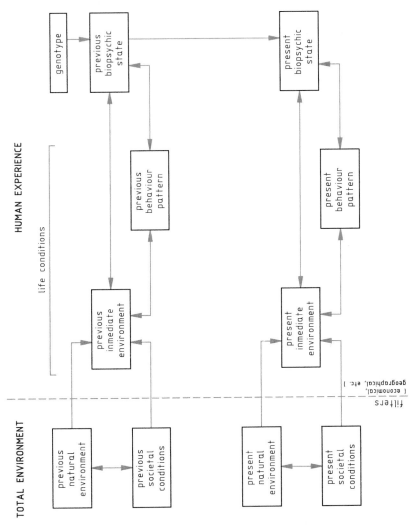

Figure 5.2 Interrelationships between genotype, present and past experience, and biopsychic state

fit neatly into any of the categories, the classification is a useful one. The broad characteristics of the four phases are now described.

Phase one: The hunter–gatherer phase

This is by far the longest of the phases (Figure 5.3), and for many thousands of generations of our ancestors, up to the time of the domestic transition, it represented the only lifestyle and economy known to humankind. We discussed some of its characteristics in Chapter 4.

Phase two: The early farming phase

This covers all forms of farming economy from the first agricultural and horticultural systems up until the time that developments in the high-energy, phase four societies brought about significant ecological changes in farming practices. From the time that cities first came into existence, the early farming phase coexisted alongside the early urban phase.

Phase three: The early urban phase

This dates from about two hundred generations ago, when for the first time some humans began to live in cities, and it persisted until the time of the industrial transition, which was properly underway in Western Europe six or seven generations ago. The early urban phase includes all human populations living in cities during that period. For sustenance, these populations were dependent on early farming communities. The early urban phase was associated with important developments on the societal level, including the institutionalisation of warfare and the division of human populations into numerous, and ever-changing kingdoms and empires. It was also associated with the continual growth in trade in raw materials and manufactured commodities between different societies that were often separated by many hundreds of kilometres.

Phase four: The high-energy phase

This phase began with the industrial transition and it is, ecologically and economically, the dominant phase in the modern world today. It is characterised by very high and increasing rates of use of material resources and of extrasomatic energy (mainly in the form of fossil fuels) which is used for driving various kinds of machines. The high-energy phase, as defined here, will be by far the shortest of the four phases. Its fundamental ecological characteristics are unsustainable. If the human species does not become

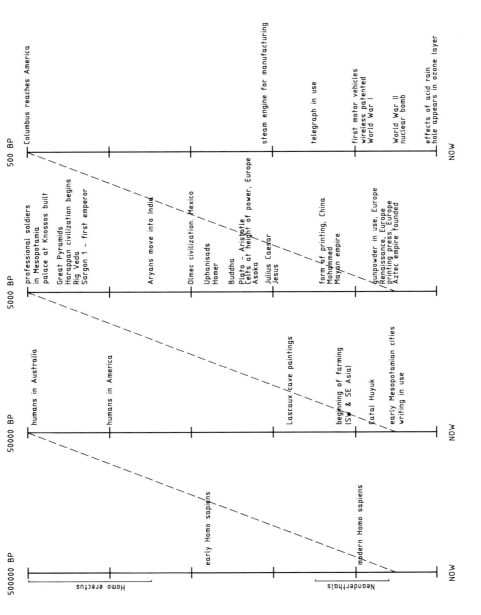

Figure 5.3 Some major developments in the history of humankind, from 500,000 years before the present (BP) to the present day. Diagram illustrating the sequence of key cultural developments in this history of modern humankind

103

extinct beforehand, there lies ahead a fifth ecological phase of human existence.

HUMAN POPULATION – DEMOGRAPHIC ASPECTS

Estimates of the total human population at various times in the history of humankind are necessarily very approximate, but the overall picture is clear enough. The number of people alive on earth today (about 5000 million) is probably about one thousand times greater than the number living when the domestic transition began in south-western Asia ten to twelve thousand years ago. At the beginning of the early urban phase, about 3500 BC, the total population of the Earth was probably around 100 million, and by the beginning of the high-energy phase it was about 1000 million. The changes in the total population over the past 10 thousand years are depicted in Figure 5.4, while Figure 5.5 shows the changes over the past 2 thousand years.

These population perspectives can be expressed in a number of different ways. For example, estimates can be made of the rate of population increase at different periods in human history, as shown in Table 5.1.

Another way of describing the trends is in terms of population doubling time. During the early farming and early urban phases the average doubling time for the global population was around 1500 years. In 1650 the doubling time was about 200 years. By 1850 it was 80 years, in 1930 it was 45 years, and in 1975 it was 36 years. Finally, we may note that the population is now increasing about 10 times as fast as during the period of the transition from the early urban to the high-energy phase – that is from 1650 to 1830, and about 40 times as fast as the period from the domestic transition to the beginning of the high-energy phase.

We shall discuss in Chapter 10 the main biological factors which lie behind the changing level of the human population since the introduction of farming. Here let us simply note that, while the early farming and early urban societies offered significant protection from the causes of death typical of the primeval phase, they were also associated with life conditions which favoured other causes of sickness and mortality, mainly in the form of contagious diseases, malnutrition and starvation. This was especially the case for the early urban societies. The situation in the modern high-energy societies is entirely different, in that the chief causes of death in early farming and early urban societies have been largely overcome through improvements in life conditions and through various cultural adaptive processes. As a result, there has been a great increase in life expectancy at birth, which is now above 76 years in some populations. A far higher proportion of babies born now grow up to reach reproductive age, and thus contribute to population growth, not only by surviving longer

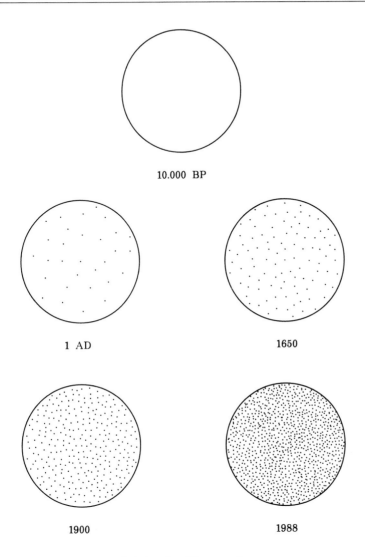

10.000 BP

1 AD

1650

1900

1988

1 dot = 5 million people

Figure 5.4 Human population changes over the past 10,000 years

themselves but also eventually by adding their offspring to the population pool.

There has been a tendency to over-emphasise the role that vaccination, chemotherapy and the use of antibiotics has played in the lowering of death rates in the recent high-energy phase of human history. Certainly these

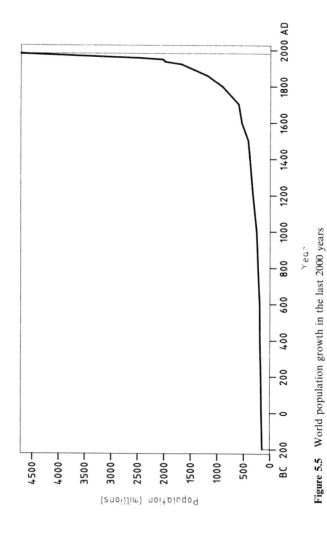

Figure 5.5   World population growth in the last 2000 years

Table 5.1 Rate of population increase at different periods of history

Period in human history	Additional number of people per year
Primeval (hunter–gatherer) phase	50
Early farming and early urban phase	50,000
From 1650 to 1960	7,000,000
From 1960 to 2000	90,000,000

cultural adaptive measures have played a part, but a far greater contribution has been made by the new standards of public and private hygiene – standards which are necessary to counteract the effects of high population density on the susceptibility of humans to contagious diseases. Improved nutrition has probably also played a very important part.

The rate of population growth or decline is also affected, of course, by the fertility rate – that is, by the number of babies produced by each adult female in the population. We can recognise in the high-energy phase of human society two sub-phases in this regard. In the early days of this phase, birth rates were high, and this fact, together with declining death rates, resulted in relatively rapid growth of populations. In the first decade of the present century, for example, the crude birth rate in England and Wales was about 30 per 1000.

However, this pattern of high birth rates and low death rates with consequent rapid population growth did not persist in most of the developed regions of the world. It gave way, in the second sub-phase of the high-energy phase, to a pattern characterised by low death rates, low fertility rates, and only small annual increases in population. The crude birth rate in England and Wales in 1976 was 11.9 per 1000.

The major factor determining fertility rates in the high-energy societies, in sharp contrast to the situation with respect to mortality rates, is personal choice – that is, the decision whether or not to have children. Personal choice is itself influenced, of course, by cultural variables, including economic pressures and religious beliefs. Another influence is technology and the availability of contraceptive devices (although the main technique accounting for the fall in fertility rates in England in the early part of this century is said to have been *coitus interruptus*). Advances in biomedical research have now resulted in the widespread use of hormonal contraceptive pills.

In many developing regions of the world today, where death rates have fallen markedly as a consequence of certain influences emanating from the high-energy societies, the birth rates remain high. This situation is resulting in a steady increase in the proportion of the world's population living in the developing regions (Figure 5.6). In 1982 the population of the world as a whole was growing at a rate of 1.7 per cent per year. The rate in developed regions was 0.6 per cent per year and in developing areas it was 2.2 per

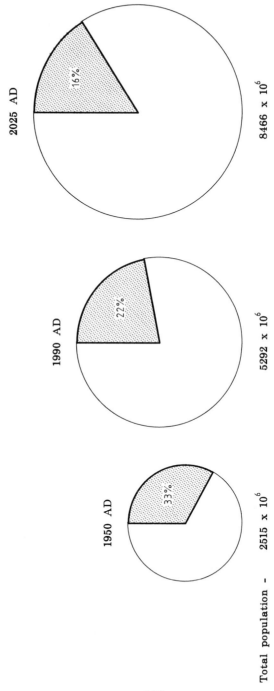

Total population -   2515 x 10⁶

Figure 5.6   Recent and predicted growth of population, and shares of more developed (shaded sections) and less developed regions

cent of more per year. It has been estimated that by 2000 AD, four-fifths of the world's population will be living in today's developing countries.

These differences in birth rates are also reflected in the different age structures of human populations in developed and developing regions, as shown in the population pyramids in Figure 5.7. The much higher proportion of young people in the developing regions is due partly to higher birth rates and partly to the fact that a significant increase in life expectancy in these regions has been a relatively recent development. An import implication of the present age structure in the developing areas is the fact that the high proportion of young people will result in an increase in the number of births in the population when this group reaches maturity, even if by that time they are planning to keep their families small.

It is self-evident that the population of the human species on Earth cannot continue to increase indefinitely. At some time it must stop growing, and we can only hope that this change will come about deliberately, and not as a consequence of large-scale catastrophe.

An important demographic change which has come about quite recently is the great increase in the proportion of people living in cities. Even up to the mid 19th century the great majority of the population of industrialising countries lived in rural settlements, and on the global scale only about 2 per cent of the human population were urban dwellers. In 1987 the proportion of the world's population resident in cities is around 40 per cent, and it is predicted that by the year 2000 it is likely to be 60 per cent.

People on the move

While it is probably true to say that the great majority of people that have ever existed have spent all their lives within, say, 500 kilometres of their place of birth, it is also a fact that migration, often over very long distances, has been one of the most outstanding and significant features of human history. Some of these movements have been peaceful, but others have involved a great deal of violence and homicide; and while most of them have been voluntary, others have been forced on people by other dominant human groupings, such as autocratic governments and slave-traders.

We know that at least by 500,000 years ago populations of *Homo erectus* had spread out, from whatever starting point, to cover an area from Java in the east, to France and Kenya in the west. And our own kind of humans, *Homo sapiens sapiens* had set up residence in all five continents at least by 30,000 years ago – and possibly considerably before that time. This does not mean, of course, that individual human beings necessarily covered great distances; the expansion was clearly to some extent an incremental process. This applies, for example, to the migration of the Danubian farming people who worked their way up the river valleys from the south to the north of

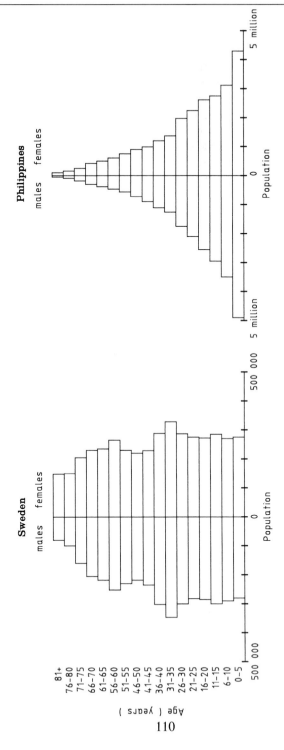

Figure 5.7 Population by sex- and age-groups in Sweden and the Philippines, 1980

Europe (see page 120). It has been estimated that their average rate of progress was less than 1 kilometre per year.

Movement by boat became a significant factor in human migratory movements from an early date. Already by 4000 BC it was important in the Mediterranean; and during the 3rd millennium BC the builders of the megalithic tombs had spread northwards by boat from Spain along the coasts of western Europe to the British Isles, and then eastwards as far as the Baltic Sea. It also seems likely that the Sumerians who built the earliest cities in Mesopotamia between 3500 and 3000 BC had migrated to the region by sea, presumably along the shores of the Persian Gulf.

It is clear that at the time when the first civilizations were coming into existence about two hundred generations ago the racial distinctions between human populations in different parts of the world, involving colour of skin, hair and eyes, general stature, and facial characteristics, were already well established, as indeed they had been for tens of thousands of years. Moreover, it is also clear that there existed throughout the world at that time a wide range of quite different languages. Consequently, the migrations have always resulted in a redistribution and mixing of both genetic and cultural traits. In view of the amount of migratory movement that has taken place over the past 5000 years, it is perhaps remarkable that the racial differences between populations in different regions have persisted to the extent that they have, and indeed that so very many distinct languages are still spoken the world over. These facts generally seem to indicate that, with a few notable exceptions, the proportion of people actually participating in these migrations has usually been very small.

In the Pacific region, long-distance migration by boat was underway well before urban centres came into existence in the region. The migrants were basically of Mongoloid origin, although with some Melanesian admixture, especially in the west. They possessed remarkable navigational skills and, starting from the land masses in the northwest corner of the ocean, they spread south-eastwards, so that virtually all the inhabitable islands were eventually occupied, even though separated from each other by many hundreds of kilometres. By the 4th century AD these people had reached Easter Island, and New Zealand was first occupied between 740 and 1000 AD. Similar people moved westward and populated Madagascar.

A particularly notable episode was the migration of people speaking Indo-European languages that began late in the 3rd millennium BC. They apparently originated from somewhere to the north-east of the Black Sea and most of them are believed to have been fair-skinned with blue eyes and fair (or red) hair. By 2000 BC a group of them, known as the Hittites, had reached Anatolia. Further waves continued to move west into Europe, and their language ultimately formed the basis of all the main European languages, from Celtish, Latin and ancient Greek, to modern French,

Italian, English and German. About 1500 BC groups of Indo-Europeans, calling themselves Aryans, migrated eastwards into India, where they encountered, and possibly destroyed, the Harrapan civilization in the Indus Valley, and eventually spread through most of the Indian subcontinent where they became the dominant class. Sanskrit and modern Hindi are Indo-European languages.

For 3000 years or more, the Eurasian steppes – that is, the grasslands extending from the plains of Hungary in the west to the Gobi desert in the east – were the source of wave after wave of barbarian invaders and migrants moving outwards in all directions, except to the north. The early civilization of Mesopotamia was continually subject to raids by people from the steppe-lands to the north-east and, when successful, the invaders often set themselves up as a dominant ruling class. In the second century BC bands of Huns from Mongolia were constantly invading China, and in the 3rd century AD they were moving into Europe. They reached the Volga in 250 AD, and Gaul and Italy in the 4th century, and they were not finally stopped in Europe until the death of their leader, Attila, in 453 AD. Further waves of people from the Eurasian steppes invaded Europe in the 7th and 8th centuries. In the 13th and 14th centuries Mongol tribesmen under Genghis Khan and his successors moved into and conquered populations over vast areas to the west, the south and the east.

While clearly these vigorous people from the Eurasian steppe-lands were highly successful biologically, militarily and politically, it is not known how many of them were involved in the migrations, nor how great was their influence on the genetic structure of the populations which they conquered.

In terms of sheer numbers, none of the migrations so far mentioned rivalled two migratory movements of the late 19th and early 20th centuries. One of these involved massive movements of people from China north into Manchuria and south into south-east Asia. Although precise information is not available, this movement certainly involved many million persons. The other great and demographically significant, movement consisted of the spread and expansion of Caucasians from Europe to all corners of the globe. This began with the exploits of the navigational adventurers from Portugal, Spain, Britain, France and Holland in the late 15th and early 16th centuries and, in particular, with the European discovery of the American continent and, 2 centuries later, of Australia and New Zealand. Europeans began to settle in North America in the 16th century and in South America early in the 17th century. In Australia and New Zealand European settlement began in 1788 and 1790 respectively. In southern Africa the Dutch started to settle in 1632, and the English in 1788.

In North America and Australia the Europeans largely displaced the local native populations. Their biological advantage was partly due to their technology and weaponry, but it was also the consequence of the fact that they introduced into the local populations a series of devastating infectious diseases, diseases to which they themselves were, for historical reasons, relatively resistant. In Mexico, for instance, smallpox wiped out at least half of the local population in the first few years after initial European contact. The same thing happened throughout the world when Europeans established contact with populations that had been for a long time isolated from the main Eurasian population mass. A classic example was the measles epidemic in Fiji in 1870 which killed 25 per cent of native Fijians.

Associated with the voluntary migration of Europeans to the Americas, was the involuntary migration of Africans to the same region as slaves. It has been estimated that between 1451 and 1870 about 11 million slaves were taken from Africa, of which 9.6 million were still alive when they reached the American coast. In 1850 about 11 per cent of the population of the USA was black.

Between 1850 and 1960 – the great period of voluntary European migration – 60 million people left the continent to settle in far-away lands. This figure represents about a fifth of the population of Europe at the beginning of this period.

Largely as a consequence of these developments, the Caucasian population of the world increased 5.4 times between the years 1750 and 1930, while in the same period the Asian population increased 2.3 times and the African population less than 2 times. By 1930 the proportion of Caucasians who did not live in Europe was one-third; and in 1970 it was more than half. At present more than one-fifth of Africans live outside Africa.

FURTHER READING

Borrie, W.D. (1972). Population, environment and society. *Sir Douglas Robb Lectures.* Auckland University Press, Auckland.

Davis, K. (1965). The urbanisation of the human population. *Scientific American*, **213**(3), pp.41–53.

Davis, K. (1974). The migrations of human populations. *Scientific American*, **231**(3), pp.93–105.

McNeill, W.H. (1976). *Plagues and peoples.* Anchor Doubleday, New York.

CHAPTER 6

FARMING

Around ten or twelve thousand years ago cultural processes gave rise to a development that was to have far-reaching consequences for humanity and for the biosphere: it was the introduction of *farming*. Since in essence this development involved the domestication of certain plants and animals and of human beings themselves we shall refer to it as the *domestic transition*.

Although farming took on many different forms in different places around the world, with respect both to details of technique and to the kinds of animals or plants that were farmed, all early farming activities consisted in essence of the deliberate redistribution of plant and animal species in a given area, aimed at increasing the local concentrations of species of food value to humans, and to lower concentrations of species of little or no food value. As a result, instead of covering big distances in search of food, people spent most of their time in one place, tending the desired plants and animals and keeping out unwanted species. Special techniques were developed in different regions, such as hoeing, irrigation, and eventually ploughing and manuring, to enhance the rate of plant growth.

The end result of this change in subsistence behaviour was that a given area of land yielded much more food for humans than had been the case in hunter–gatherer ecosystems. Thus, a much larger proportion of the energy fixed by photosynthesis in the local area was available, as somatic energy, to pass into and flow through human beings; and, as a result, farming systems could support much higher population densities of humans. As indicated in Chapter 4, population densities of hunter–gatherer communities ranged from around 0.02 to 0.2 persons per km^2. In early farming societies they ranged from 25 to 1000 persons per km^2. It is even claimed that one system – peasant farming in southern China – could support 7500 persons per km^2. It is worth noting, however, that the amount of food produced per hour of human effort in early farming societies was in general not very different from that acquired by hunter–gatherers in the same length of time.

115

Two basic techniques were, and still are, used for the cultivation of plants for food. One of these, known as *seed agriculture*, involves sowing seeds at a certain time of year, and later, after the growth of the plant, harvesting the new grain within a relatively short period. In the other basic technique, *vegeculture*, plants are reproduced by vegetative propagation, which involves cutting off parts of the plant, (e.g. rhizomes) and replanting them elsewhere. Vegeculture is practised especially in tropical regions, and the three main centres of tropical vegeculture are south-east Asia, West Africa and South America. In vegeculture harvesting may be a relatively continuous process going on at all times of year. Since roots stay healthy in the ground, there is less need for storage. Vegeculture has been used for many tropical roots, such as yams, sweet potatoes, manioc, arrowroot and taro. A very different form of farming is the kind of *pastoralism* where normadic people move with their flocks or herds of domestic ruminants over great distances. This is especially characteristic of arid and semi-arid areas. Of course, many practices fall between these extremes.

THE BEGINNINGS

Present evidence suggests that groups of people started farming independently in at least three regions of the world: south-western Asia, south-eastern Asia and Middle America.

The earliest evidence of agriculture based on the cultivation of seeds, notably wheat and barley, and the domestication of goats, sheep and cattle is found in fairly high country in a broad area known today as the Fertile Crescent, extending from Greece to a region about 2400 kilometres to the east and to the south of the Caspian Sea, as well as in the uplands flanking the valleys of the Tigris and Euphrates rivers (Figure 6.1).

It is likely that the shift from an economy based on hunting and gathering to one in which human populations were dependent mainly on farming was a slow process – possibly extending over a thousand years or more. There is evidence that people living in southern Egypt were collecting and grinding grain from barley nearly 18,000 years ago, and their tools included not only grinding stones and some mortars and pestles, but also objects that appear to be the blades of sickles, presumably used for reaping barley and perhaps other grasses. It is not impossible that these people were already cultivating barley.

By 13,000 to 11,000 years ago some people in south-western Asia (Palestine and Syria) were living in small hamlets. They, too, used sickles for cutting stems of wild cereals, and again it is possible that some of the 'crop' had been deliberately planted near their homes. Certainly, by around 9000 years ago the inhabitants of this area were cultivating wheat and barley and keeping sheep and goats. In one farming settlement located in

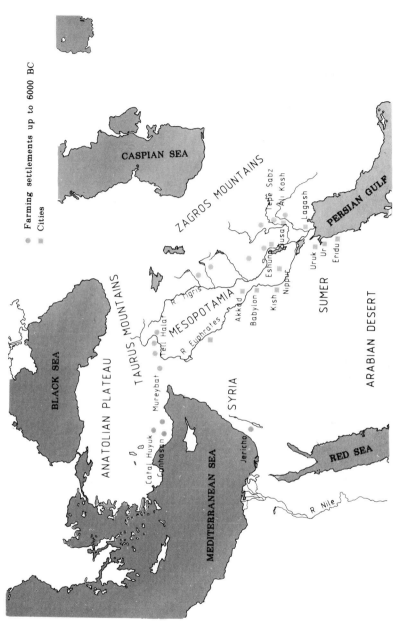

Figure 6.1 Early sites of farming and urbanisation in south-western Asia

Syria, called Abu-Hureyra, the population grew to be several thousand. The food of these people consisted mainly of wheat, barley, lentils, gazelles, goats and sheep. They appear to have traded with communities in other regions, and excavations at the site have revealed jadeite, serpentine, agate, malachite and obsidian from Turkey, as well as turquoise from Sinai, soap stone from the Lagos Mountains and cowrie shells from the Mediterranean or the Red Sea.

Another especially interesting place is Çatal Hüyük, which lies just south of the Taurus Mountains in southern Anatolia and where, between 7000 and 6000 BC, there existed a thriving community consisting perhaps of 5000 people. Their economy was based on the cultivation of barley, wheat, peas and lentils, and they kept sheep, goats, and dogs and, later in the period, cattle. They also hunted wild cattle, deer, asses, sheep, pigs and leopards. The rectangular mud-brick houses at Çatal Hüyük were built very close together and usually had a store room containing a bin for holding grain. The entrances to the houses were in the roof. The women and children wore necklaces, armlets, bracelets and anklets made of beads as well as pendants made from a wide range of different kinds of stones and shells and, towards the end of the period, copper and lead. Cosmetics were apparently widely used and consisted of red ochre, blue azurite, green malachite and possibly galena. Mirrors were made of highly polished obsidian. There is also evidence of a high level of technical competence in the manufacture of textiles, and at least three different styles of weaving were practised, using wool from sheep.

In southeastern Asia the domestication of plants for food production was well established by 7000 BC, and it is likely that already by 9000 or 10,000 BC people living in Thailand had an advanced knowledge of farming methods. Farming in this region was different from that in southwestern Asia, due to differences in local fauna and flora and in the climate. Instead of cultivating wheat and barley, these farmers grew various roots, such as taro and yams, as well as cucumbers, peppers, bottle gourds, and different kinds of beans. They also deliberately encouraged the growth of banana, coconut, sago and bread-fruit trees. Pigs and poultry were domesticated in this region.

The first signs of farming in northern China date from the 6th to the 5th millennium BC, when people practised seed agriculture with millet and also kept pigs.

It is uncertain where rice was first domesticated, although so far the earliest evidence of it comes from Thailand and is dated around 3500 BC. The cultivation of wet rice (as distinct from upland rice, which like other cereals, relies on rainfall) eventually came to involve fairly elaborate methods, including irrigation, transplanting, terracing, the levelling of fields and the construction of embankments, although less intensive cultivation is possible without these techniques.

In the Americas, it is likely that maize had been domesticated by 6000 or 5000 BC in the region which today comprises southern Mexico, Guatemala and Honduras, and by 3000 BC squash, beans, avocados, gourds, pumpkins and chillies were also cultivated. However, hunting and gathering remained the main source of food in this region at least until about 3000 BC. In the coastal areas of Peru in South America, squash, beans, chillies, peppers and cotton were grown by the 5th millennium BC, although fish was also an important source of nutrition in these parts. In the lowlands to the east of the Andes, manioc, sweet potato and arrowroot were farmed, and on the Andean plateaus the potato became established as the main crop around 1000 BC.

It is not known whether farming in Africa had independent origins. We noted above the possibility that people in southern Egypt may have cultivated barley long before it was grown in the Fertile Crescent. In West Africa vegeculture of root crops – mainly the indigenous yam – was practised by the 5th millennium BC, and cereal production was carried out in the savannah country north of the tropical rain forest by the 3rd millennium BC. The climate in this region was unsuitable for wheat and barley, and the crops grown were local millets and sorghum.

We do not know why some groups of humans adopted farming as a means of acquiring food. The reason is unlikely to have been because farming was seen as easier or more enjoyable, since in general it was more arduous and often more monotonous than hunting and gathering. A possible explanation is that it began in a haphazard way, at a time when the climate was especially favourable for hunting and gathering. Because food was plentiful, people found themselves living relatively settled lives, eventually building themselves permanent homes of mud or stone. In these circumstances some of them may have experimented with sowing seeds of wild cereals, or propagating plants by vegeculture. The sedentary lifestyle would also have allowed them to bring home orphan animals from the bush and rear them in captivity. As time went on, the techniques of cultivation of foodplants and of the farming of animals would have improved, although for a long time these domesticated sources of food would have formed only a small part of the diet. At the same time, because the settled lifestyle was less hazardous than that of the nomadic hunter–gatherer and because transient illness was less of a survival disadvantage, the populations of the settlements are likely to have increased; and the additional food provided by farming would then have become useful for supporting the larger numbers of people. Eventually the cultivated plants and domesticated animals would no longer have been merely incidental –

they would have been *necessary* for survival: and farming then became a serious business.

THE SPREAD OF FARMING

It was several thousand years before farming spread from its few centres of origin to all regions of the Earth. In fact it did not become firmly established in Australia until about 200 years ago.

When the inhabitants of southwestern Asia were beginning to settle down in little hamlets as a prelude to serious farming, the people of northern and western Europe, known respectively as Magdelenians and Kunda, were still leading a relatively mobile existence, following herds of reindeer over the open grassland that covered the plains. Then, around 8300 BC the ice sheets began their final melting, and a significant increase in the temperature of the region occurred in the course of only a few generations. As a result, the grasslands were invaded by forest, and the deer hunters were forced to adapt their lifestyle to the changed conditions. They did so by reverting to an economy based on mixed hunting and gathering, and by developing an impressive array of new techniques for extracting food from rivers and from the sea. Some of them adopted a relatively sedentary existence close to or within forests, and mainly along river valleys and by the sea shore. The people of this *mesolithic culture*, known today as the Maglemosians, were artistically inclined, decorating objects of bone, antler and amber with engravings of animals and humans and with various geometrical designs reminiscent of the art of their reindeer-hunting ancestors.

Farming spread into Europe from Anatolia, Greece and south-western Asia by two means. On the one hand, groups of people who practised agriculture migrated northwards and westwards, especially along the valleys of the great rivers, exploiting the vast beds of loess that had been laid down by the strong winds of the glacial epoch, from Serbia and Poland in the east to Belgium in the west. These people pushed along the Danube into the area which today incorporates central Hungary, lower Austria and Bohemia, and then on westward as far as the Rhineland and the Maas. By the 5th millennium BC they had reached southern Germany and Holland. They grew einkorn, emmer, barley, peas, beans and flax, and they kept goats, sheep, cattle and pigs. Meanwhile, other farming people were also moving up through Spain and Switzerland to France and eventually Britain. By 2500 BC some of them had reached the southern edges of the vast coniferous forests of Scandinavia and Russia.

The other means by which farming spread was by acculturation, as distinct from colonisation. The Maglemosian people eventually took it up, adapting it to their local situation and also to their own cultural background. Needless to say, these two processes were not likely to have been entirely separate. The Danubians moving north and west will have met, and probably mixed and interbred with, local people.

About the same time as farming was being introduced into western Europe, it was also creeping southward down the valleys of the Tigris and Euphrates Rivers where it depended not on rainfall, but on the practice of irrigation. Here it would later provide the economic base for the early cities in Sumer and, later on, for the Akkadian and Babylonian empires.

The earliest definite evidence of farming in Egypt, in this case the cultivation of wheat and flax, comes from the Nile Delta and is dated about 4900 BC. By about 4000 BC, farming was carried out much further west along the North African Coast. It did not spread into southern Africa, south of the tropical forests, until the Bantu occupation of the area, which took most of the 1st millennium AD.

Farming also spread eastwards from the Fertile Crescent, and there is evidence of farmers in northwestern India around 3500 BC. By 3000 BC there were farms on the plains of the lower Indus where use was made of the summer floods to grow wheat and barley. From here farming spread southward into the Indian Peninsula, although it apparently did not reach the upper Ganges area to the east until about 1100 BC, and the middle Ganges until about the 8th or 9th century BC. The earliest signs of rice in the Ganges Delta are dated at around 700 BC. Available evidence suggests that early agriculture in India was the result of diffusion from southwestern Asia, although it also involved the local domestication of rice and cotton as well as the cultivation of some unexplained imports of crops from Africa.

The southeastern and eastern Asian farming complexes – that is tropical vegeculture and wet rice cultivation – spread early on from the centre or centres of origin in all directions over the mainland, and also into eastern Melanesia and Polynesia. In most areas, wet rice cultivation displaced vegeculture and eventually came to be the main source of sustenance for the human populations of the Far East.

In the Americas, the cultivation of maize, squash and beans had, by 500 AD, spread as far north as the Great Lakes and as far south as the Rio de la Plata, between Argentina and Uruguay.

KINDS OF FARMING AND CHANGING TECHNOLOGY

Apart from the distinction between the two broad categories of plant farming – seed agriculture and vegeculture – various other important differences exist between the techniques of preindustrial farming as practised at different times and in different places. It is likely that all regimes for the cultivation of food plants were initially based on shifting agriculture. A small area of forest land would be cleared of trees or other unwanted plant species, and the desired crops would be planted or sown. After a number of seasons, yields would fall because of depletion of nutrients in the soil (this, in turn, being due to the fact that plant material was removed from the plot for human consumption, thereby breaking natural nutrient cycles); and the farmers would then clear another site, and so begin all over again. This procedure would be repeated a number of times, and eventually the original plot would have recovered its fertility and could be used again. This system, known as *shifting* or *slash-and-burn agriculture*, was used both for vegeculture and seed culture.

In the case of the cultivation of wet rice shifting was unnecessary, because irrigation brought in a fresh supply of plant nutrients each season. Irrigation was also used for cultivating other grain crops. By soon after 3000 BC it formed the basis of the agricultural production which supported big urban populations in the great alluvial valleys of the Tigris and Euphrates rivers, the Nile, the Indus, and later, around the 13th or 14th century BC, the Yellow River in China.

The primitive method of sowing grain by dropping the seeds into holes made in the ground with a pointed stick gave way early on to hand furrowing, a technique which lasted for many millennia until the invention of the wooden plough, a device that was at first drawn along by men, but later by oxen. It is not known when it was first introduced, but it was definitely in use both in Mesopotamia and in Egypt by 3000 BC.

The plough came into use in Northern Europe some time between and 3000 and 2000 BC. The later development of the heavy wheeled metal plough, fitted with a mould-board (which turns over the sliced soil), further increased the effectiveness of the device. It is noteworthy that in northern Europe one of the advantages of ploughing is that it aids drainage, while in the southern part of the continent its value lies partly in the fact that it reduces water loss through evaporation.

In the early days of cultivation of cereal crops in southwestern Asia and in Europe and India, shifting agriculture was necessary because of the inevitable decline of soil fertility after a few harvests. Eventually, however, this practice was replaced by the alternating two-field system. This consisted in essence of a drastic shortening of the period of fallow, made possible mainly through the effect on soil fertility of the manure of farm animals. This development, as well as other improvements in the methods of cultivating soil, led to bigger yields per unit area, and it allowed people to stay permanently in the one place, and at higher population densities than had been possible previously.

By the time of the Roman Empire, the two-field system, in which the fields alternated between spring- or winter-sown grain and fallow, was practised in some regions, although there was still much shifting agriculture. By the 6th century, the two-field system existed over most of the continent of Europe. By the 8th century the three-field system had come into use in some areas. This involved using one field for a winter-sown cereal crop, one for a spring crop, while the third field lay fallow; this system resulted in four harvests in 2 years from an area which would have yielded only three harvests under the two-field system.

Although some modifications in the techniques of farming were introduced in Europe after this time, such as the use of horses as draft animals and the introduction of horse collar and breast plate, the fundamental characteristics of the farming of cereal crops remained basically unchanged until well into the 19th century. With regard to other kinds of crops, the most important developments in European farming before the 19th century were the introduction, about 1500 AD, of maize (or 'corn') and about 1570 AD of the potato. The former came from the central American civilization, and the potato from the highlands of Peru. Both crops eventually made important contributions to the food supply of the growing European population, the potato mainly in the north and maize in the south.

SOME ECOLOGICAL CONSIDERATIONS

Whether or not a farming ecosystem continues to be satisfactorily bioproductive depends on several factors. These include the nature and the depth of the soil in the system, the degree to which nutrients are returned to the soil. Some agricultural systems, such as the mixed farming system of northern Europe and the wet rice system in the Far East, have shown themselves to be remarkably sustainable over long periods of time. In other regions farming has resulted in a progressive decline in bioproduction, sometimes to such an extent that the land has become permanently less productive than it was before human intervention. Examples include the irrigation-based agriculture of Mesopotamia, early farming systems around Carthage in North Africa, terraced farms on hillsides in Greece and southern Italy, and, in more recent times, large areas of semi-arid land in Australia.

The so-called 'marginal' lands are especially vulnerable to ecological damage. Although these areas, which are mainly in arid and semi-arid parts of the world, are characterised by relatively low biological productivity, they still play a vital role in the economies of many countries and the lives of millions of people. They contain more than half of the Earth's stock of cattle, more than a third of its sheep and two-thirds of its goats.

Today almost all the world's marginal lands are in danger of losing their biological productivity as a result of increased pressure from animals and people. Overgrazing by stock is not the only problem. The constant search for wood for cooking purposes is having serious environmental impact, because shrubs and trees play an important role in maintaining the health of arid and semi-arid ecosystems. They protect soil against the direct impact of rain, and thus ensure better water regulation in the soil. Moreover, the fallen leaves and branches enrich the humus content of the soil, and provide a habitat for birds and other animals which play a significant part in the functioning of the ecosystem.

The main causes of degradation in food-producing ecosystems have been erosion and chemicalisation. As discussed in Chapter 2, erosion is a natural phenomenon; it is the process by which, as a result of the action of wind and rain, fragmented rock (sand, gravel, clay etc.) eventually makes its makes its way from its site of origin to the ocean beds. Natural vegetation tends to slow down this process, resulting in the accumulation in some areas of many metres of soil. In more ecologically vulnerable areas, such as the marginal lands mentioned above, and hillsides in the Mediterranean region and around the ancient city of Teotihuacan in Mexico, overgrazing, the over-use of wood and unwise farming practices have sometimes resulted in a massive increase in the rate of erosion, so that soil accumulated over many millennia has been lost within a few years.

Chemicalisation is the term used for the accumulation in the soil of certain chemical substances, mainly sodium compounds, in unnatural concentrations and which interfere with plant growth. A classic example in history is provided by the eventual failure of the Mesopotamian agricultural system in the Tigris and Euphrates valleys, the system which supported the populations of the early Sumerian and Akkadian cities. It is believed that one of the main factors responsible for the collapse of this system was the excessive accumulation of sodium chloride which was brought into the system in dilute solution in river water and which was left behind in the soil as the water evaporated. Deforestation can also result in salinisation by increasing the level of the water table, so that evaporation results in the concentration near the surface of salts present in solution in the underground water.

Another kind of change which can affect the production of a particular food source, plant or animal, is *disease* due to parasitic or pathogenic organisms. In human history this has been a frequent cause of serious, but temporary food shortages, sometimes of severe famine. One reason for this is the fact that high population densities of any particular species of plant or animal are especially susceptible to diseases of this kind. Important examples affecting plant foods in human history have been wheat rust, ergot (a disease of rye) and potato blight. This last was responsible for the great famine in Ireland of 1845 and 1846, which directly or indirectly caused hundreds of thousands of deaths and gave rise to human distress on an immense scale. It also had long-lasting and world-wide political repercussions.

The adaptive reactions of human communities to disasters of this kind have ranged from elaborate rituals aimed at appeasing gods to the

124

application of various chemical substances which, through trial and error, have been found to be helpful. The application of sulphur dust by the farmers of Ancient Greece to prevent or cure wheat rust is an example of the latter.

Crop failure due to drought has also been a frequent cause of under-nutrition in human history. It is said that in China severe famine struck one region or another, on average, once a year over the last 2000 years. Human populations which are nutritionally dependent on a single food source are obviously much more vulnerable to the effects of abnormal weather or plant diseases than are those which have access to a broader range of foodstuffs. Hunter–gatherers are less likely to be severely affected by drought than are farming communities that depend for their sustenance on one annual crop of a single cereal.

From the biological standpoint one of the most obvious impacts of farming (apart from its effect on the size of human populations and on the lifestyle of individuals) has been its influence on the distribution of different kinds of plants and animals on the surface of the planet (Figure 6.2). Most of the plant species now in use in farming systems had been domesticated at least 4000 years ago, but until moderately recently many of them were confined to the regions in which they were first used. In general, before the 15th century diffusion of food plants had been a relatively slow process. Exceptions to this generalisation include rice, which originated in eastern Asia and which was already grown in Mesopotamia in the 1st millennium BC, and citrus fruits which were introduced into the western Mediterranean from the Far East at an early date.

The discovery of America by Europeans was an especially important development in this context, resulting in the introduction into Europe not only of maize and potato, but also of squash, gourds, pumpkins, peppers, chillies and the turkey. It also caused movement in the opposite direction, involving the introduction into the American continent of the cereal crops of Europe, and of cattle, sheep and pigs. Later on, all the main European food sources of the northern hemisphere were introduced to New Zealand and Australia.

Just as new plants and animals were introduced into farming ecosystems, so were local native ones displaced. In Europe, the most striking example of this was the displacement of the dominant group of organisms, namely, the trees of the great forests that had enveloped so much of the continent when the Danubian farmers began moving in around 5000 BC. These farmers cleared small patches of the deciduous forests growing on the light loess soil which they preferred for cultivating their crops, and as the fertility of the soil eventually declined, they moved elsewhere and the forest regenerated. But as the intensity of farming increased, less regeneration was possible, and some fertile regions remained more or less permanently cleared. In the

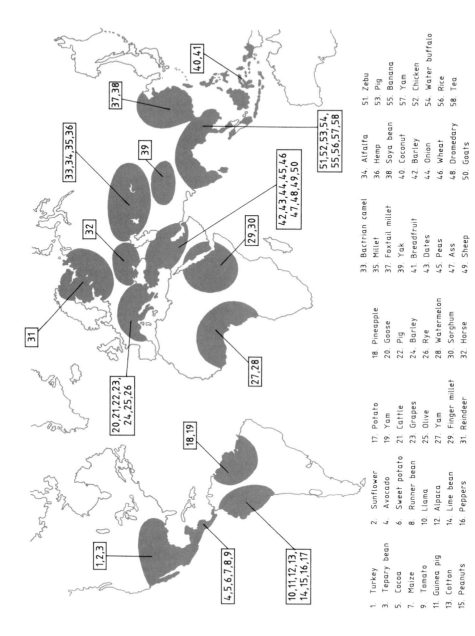

Figure 6.2 Regions of origin of domesticated plants and animals

126

less fertile areas in northern and western Europe where there was a high rainfall deforestation and pastoralism led, early on, to the permanent clearing of areas which became open moorland covered with heath and other low shrubs. However, even in Roman times dense forests still covered most of central and western Europe, and it was not until the early part of the 2nd millennium that 'the great age of land clearance' began – associated with a significant increase in the human population of the region.

It was not only the need for land for food production that brought about the disappearance of forests. As time went on, the demand for timber as fuel and for various other purposes became increasingly important as a motive for felling trees. The pace of industrial activities was quickening. Wood ash, for example, was needed for glass works and for making soap; and timber was used for props in the mining of tin, copper and iron, and charcoal was used for smelting in the metal industry. By the 16th century there were complaints in many places about the shortage of timber.

In the Mediterranean region the clearance of forests came about earlier than it did in the north. The process of forest clearance was already well underway at the time of Homer in the 9th century BC, who likened the noise of a battle to 'the din of woodcutters in the glades of a mountain'. Early in the 4th century BC Plato, referring to the disappearance of forests in Attica, wrote: 'What now remains compared with what then existed, is like the skeleton of a sick man, all the fat and soft earth having been wasted away, and only the bare framework of the land being left'.

The earlier disappearance of trees in the Mediterranean area came about partly because the evergreen forests of the region were easier to clear than the deciduous forests further north, but more particularly because the ecological conditions were less favourable to their rapid regeneration. Among the components of these ecological conditions, along with the nature of the climate and the soil, were the ubiquitous goats which roamed the cleared areas in large numbers. It has been suggested that they effectively destroyed any seedlings that might otherwise have grown into trees to replace those that had been removed by humans. As a result, much of the evergreen forest in the Mediterranean region was transformed early on into the semi-natural brushwood which is known as garigue or maquis. Some authors have suggested that deforestation in Greece and in Italy was an important factor contributing to the decline of Roman and Greek civilization.

FARMING IN THE HIGH-ENERGY SOCIETIES

Despite enormous variation from time to time and from place to place in patterns of societal organisation and land tenure and some gradual increases in yield as a consequence of improved techniques, the basic ecological characteristics of farming remained unchanged throughout most of its history up until the 19th and 20th centuries. But the industrial transition to the fourth, high-energy, phase of human existence ushered in a new era in farming, associated with fundamental changes in agricultural practice, especially in cereal production. This development involved, first and foremost, the use of machines powered by fossil fuels to perform work previously done by humans or draft animals (e.g. ploughing, sowing and harvesting). Another feature of the transition has been a progressively increasing application of artificial fertilizers (mainly nitrogenous, phosphate and potash fertilizers).

The phosphate and potash fertilizers are derived from natural deposits in certain areas of the world. World resources of phosphate rock are considered to be sufficient to last for about 200 years, and potash reserves may be sufficient to last about 5000 years. Nitrogen fertilizers are now made synthetically from atmospheric nitrogen; and although this means that there need be no shortage of nitrogen, the methods used are energy costly and this fact may create problems in the future. The amount of fertilizer used at present is much greater in the developed countries, and the overall global use of artificial fertilizers has increased about five-fold since 1950.

Other changes have included the widespread use of synthetic pesticides to control parasites and diseases due to micro-organisms and the cultivation of new high-yielding varieties of certain crops. All in all, these changes have resulted in considerable increases in yield per unit area. Thus, in the USA, for example, the yield of maize (corn) per hectare increased almost three-fold during the period 1900 to 1980, due mainly to the application of artificial fertilizer and the introduction of new hybrids.

A more striking outcome, however, has been the great increase in yield per hour of human labour. In the early farming phase a typical farming couple produced, like hunter–gatherers, sufficient food for themselves and their families and sometimes a small surplus to contribute to the diet of non-farmers. In the high-energy phase the situation is very different. In the United States one farm worker in the 1970s produced sufficient food for 50 people. Australia is an extreme case, where one farmer now produces enough food for 85 people, two-thirds of whom live outside Australia. It is worth noting, however, that this individual farmer is often at work for 10 hours or so per day, unlike his or her farming ancestors of 200 years ago, who were probably in the fields on average 3–4 hours per day. Moreover, his work is dependent on the work of countless other individuals involved in the design and manufacture of tractors and other machinery, in extracting or preparing artificial fertilizers and in transporting material, often over many thousands of kilometres, to and from the farm.

In the modern high-energy phase of society, therefore, the great majority of human beings do not participate in direct subsistence activity and so are far removed in their experience from the realities of food acquisition and production. Nevertheless, they all have to eat, and most of them engage in indirect subsistence activity in order to earn money with which to purchase food.

The average person in typical high-energy societies consumes, directly and indirectly, four-fifths of a tonne of cereal grain per year; but only about 10 per cent of this is eaten directly, in the form of grain itself. Most of it is used to feed animals, and is thus later consumed in the form of meat, eggs and milk. Through this process, only about 10 per cent of the food calories initially contained in the grain reaches human beings. The cereal-based farming systems of the high-energy societies also produce a broad range of vegetables and fruits for human consumption.

The situation has been different in the developing regions of the world, which include most of the rice-growing areas. Here farming has remained labour-intensive. Nevertheless, considerable increases in yield have been achieved in some regions of the Third World as a consequence of the so-called *Green Revolution*. This began in the 1960s and it continued to have an important influence on agricultural trends during the 1970s. It was the result of scientific advances in the high-energy societies and is based on the development of high-response varieties (HRV) of wheat and rice, and also to some extent of maize and millet, as well as the increasing use of artificial fertilizers and pesticides. In the case of wheat, new high-yielding 'dwarf' varieties developed in Japan were introduced into various developing countries. Big doses of fertilizer, which in the conventional strains of wheat produce heads heavier than the plants can support, result in similar heavy heads of grain in the dwarf varieties. In the case of these new varieties, however, these heads were effectively supported by the shorter, sturdier stems. Following the establishment of the International Rice Research Institute in the Philippines, similar new varieties of rice were produced.

The use of the new varieties resulted in an increase in the Asian food supply of around 16 million tonnes in the mid-1960s, enough to feed 90 million people. In India, for instance, there was a doubling of the wheat crop in a 6-year period; and there was also a remarkable increase in Pakistan, and some increase in the Philippines, Sri Lanka, Indonesia, and Malaysia. Another country that was much affected was Mexico, where the Japanese dwarf varieties of wheat were first tried out.

Unfortunately, the relief provided by the Green Revolution to the problem of food shortages in developing countries where the human populations are still growing rapidly can only be temporary. These agricultural systems have reached their new limits of production, and further major improvements in yields seem unlikely. Moreover, the new methods are dependent to an extraordinary degree on continual inputs from outside the local system – especially of energy-costly artificial fertilizers and pesticides. The populations which are dependent on them are therefore often very much at the mercy of political, economic and ecological events in societies far beyond their borders. Another problem is associated with the tendency for the changes in farming practices in these developing areas to benefit the rich rather than the poor. Although the use of high yielding varieties could well be adapted to labour-intensive conditions, in practice it has often resulted in a boost in capital-intensive and energy-intensive mechanisation, giving rise to widespread unemployment. In many situations the introduction of the HRV varieties has made the rich landlords richer and the poor peasants poorer.

From the ecological standpoint, one of the most significant aspects of the modernisation of agricultural systems is the change that has come about in the energetics of crop production. The difference between early farming systems and high-energy agriculture lies partly in the fact that in the latter the input of human and animal *somatic energy* has been largely replaced by *extrasomatic energy*, mainly in the form of liquid fossil fuels, used in machines on the farm (and in the manufacture of the machines elsewhere in society). There is also a significant energy cost inherent in the use of artificial fertilizers when account is taken of the energy used in their extraction or synthesis, in their transport to the farm, and in their mechanical distribution onto the land.

In the early farming societies, a typical ratio of *energy input* (mainly human and/or animal labour) to *energy output* (energy value of the product) would have been between 1:15 and 1:20. Today the ratio in the USA, United Kingdom and Holland ranges between 1:0.5 and 1:0.7. Ninety per cent at least of the energy input in these systems is in the form of fossil fuels. By the time the food reaches the home of the consumer, further energy has been used in transport and in wrapping and, in some cases, in preparation of the food for the consumer. In the USA these factors bring the energy input to energy output ratio down to 1:0.2.

OVERVIEW OF GLOBAL FOOD PRODUCTION IN RECENT YEARS

The total amount of food produced for human consumption has increased dramatically during the past century in response to population growth. While some of this increase has been due to improved farming techniques, it has mainly been the result of increases in the area of cultivated land. Between 1870 and 1960, for example, the arable area, in millions of hectares, increased in selected regions as follows: Europe, from 141 to 157; China, from 82 to 113; India and Pakistan, from 69 to 151; North America, from

Table 6.1 Average daily food energy supply per capita, as a percentage of average requirement (1972–1974)

World	107
All industrialized countries	132
All developing countries	96
Africa	91
Latin America	107
Near East	100
Far East	92

Table 6.2 Rate of change in grain production

Decade	Total (%)	per capita (%)
1950–60	+34	+13
1960–70	+30	+ 6
1970–80	+31	+ 9
1980–90	+17	− 2
1990–2000	+ 9	− 7

81 to 183; Argentina and Uruguay, 0.4 to 24; and Australia, from 0.4 to 12.

The overall food supply between 1972 and 1974 in the world and in different regions is shown in Table 6.1, expressed in terms of the percentage of the average human requirement.

Although the total amount of grain produced in the world as a whole has continued to increase each decade, the rate of increase has fallen off considerably over the past decade. In fact, overall production fell sharply in 1987 and 1988, and the production per capita has decreased each year since 1984. The rate of change in total and per capita grain production by decade since 1950, together with an estimate for the decade 1990–2000, are shown in Table 6.2.

Unless there comes about a sudden increase in mortality, the widening of the gap between population growth and food production is set to continue.

Sustainability of production and some predictions

From the beginning of farming until about the middle of the present century, the area of land cultivated for crops grew at a rate which more or less corresponded to the rate of growth of the world's population. About 11 per cent of the world's land surface is now under cultivation, and for various reasons it is unlikely that this area can ever be greatly increased, and already the rate of expansion of crop land has slowed down markedly. It has been estimated that in the late 1950s crop land was increasing at a rate of about 1 per cent per year, in the 1970s at about 0.3 per cent, and in the 1980s at 0.2 per cent, and that in the 1990s it will be increasing at 0.15 per cent per year. In fact, in some regions of the world, inhabited by one-third of the human population, the area of crop land is already shrinking. The increase in food supply for the growing world population in recent decades has been mainly the result of an increasing yield per unit area.

Many authors believe that a progressive decline in the area of bioproductive land over the next few decades is inevitable unless there come about some fundamental changes in societal arrangements and farming policies. One of the important factors contributing to this decline is soil erosion, which is now taking place at about three times the natural, or pre-agricultural rate. It has recently been estimated that the excess erosion of top soil (rate of soil loss minus rate of soil gain) in the croplands of the world is at present about 25,400 tonnes per year. It is predicted that if this trend is not soon halted there will be widespread food shortage and famine.

There has been a good deal of discussion and debate during recent decades about the potential carrying capacity of the Earth. What is the maximum number of people that could possibly be supported by the biosphere? Views range from those of authors who argue that the present population of around 4000 million is already above that which could be fed on a typical North American diet, to those who believe that the Earth's ecosystems could support nearly 50,000 million people. The prevailing view at present is that it might be possible to double global food production, but not to treble it. It is possible, but by no means certain, that the situation might to some extent be relieved by advances in biotechnology, such as hydroponics, greater use of micro-organisms as nitrogen fixers and as agents of organic synthesis, and new forms of cereals that fix nitrogen and have a higher capacity for photosynthesis than existing forms.

In speculating about the carrying capacity of the Earth it is necessary to take into account not only food supply, but also the technometabolism of the human population. In other words, the total number of people that could be supported by the ecosystems of the biosphere will be very much affected by their patterns of use of resources and energy, and especially of waste production (see page 251).

Forests

Serious concern has been expressed over recent years about trends in the forests of the Earth. Behind this concern lies the fact that more trees are destroyed every year than are planted, and the annual deficit is about 11 million hectares of forest.

As discussed in earlier chapters, extensive deforestation began in Europe around 1100 AD and continued until the 14th century, when it declined after the plague. Deforestation began again around 1500. Eighty per cent of central Europe had been covered with forest around 900, and only 25 per cent in 1900. The European forests reached a minimum at about the time of the First World War. By this date the forests of North America had also declined by about 60 per cent, although some reforestation has taken place since then, covering an area of 0.5 million km^2.

Progressive deforestation has been taking place in many other parts of the world. Most of North Africa and the Middle East as well as a great deal of continental Asia, Central America and the Andean regions of South America are now virtually treeless. Problems associated with deforestation are also looming large in parts of Central Africa and on the Indian sub-continent.

The developed countries, with 30 per cent of the world's population at present consume roughly 88 per cent of all industrial wood. The per capita consumption of wood in Britain each year is $0.72 m^3$. The average person in the developed countries uses about 127 kg of paper each year, as compared with 5 kg for every individual in developing regions. At present most of the timber and paper used in the developed countries is provided by the temperate forests of Canada, Finland, Norway, Sweden and the USSR. In the developing areas, 80 per cent of all wood consumed is used as firewood; and the per capita consumption for this purpose varies between $0.35 m^3$ per capita in India to $1.3 m^3$ in forest-rich countries like Indonesia. Some estimates predict that by the year 2000 the demand for wood the world over will have doubled, resulting in a serious shortfall in supply.

It has been estimated that tropical forest, which accounts for about 69 per cent of forest productivity in the world, is being destroyed at an annual rate of 4.1 million hectares in Latin America, 2.2 million hectares in Asia and 1.3 million hectares in Africa, giving a total of 7.6 million hectares per year. At this rate, the world's remaining tropical forests are likely to be reduced from the 1200 million hectares which they occupied in 1970 to less than 1000 million hectares by the year 2000 AD. Some authors believe that the rate of decline of tropical forests is much greater than this and it has even been suggested that all Asian forests will have disappeared by that year, and all those in Latin America by 2020 AD.

Mention must also be made of the fact that in the high-energy societies of the northern hemisphere today vast areas of forest are either dead or dying, apparently as the result of atmospheric pollution with acids and other noxious compounds produced by industrial processes and transport systems (see page 165).

PLANT CULTIVATION AND ANIMAL BREEDING FOR NON-UTILITARIAN PURPOSES

Before concluding this chapter it is worth drawing attention to the fact that for a very long time some humans have considered it worthwhile to devote considerable effort to raising and caring for various plants and animals that contribute nothing whatsoever towards human survival. The main motivation, especially in the case of plants, seems to be an aesthetic one. In Abraham's time, trees had been planted on the terraces of the ziggurat in the ancient city of Ur, and these were kept alive by water carried up from the Euphrates River. The Hanging Gardens of Babylon have been classed as one of the 'Seven Wonders of the World'. They, too, were irrigated with water from the Euphrates. In ancient Rome flowers, shrubs and trees grown simply for pleasure were a characteristic feature of the gardens surrounding the villas of the patricians. These gardens contained a wide range of different kinds of plants, including roses, periwinkles, poppies, rosemary, violets, as well as box, fig, mulberry, quince and pomegranate trees.

In England, the cultivation of flowering plants and shrubs for purely aesthetic reasons and the design of ornamental gardens began to become popular in the late 15th and early 16th centuries, and it eventually became an almost consuming passion of the English, rich and poor alike. And there must be few homes in the high-energy societies today that do not contain their complement of living plants. Indeed, almost every dwelling in the squatter settlements of Hong Kong, Mexico City and no doubt many other places has its own little collection of potted plants, carefully tended and watered by the human occupants. The recent controversy in North America about plastic trees is also interesting. Some people object strongly to the idea of substituting the synthetic object for the real living tree; but it is pertinent that these artificial plastic objects are made to look, as nearly as possible, like trees – whereas they could be made of any other shape or colour.

With respect to animals, the Pharaoh's of ancient Egypt and the kings and emperors of Mesopotamia had their personal collections of wild animals. Later, exotic animals came to be seen as appropriate gifts from one ruler to another all over the world. Since the 12th century AD, the Kings of England owned collections of lions, leopards and other alien creatures; and zoological gardens eventually became very popular institutions with the population at large. The breeding of dogs and cats for non-utilitarian purposes has also long been a feature of human society; and in the modern world a high proportion of households possess an aquarium if not also one or two caged birds.

FURTHER READING

Baker, H. 1970. *Plants and civilization* 2nd edn. Macmillan, London.
Brown, L.R. and Wolf, E.C. (1984). *Soil erosion: the quiet crisis in the world economy.* Worldwatch Paper 60. Worldwatch Institute, Washington DC.

Carefoot, G.L. and Sprott, E.R. (1969). *Famine on the wind: plant disease and human history.* McGill-Queens University Press, Montreal.

Heiser, C.B. (1973). *Seed to civilisation: the story of man's food.* W.H. Freeman, San Francisco.

Eckholm, E.P. (1982). *Down to earth: environmental and human needs.* W.W. Norton, New York.

Leach, G. (1976). *Energy and food production.* IPC, London.

Lieth, H. and Whittaker, R.H. (eds.) (1975). *Primary productivity in the biosphere.* Ecological Studies 14, Springer-Verlag, Berlin.

Reed, C.A. (ed.) (1977). *Origins of agriculture.* Mouton, The Hague.

Salaman, R.N. (1949). *The history and social influence of the potato.* Cambridge University Press, Cambridge.

Thomas, V.C. (ed.) (1956). *Man's role in changing the face of the Earth.* University of Chicago Press, Chicago, IL.

Ucko, P.J. and Dimbleby, G.W. (eds.) (1969). *The domestication of plants and animals.* Gerald Duckworth, London.

CHAPTER 7

TECHNOLOGICAL DEVELOPMENTS AND THE METABOLISM OF SOCIETY

As discussed in previous chapters, the aptitude for culture added an extra dimension to the metabolism of human populations – *technometabolism* – consisting of the inputs and outputs of materials and energy resulting from technological activities. The main component of technometabolism before the domestic transition resulted from the use of fire – the inputs being wood containing energy in chemical form, and the outputs carbon dioxide, other products of combustion and energy, mainly in the form of heat. Small amounts of wood, stone and fibre were also used for making simple utensils, weapons and ornaments.

After the domestic transition, people experimented with new ways of modifying substances in the environment for the purpose of manufacturing various kinds of ornaments and tools. The main developments involved the use of fire for changing the chemical or physical structure of certain natural materials. In fact, long before the domestic transition, at least one group of hunter–gatherers had discovered the hardening effect of heat on wet clay: an ancient kiln discovered near the Pavlov Hills in Czechoslovakia contained more than 2000 clay pellets (some showing finger marks) and a range of pieces of the clay modeler's art – including the heads of bears and foxes.

It is not known when or where the art of making earthenware pots was first practised, although it is clear that farming existed for thousands of years before this happened. Pottery was not introduced into Jericho, for example, until around 2000 years after the original establishment of this early farming settlement. Pottery developed independently in the Americas, although in Peru farming and fishing communities thrived for many centuries without the potters' craft, using gourds for holding liquid.

Pottery depends on the fact that when moistened clay is heated to around 450 to 500°C, a chemical change takes place that renders it hard and waterproof. If it is heated to 1400°C it vitrifies – that is, the silica in the clay takes on a glassy form.

The work of potters consists of a number of distinct phases. First they have to select an appropriate kind of clay. Then the clay is moistened and made into the desired shape, and finally this shaped clay is exposed to heat. In the early days in the Middle East clay was baked in ordinary fires, often covered with green leaves to increase heat. It was probably not until about the 6th millennium BC that the kiln first came into use in the region, providing more controlled conditions and higher temperatures, in excess of 10°C. Certainly by 6000 BC, the techniques of pottery at Çatal Hüyük were relatively well advanced, and the potters knew, for example, how to produce red or black pottery at will (the clay turns black in the presence of oxygen and red in its absence).

The next important development in the technology of pottery was the invention, perhaps around 3000 BC, of the potter's wheel. In this technique, the lump of wet clay is placed in the centre of a fast turning wheel (turning at least 100 times per minute). With light pressure from the potter's hand the clay rises easily and it can be made to take on any circular shape that is desired. Since this development, the potter's art has remained virtually unchanged to the present day, save for relatively minor refinements made in China and in Europe over the centuries.

We noted earlier that before the domestic transition hunter–gatherers often put more work into the manufacture of utensils than was necessary simply to render them functional – apparently purely for aesthetic reasons. The same applies to pottery. From very early on, pots made for the purpose of holding liquids were decorated with simple geometrical designs in various colours: and later figures of animals and humans appear in the designs – as in the case, for instance, of the superbly decorated and colourful vases from the Minoan civilization of around 1800 BC and the Athenian vases from the 6th and 5th centuries BC. About 700 AD the technique was developed in China for making the white, transluscent and metallically resonant porcelain. This technique was imitated in Baghdad, Spain and Persia and, much later, in Delft in the Netherlands and by Josiah Wedgwood in England. All this human effort was quite unnecessary, of course, in terms of the practical function of the manufactured object.

METALLURGY

At around the same time as the people in southwestern Asia were developing the art of pottery, some of them were also beginning to make things with metal. As in the case of the Palaeolithic mammoth hunters experimenting with clay, the initial motivation seems to have been aesthetic rather than utilitarian. Both gold and copper exist in nature in pure metallic form, and people discovered that they could be transformed into desired shapes by hammering. In Çatal Hüyük small shaped pieces of copper and of lead have been found, strung like beads on the fringes of pieces of clothing. Graves excavated at Varma on the Black Sea and dated around 4300 BC have been found to contain large numbers of copper objects, as well as many beautiful articles of beaten gold.

Gold and silver were already greatly valued in Mesopotamia in the 3rd millennium BC, and increasing quantities of these minerals were imported into the region to satisfy the desires of the local rulers. Queen Shub-ad's tomb in the royal cemetry at Ur contained 48 silver vessels. By far the richest deposits of gold were in Egypt, and gold became a key factor in the foreign policy and economy of the Egyptian empire.

In the Americas copper in its native form was used extensively from around 3000 BC by people living around the Great Lakes in the north for making ornaments and implements. They shaped it by heating, which rendered it rather more malleable, and by hammering and cutting it with stone tools. It was polished by rubbing with stone. Further south, in Central and South America, native gold, silver and copper, as well as platinum, were used to make ornaments from the 1st millennium BC, and copper was used from around 500 AD. The techniques of the goldsmiths in the Mayan, Aztec and Inca civilizations were very advanced.

Although iron can also be found in uncombined or native form in nature, no artefacts made directly by reshaping native iron have been found from southwestern Asia or from the early American civilizations. This may be either because iron was not used, due to the fact that it is much harder than copper, lead, silver and gold, or because it reacts readily with other elements and so disintegrates relatively rapidly.

It is not known precisely when or where people in southwestern Asia discovered techniques for extracting metals from their ores by heating. The copper ore, malachite, occurs in many areas of the Middle East, and it was used as a pigment at least from the 5th millennium BC, especially as a cosmetic for painting the lower eyelid. The extraction of copper from this ore, however, requires an intense heat of at least 1084°C and an oxygen-free atmosphere. It seems likely that the discovery of the basic technique for achieving such temperatures was made in kilns used for manufacturing pots. There is evidence of smelted copper in Iran from around 4500 BC, although the sophistication of artefacts from that period suggests that there already existed a deep-rooted tradition in the relevant techniques probably going back a considerable time. The oldest known furnace designed specifically for extracting copper from malachite exists in southern Sinai and is dated about 3500 BC. It would have provided a temperature of 1180 – 1350°C, and it used charcoal to ensure absence of oxygen. The high temperature was maintained by means of a forced draft. Copper obtained in this way was later remelted and poured into moulds of the desired shape. This development provided the essential basis of the metal industries from that time to the present day.

According to present evidence, copper smelting reached Italy sometime between 3000 and 2500 BC, Britain by 1900 BC and Scandinavia by 1500 BC. It was practised in India by 3000 BC and in southern Russia by 2000 BC.

One of the most important refinements of technique in metallurgy was the discovery that alloys – that is, mixtures of more than one metal – were for many purposes more useful than a single pure metal. The first metal to be deliberately added to copper was apparently arsenic, the copper-arsenic alloy being, after hammering, much harder than pure copper. Bronze, the alloy of copper and tin, was in use in Sumer around 3000 BC, although initially the inclusion of tin with copper was accidental, since the copper ores which came from Oman naturally contained some tin. Later tin was added deliberately to copper to produce true bronze, which is easier to cast than pure copper and is also somewhat harder.

Recent archaeological work has shown that people living at a place called Ban Chiang in northern Thailand about 2000 BC were skilled in manufacturing articles in bronze, containing about 10 per cent of tin; and the Shang people who settled on the flood plains of the Yellow River in the Henan Province in Central China around the 16th century BC made many objects out of bronze, some of them small and delicate and some quite massive.

Some authors have argued that metallurgy, including the art of alloying, was discovered independently in China. While this may well have been the case, the 1000 or so years which elapsed between the establishment of well-developed bronze industries in southwestern Asia and the Mediterranean and its appearance in the Yellow River civilization allowed plenty of time for the transmission of this technology by cultural diffusion.

It is worth drawing attention to the three basic ways that metals have been perceived to be of value to human beings. First, they have been prized for aesthetic reasons. As discussed above, the first uses of copper and lead were for decorative purposes, and for millennia gold and silver had been used mainly for making things that were pleasing to the eye. Second, metals came to be used for practical purposes, especially in the manufacture of implements for cutting, of weapons for killing, and of bowls, drinking vessels and shields, and later in human history they became important in the manufacture of vehicles, buildings, and ever more sophisticated and destructive weapons. These two uses of metals – the aesthetic and the practical – are not, of course, mutually exclusive, in that many an item made for some practical purpose has an aesthetic dimension, as in the case, for example, of the extraordinarily beautiful dagger found in Tutankhamen's tomb, with its blade of iron and hilt of gold.

The third important use of metals has been for purposes of exchange. It is possible that this function was initially linked with the aesthetic factor: that is, because gold and silver were prized for their beauty, they were sought after and considered valuable. Later, because of their ease of handling and their durability, they came to be used in a more systematic way as a symbol for worth. Already by 2400 BC, in the reign of Manishtusu, King of Kish, silver was a recognised standard of exchange; one *mina* of silver was equivalent to 60 *gur* of grain. And when Abraham purchased the cave of Machpelah, he weighed out 400 shekels of silver; and Jacob bought a field at Padan-Aran for 'an hundred pieces of money'. As mentioned above, gold became an essential factor in the foreign policy of ancient Egypt where the Pharoahs held the monopoly of the mines, and the enemies of the Egyptian empire were constantly demanding gold as the price for peace.

Despite the fact that iron ores are very widely distributed in the Earth's crust, the smelting of iron was not developed until about 1000 years after the earliest smelting of copper. This was partly due to the fact that pure iron melts at 1535°C compared with 1083°C for copper.

This higher temperature was not finally attained until the development of the blast furnace of the Middle Ages. At the lower furnace temperatures used for smelting copper, iron yields only a spongey mass called *bloom*. It was discovered, however, that if bloom is subjected to repeated hammering, the non-ferrous component, or *slag*, can be driven out, leaving a bar of almost pure iron. This can then be reheated and hammered into a desired shape. The technique for making objects of *wrought iron* in this way was developed in the Hittite Empire during the latter part of the 3rd millennium BC. A disadvantage of the process is the fact that it is not possible to produce a very sharp edge to the manufactured article. However, around 1400 BC a subject people of the Hittites found that sharpness could be achieved by repeatedly hammering and reheating this iron in direct contact with charcoal. This treatment produces the alloy of iron and carbon, known as *steel*. Later, it was discovered that further hardening could be attained by plunging the hot metal into cold water, a process known as *quenching*. About 200 years later, the practice of *tempering* was developed which involves reheating the metal to 700°C after quenching, rendering it less brittle.

After the downfall of the Hittite Empire about 1200 BC, the techniques of the Iron Age spread relatively quickly in all directions. By around 1000 BC, most of the familiar metal tools of the modern carpenter, such as chisels, files, and saws were already in existence.

In China, iron smelting began about 1000 BC. Because the Chinese possessed a different kind of bellows that produced much higher temperatures in their furnaces, they were able to melt iron and, by pouring it into moulds, to manufacture articles of *cast iron*. By the end of the 3rd century BC, at the time of Qin Shihuang, the First Emperor of China, metallurgy in China had reached a high degree of sophistication, and up to 15 different metals were used in alloys, most of them deliberately added.

The Iron Age in India began about the same time, although little is known of the early techniques used. It was apparently in India, in the region of Hyderabad, that the technique was first developed in which pieces of wrought iron were heated in a crucible with pieces of wood and leaves of certain plants, producing *wootz*, an extremely hard form of steel. The technique was later used further west in the production of the famous *Damascus steel*.

Iron was a major factor in the rise of Greece as an important power, and formed the basis of the armoury of renowned hoplites of the Greek army. It was also very important in the expansion of Roman power in the Western world.

Meanwhile, the aesthetic metals, silver and gold, continued to be of importance in the ancient world. Silver mined at Rio Tinto in Spain by the Carthaginians is said to have formed the mainstay of their empire in the 5th century BC, and later this same source of silver was of great importance in the economy of the Roman empire.

A significant development around 1500 AD, following the voyages of Christopher Columbus and other seafaring adventurers, was the introduction into Europe of enormous quantities of gold from Middle and South America. Because humans continued to place great value on this metal, despite its relative lack of practical uses, this influx had immense impact on international affairs and on the relationships between European powers. It also acted as a stimulus to trade and commerce in the whole region. Three hundred years later, the symbolic meaning given to gold by human culture was responsible for the great goldrushes in California and southeastern Australia, resulting in the mass migration of Europeans and, in the case of Australia, of Chinese, into the gold-rich regions.

Returning to the more useful metals, various refinements were introduced in the 18th and 19th centuries in metallurgical techniques, including the use of coke as a fuel for blast furnaces and the rediscovery at Sheffield of the wootz technique. Another important development was Bessemer's process for producing large quantities of malleable workable iron with a low carbon content.

Iron in one form or another, and usually combined with various other substances, has come to be of supreme importance in the material world of modern high-energy societies, where it is used for all manner of purposes. The annual per capita consumption of iron in the USA today is about 0.45 tonnes and it is slightly less in Australia and Britain.

Other metals are also used now for a wide range of different purposes. After iron, the most used metal is aluminium which, after oxygen and silicon, is the commonest element in the Earth's crust (representing 8.3 per cent by weight; iron is 5 per cent). The annual usage of aluminium now amounts to 4 kg per person on the global level.

PITCH, CEMENT AND CONCRETE

The built environment with which we are familiar today would be inconceivable without the use of certain binding materials used for joining stones or bricks together or for making floors, highways and solid blocks used in various kinds of construction work.

The very earliest stone structures made by humans, consisting of dwellings, tombs or temples, were built with stone blocks laid one above the other without the use of any cementing material, and the stability of the walls depended entirely on the appropriate shaping and placing of the stone masses. Two particularly elegant examples of this method of building are the domed chambers of Mycenae and the Gallarus Oratory on the Dingle Peninsula in County Kerry, Ireland.

In ancient Egypt walls were made of dried (but not baked) mud bricks. After each row of bricks had been laid down, a layer of moist mud, sometimes mixed with chopped straw, was applied. After drying, the wall consisted of a solid mass of dried clay. This method was, of course, useful only in dry climates, since in wet areas the clay would eventually be washed away by water. It is still used today, and in Kuwait for example many buildings are constructed in this way. The Egyptians later used a mixture of burnt gypsum and sand for binding stones.

In the early Sumerian cities the naturally-occurring form of *pitch* known as *bitumen* was used for binding blocks of stone. Deposits of this material are found on the surface of the Earth's crust in parts of the Middle East. It consists mainly of hydrocarbons of organic origin, and it is viscous and soft when heated, but firm when cool. Similar material can be made from wood (wood pitch) and coal (coal tar pitch), being the residue left after the distillation of wood or coal. Pitch was used in Babylon for binding together burnt bricks and also at Mohenjo-dara in the Indus Valley (2500–2000 BC), and it is widely used at the present time, especially in the construction of roads.

In Crete, and later in Greece, mortar for building purposes was made by heating limestone (calcium carbonate) to produce lime (calcium oxide), which was then mixed with sand and water. This technique was borrowed by the Romans who applied it in the construction of buildings at Pompei around 300 BC. Later the Romans used a great deal of *concrete* in their buildings: which consisted of a mixture of lime, sand, water and a volcanic earth known as pozzolana.

There was a decline in the technology of cement and concrete during the Middle Ages, but by the 14th century excellent mortar was again in use in Europe. The 19th century witnessed further important advances in the art of cement-making and in the understanding of the roles of the different components. Portland cement is a product of this era, and it is very widely used in the modern world. It consists essentially of a mixture of certain carefully selected limestones and clay which has been heated to a high temperature and then ground to a fine dust. It sets hard when mixed with water and, like the concrete of the Romans, it hardens under water. Mixed with sand and water it is used as mortar; and mixed with sand, gravel and water, as concrete.

The rate of use of cement by the human population of the world has been increasing rapidly over recent decades. For example, in 1970 the global use of cement has been estimated to have been $568,910 \times 10^3$ tonnes, and in 1980 it was $920,000 \times 10^3$ tonnes. In 1980, the per capita use of cement, globally, was about 250 kg and in the USA the per capita use in 1972 was estimated to be 364 kg.

SYNTHETIC PLASTICS

Recent decades have seen the growth of a major new industry – the production of synthetic materials used for a wide range of purposes, including the manufacture of clothing, utensils, pipes and countless other commodities. This industry dates back to the middle of the last century, when a hard flexible transparent substance known as celluloid was made by mixing nitrocellulose and camphor. In 1904 'Bakelite' was prepared from formaldehyde, phenol and ammonia; and in 1912 'Cellophane' was made by treating cellulose with caustic soda and carbon bisulphide. Nylon, a synthetic polyamide, made its appearance in 1936, and has been widely used in synthetic fabrics. Since that time many other kinds of synthetic polymers have come into use. The basic raw materials used in the manufacture of these synthetic plastic materials are coal or petroleum, and a range of gases – especially oxygen, nitrogen, hydrogen, chlorine and fluorine. The plastic materials are moulded at high temperatures and at high pressure.

The most widely used types of plastic today are the following:

Acrylonitrile-butadiene-styrene (ABS). This is a tough and mechanically strong plastic used in telephone handsets, electrical appliances and various items of car trim.

Low density polyethylene (LDPE). This is the most used plastic wrap for food.

High density polyethylene (HDPE). Used for making bottles for milk, bleach, detergent and fruit juice. It is a stiff crack-resistant plastic.

Polyester in a resin form is combined with glass fibres to produce 'fibreglass'. It is also used in fabric.

Polyethylene terephthalate (PET). A lightweight, tough and shatterproof, and heat-resistant plastic suitable for such packaging applications such as carbonated soft drinks. It is also used for packaging frozen foods that can be heated in microwave or conventional ovens.

Polypropylene (PP). A lightweight heat and chemical resistant plastic with a high surface gloss. It is used as a fibre in ropes, carpet and woven fabric, and in machine components such as washing machine agitators and toilet cisterns.

Polystyrene (PS). The most easily moulded of plastics. It is used widely as refrigerator and washing machine components and, in the form of foam, for disposable dishes, caps, meat trays. PS foam or beads are used as thermal insulation and for packaging fragile goods.

Polyvinylchloride (PVC or vinyl). Used in pipe systems for water supply, drainage and gas reticulation, electrical insulation, rainwear, and footwear, credit cards, and bottles.

Polyurethane. This is widely used as a flexible foam for cushioning in domestic furniture, cars and aircraft, and for insulating refrigerators and storage tanks. It is also used in car bumpers and ski boots.

Most other plastics fall into the following two groups: *engineering plastics* – including nylon, acetal, acrylic and fluoroplastics, and *thermosetting plastics* – used in textile treatment, the manufacture of plywood, particle board, decorative laminates and paints.

The domestic consumption of plastics is still rising in the high-energy societies. In Australia, for example, the amount of plastic used increased by nearly 30 per cent between 1984 and 1988 and usage is currently increasing by about 5 per cent per year. In 1989 the per capita consumption was 74 kg, 32 per cent of this being used in packaging. However, apparently because of environmental concerns, there has been a recent 17.6 per cent decline, between December 1989 and February 1990, in the sales of disposable plastic bags (such as freezer bags and kitchen tidy bags).

There has been considerable debate recently about the environmental impacts of plastics. On the one hand, it is argued that they are 'biosphere-friendly', because it takes less energy to produce a plastic product than a comparable one made from glass or aluminium. In Australia the manufacture of plastics accounts for 2.7 per cent of the total extrasomatic energy used.

On the negative side, the lack of degradability of plastics means that they represent hazards for sea birds, marine mammals and other creatures. In many parts of the world discarded plastic materials scattered over city streets or the countryside are an aesthetic disaster. In some cases the processing and manufacture of plastics results in the release of toxic chemicals into the natural environment.

MECHANICAL DEVICES AND MACHINES

Introduction

The history of human technology and the development and application of mechanical devices by humankind will be discussed in three parts. First we will consider the sources of power (or energy) used for driving mechanical devices, and then the key scientific discoveries and principles on which these devices depend. Finally, we will briefly discuss the intended uses of mechanical devices.

Sources of physical power

Devices depending on direct human effort

Very early on in the history of the human species some basic mechanical principles were discovered which have played an immense role in techno-logical devices ever since. Perhaps the most significant of these is the principle of the *lever*, and it provides the basis of nearly all mechanical devices used for moving objects. No information exists on its origin, but the principle was clearly described in Greece during the 3rd century BC. Archimedes is credited with saying: 'Give me but a place to stand, and I can move the world'. In fact, hundreds of years before Archimedes people living in Greece were using the principle of the lever in their beam-presses to express juice out of grapes and olives.

Four other mechanical devices related to the lever were also well established by the time of Archimedes. They were the *wedge*, the *screw*, the compound *pulley* and the *wheel and axle*. These devices, like the simple lever, involved the transformation of a small free-acting force through a long distance into a greater force acting through a short distance.

146

Another important principle discovered early on is that of the spring, which is a device for accumulating energy and releasing it suddenly when required. The bow, used for shooting arrows, provides the first known example of the application of this principle by human beings. Later uses included the various kinds of cross-bow and catapults. The spring as a source of lasting power in small machines was not developed until much later. Its first use in this way was in clocks in the middle of the 15th century AD.

The principles of the lever and the spring find widespread application in the modern world, both in machines which depend on human effort and in machines powered by various other sources of energy.

Devices employing other (non-human) sources of energy

The source of power used in the early applications of the lever and spring was the somatic energy of the human body, derived immediately from food consumed and ultimately from sunlight. One of the most momentous consequences of culture has been the development of devices which use other, non-human, sources of energy to do work which would otherwise have been done by humans or, in some cases, work of a kind which could never be done by humans. One of the earliest examples is the ox-drawn plough, which was in use in the 2nd millennium BC in Mesopotamia, and possibly much earlier. The plough, and especially the later heavy metal plough, had major impact on the ecological relationships between human populations and the biosphere, by facilitating tillage, increasing the yield of crops and, in northern Europe, enabling agriculture to spread into areas with heavy soils.

Later, horses were used for pulling carts and, in warfare, for pulling chariots. These uses of horse power depended, of course, on the invention and development of the wheel.

The ox and the horse, as sources of power, played a key role in the civilization of medieval Europe, and it has been estimated that the average European was provided with five times as much motor power from beasts of burden than was the average Chinese. In 18th century England, and probably much earlier, there was a higher ratio of domestic beasts per cultivated acre than in any other country except Holland.

When horses were first used as draught animals they exerted about four times as much power as human beings; but since they consumed about four times as much food as humans, their use, at least in terms of straight energetics, did not make all that much sense. Initially, the harness of the horse consisted of a yoke similar to that used for oxen, but this device was not well suited to the horse's anatomy. Later the breast-band was introduced, attached between the legs to the girth. A more important improvement, however, was the transformation of the breast-band into the stiff padded

147

horse-collar. As a result of these developments, which some authorities believe originated in China, the effective tractive power of the horse was increased four or five-fold, so that in the 12th and 13th centuries this animal came to be much more widely used in Europe. Eventually, it almost entirely displaced the ox as the draught animal on that Continent.

Domesticated horses were also used for carrying humans from place to place. The use of the horse for riding first became important around 800 BC, and was possibly introduced into southwestern Asia from the Eurasian steppe-lands, although this is not certain. An Egyptian painting suggests that people were riding horses in 1400 BC, and recent finds at Dereivka on the Dnieper River suggests that they may have been doing so as long ago as 4000 BC.

Animal power has also been used, in combination with various mechanical devices, for a number of other purposes. For example in the 5th century BC donkey-driven mills were used to crush ore from the silver mines at Laurion in Greece, and donkeys were later harnessed to mechanical equipment for grinding corn, crushing grapes and lifting water.

In mechanical devices employing animal power, the energy source is still *somatic*, although it is *animal somatic* energy rather than *human somatic* energy. However, a number of devices developed in the early days of civilization made use of *extrasomatic energy*. Some of these exploited wind power. From around the 4th millennium BC small wind-driven boats sailed up the Nile and at least by 2500 BC they were sailing across the Mediterranean. Sails, sometimes supplemented with oars, were the basis of oceanic transport of people and material up until the 19th century AD.

Another use of wind power was in windmills, used mainly for pumping water and grinding corn. These did not reach Europe before the 12th century AD, although they had been in use in Persia during the 7th century AD. Watermills, however, were known to the Greeks and the Romans and were used for grinding corn in the first century BC; but they were not widely used until the Middle Ages. However by the 11th century AD they were to be found everywhere in Europe, driving grindstones and turning millstones and edge-runners, which were used for such purposes as mashing apples for cider, pressing olives for oil, and pulverising charcoal for gunpowder.

The next important technological development involving a new source of extrasomatic energy, and one of major significance in human affairs, was the invention of gunpowder. Roger Bacon, who lived from 1214 to 1292, wrote a formula for gunpowder as follows: 7 parts of saltpetre, 5 parts of young hazelwood (charcoal) and 5 parts of sulphur. He states that this mixture will explode, and that it can cause an enemy to be blown up, or at least to flee in terror. By the year 1300, mixtures of saltpetre, sulphur and charcoal were prepared for use in artillery for projecting stones and, later on, balls of metal, through the air towards an enemy.

The early experiments with gunpowder represented the beginning of a branch of human endeavour which is still very much a feature of society and which is aimed at producing ever more powerful and destructive bombs. It is noteworthy that the mechanical devices employing these explosive mixtures were used solely for destructive purposes – that is, for killing other members of the human species in battle (or their horses), for destroying buildings and for breaking up rock. Attempts to use them as a source of power for driving engines have not been successful.

In the last decade of the 17th century a machine was in use in Britain which was driven by energy derived from burning coal. It was a form of *steam engine* and was used for pumping water from the bottom of deep mines to the surface. This modest development ushered in a new kind of technology which became one of the most characteristic features of the Fourth high-energy Phase of human existence and one of overwhelming ecological significance – a technology in which machines for performing various kinds of work were powered by the combustion of fossil fuels. This technology thus made use of energy that had been reaching the Earth, over hundreds of millions of years, in the form of sunlight, and which had been converted into chemical energy through photosynthesis in living organisms.

In the steam engine itself, coal is burned to heat water, converting it to steam. The pressure of the steam is used to drive various mechanical devices to provide movement, as in pumping, hammering, turning and transporting.

Experiments carried out in the second half of the 19th century with gas, oil, and petroleum as energy sources resulted in the development of the *internal combustion engine*. In this device the combustion occurs within the engine, rather than in an external furnace as is the case in the steam engine. A spark causes an explosive expansion of gases, and the resultant pressure is used to drive a piston. In the internal combustion engine the effect of the combustion of fuel is thus more direct, and there is no need for the furnace, boiler, condenser, valves and pipes of the steam engine.

The main features of the modern internal combustion engine had appeared by the year 1900, although its enormous influence on world civilization was not felt until well into the 20th century. A modification of this mechanical device is seen in engines of jet propulsion, in which gases rapidly expanding in one direction (following combustion of liquid fossil fuel) drive the vehicle in the opposite direction.

Another set of scientific advances relating to the use of extrasomatic energy that has had an enormous influence on human affairs involved the discovery of *electricity* and *electromagnetic phenomena*. The recognition of the existence of electricity goes back to the late 18th century. By around 1800 electric batteries, consisting of alternating plates of silver (or copper) and zinc, were in existence. The observation that an electric current running in a wire could deflect a compass led to appreciation that a relationship existed between electricity and magnetism, and in 1821 Michael Faraday, exploiting this discovery, showed that electrical energy could be used to produce rotary motion. The electrical motors which are in use today in so many different mechanical devices depend on this principle. Faraday then reasoned that if electricity plus magnetism could give rise to movement, then perhaps movement plus magnetism could give rise to an electric current. His experiments showed that such *electromagnetic induction* is indeed possible, and this discovery forms the basis of all modern electricity generators.

The applications of this form of energy have been very numerous. By the 1870s, electricity was used for lighting in the arc lamp. More successful in the long run, however, has been the filament lamp, which was originally invented in England around 1848, but which was more effectively developed in North America in the 1870s. Other household applications of electricity include devices for heating air and water, cooking, and numerous other devices, such as food mixers and hair driers. Another extremely important application of electricity is as the source of the spark in internal combustion engines.

While electricity is an additional source of power for human society, it has, in the main, been a secondary source. Unlike the situation with other extrasomatic energy sources, it has not proved possible to tap the 'natural' electricity in the environment for commercial use, such as that which is manifest in electromagnetic storms. The electric battery, however, can be regarded as a primary source of electricity.

By far the biggest source of electricity in the modern world is generators driven by fossil fuels. The usual efficiency of these devices, in energy terms, is nowadays about 30 per cent. Some electricity is also produced from generators driven by water falling from higher to lower land and such hydroelectricity plants contribute about 6 per cent to the overall electricity budget of the world as a whole. Wind power has also been used to drive generators of electricity, but its contribution at the present time to overall electricity production is negligible.

More recently another source of extrasomatic energy, *nuclear* power, has been developed and has become of overwhelming significance in human affairs. The fundamental scientific discoveries which ultimately led to this development were made in Paris at the end of the 19th century by Marie and Pierre Curie, who demonstrated the existence of radioactivity. Later work has shown this phenomenon to be due to the fact that the nucleus of the atoms of certain substances, for example uranium 235, are unstable, and have a tendency to release neutrons, at the same time emitting energy in the form of electromagnetic radiation consisting of alpha, beta, gamma and X-rays. The neutrons freed in this way may, by bombarding other atoms, cause the further breakdown of atomic nuclei, releasing more neutrons and giving off more electromagnetic energy; and these neutrons, in turn, may initiate further breakdown of atomic nuclei, and so on. Use was made of this kind of chain reaction in the development of atomic bombs, like those used at Hiroshima and Nagasaki. In these devices the whole reaction proceeds extremely rapidly, so that a massive amount of energy is released in an extremely short time, some in the form of alpha, beta, gamma and X-rays, and some converted to pressure waves and to heat. The nuclear chain reaction has also been exploited in fission reactors, in which the process is controlled and on-going, so that the energy is released gradually over a considerable period of time. In these reactors, much of the electromagnetic irradiation becomes transformed to heat, and this is used to convert water to steam, which in turn drives generators to provide electricity. As in the case of fossil fuel electricity generators, the efficiency in energy terms is around 30 per cent.

The most important of the fissile isotopes (i.e. elements which are capable of sustaining a nuclear chain reaction) are uranium-235, plutonium-239 and uranium-233. Only the first of these occurs naturally in appreciable amounts, and it makes up about 0.7 per cent of the uranium which occurs in nature. Another important fissile isotope is thorium-232. At present most nuclear fission reactors use uranium-235 as the primary nuclear fuel and a mixture of uranium-235 and uranium-238 (the other 99.3 per cent) nuclei to initiate the transformation to plutonium-239. Some of that plutonium is subsequently itself fissioned while still in the reactor thus contributing to the chain reaction. However, some plutonium remains when, after a year or so, the spent fuel is removed from the reactor. This plutonium, if recovered at a fuel reprocessing plant, along with unconverted and unfissioned uranium remaining in the fuel, may be recycled as fuel for the reactor that produced it; or it may be used to manufacture nuclear bombs. Nuclear power at present contributes about 2 per cent to the overall extrasomatic energy use by humankind.

Although interest in the direct use of *solar power* as an energy source goes back to the last century, it is only in recent decades that serious attention has been paid to the idea that extrasomatic energy for use in human society might be derived directly from sunlight[1]. In fact, the Earth receives directly from the sun about 28,000 times more energy than is used commercially by humankind today. As discussed in Chapter 1, 35 per cent of this energy is reflected back into space more or less immediately, 17.5 per cent is absorbed by the atmosphere and about 47.5 per cent penetrates

---

[1]   The potential energy in animals, slaves, wind, water, wood and fossil fuels is, of course, derived indirectly from the sun. Moreover, solar energy may be used directly for warming buildings in cold climates, and for such industrial processes as the preparation of salt by evaporating sea water.

to the Earth's surface. In the USA, the sunshine which falls on the roads in one day represents about twice as much energy as is derived from fossil fuels the world over in the same period.

Basically, there have been two main approaches to the use of solar power. In one, it is used as a direct source of heat for industrial processes and domestic heating, and in some cases it is used for preheating water or some other material, while another energy source is used to raise the material to higher temperatures.

The second approach involves devices designed to convert light energy coming from the sun into electric energy. In one of these, sunlight is collected in mirrors which focus it onto a boiler. High-pressure steam is produced in the boiler, and this is used to drive a generator to produce electricity. In another device sunlight is converted directly into electrical energy in *photovoltaic cells*. Although the theoretical efficiency of these cells is less than 25 per cent, their advantages include the facts that they have no moving parts, they consume no fuel, they produce no pollution, they have long lifetimes, and they require little maintenance. Moreover, they are made from silicon, which is the second most abundant element on the Earth's crust. At present photovoltaic cells are expensive to buy, but it is likely that they will become less so.

From the ecological standpoint, there exists an important distinction between the various direct and indirect forms of solar power (including windpower and hydroelectric power but excluding fossil fuels) on the one hand, and fossil fuels and nuclear power on the other, in that there are no incidental chemical by-products released into the environment in the case of the former. Fossil fuels result in the liberation of carbon dioxide, carbon monoxide, hydrocarbons, and sulphur and nitrogen oxides; and nuclear power produces highly radioactive substances. Furthermore, the use of solar power does not release additional heat to the environment beyond that which would in any case be given off as a consequence of the solar radiation of the Earth.

Some key mechanical devices and their uses

Except in the case of fire used simply for producing heat, the various uses to which these extrasomatic sources of energy are put all involve mechanical devices, of which there is now a vast array of different kinds with different purposes. Some of them perform tasks that would otherwise be carried out by humans, while others do things that human beings could not possibly do. They depend on a wide range of fundamental discoveries and inventions, from the lever and the spring to the more sophisticated developments of the last 150 years. Especially important among the more recent inventions are those involving electricity and various electromagnetic phenomena.

They have transformed society and have had an immense impact on human experience. They range from relatively simple lighting, heating and cooling equipment to radio, television and a plethora of electronic devices involving transistors, silicon chip semiconductors, electromagnetic recording tapes, and instruments for emitting or detecting various kinds of electromagnetic waves. Another key development of very recent origin is the laser, which is an electromagnetic device for converting light of mixed frequencies into an intense narrow monochromatic beam. Laser beams have found many technical applications.

The great majority of the uses to which the various fundamental discoveries and inventions have been put fall quite readily under the headings: *transport*; *destruction*; *manufacturing*; *shifting material*; *communicating* and *storing information*; *sound making*; *and measurement and observation* (Table 7.1).

The consequences of advances in human technology through the ages, and especially in the last couple of centuries, for the life experience of humans themselves and for the relationships between human society and the biosphere have been multiple and wide-ranging. Although a systematic account of these consequences is far beyond the scope of this volume, some of the more significant impacts will be mentioned in later chapters.

THE TECHNOMETABOLISM OF SOCIETY

We have already noted that early in the history of our species, the human aptitude for culture gave rise to a new dimension of the metabolism of human populations – *technometabolism* – consisting of the various inputs of resources and energy and outputs of water that result from technological processes.

To some extent, of course, other animals make use of materials in their environment other than those which they consume as food. The twigs, leaves and pieces of grass used for nest building in birds are an obvious example. Some species even make use of energy sources other than the somatic energy passing through their own bodies (apart from the direct warming effect of sunlight). An interesting example is the mallee fowl of Australia. The female of this species deposits her eggs, one by one and over a period of several months, in mounds of leaf litter that have been built by the male bird. The heat for incubating the eggs is derived in part from sunlight and in part from bacterial fermentation of the leaf litter (a process which is actually induced the previous winter when the soil is moist and when the male bird starts preparing the mound). Throughout the incubation period, which lasts around 6 months, the cock bird carefully regulates the temperature by adding or removing soil and leaf litter as necessary, and

Table 7.1   Uses of mechanical devices

Transport	Destruction	Manufacturing
carts	knives	spinning wheels and looms
bicycles	axes	jennies
motor bicycles	spears and swords	sewing machines
motor cars and trucks	bows and arrows	potters wheels
tractors	guns	numerous devices
ships, submarines	bombs	mechanical robots
balloons	nuclear and hydrogen	
airplanes,	bombs	
helicopters	laser weapons	
rockets	chemical weapons	
satellites	blasting equipment	
Shifting material	*Communicating and storing material*	*Sound-making*
ploughs	printing press	percussion and string
earthmoving equipment	typewriter, word processor	instruments
cranes	telephones	wind instruments
harvesting machines	radio, television and video	loud speakers
carpet sweepers	equipment	sirens
vacuum cleaners	records, cassettes	
pumps	computers	
	cameras	
Measurement and observation		*Other*
spectacles		ovens
telescopes		heaters
microscopes, electron microscopes		refrigerators
sextants, compasses		lamps
clocks		wine presses
cameras		can openers
geiger counters		brewing equipment
		X-ray machines
		devices used in health care

the temperature of the eggs usually remains extraordinarily close to 33.5°C throughout this time.

The regular use of fire by early humans was the first, and for a long time the only, deliberate use made by human beings of energy other than the somatic energy entering their bodies in the form of food. It was a development of great significance for humanity, not only affecting the quality of everyday experience but also greatly enhancing the adaptive potential of human populations to certain new environments. It also had a greater impact on the ecosystems of which humans were a part than did any other cultural development for several hundred thousand years.

It has been estimated that the regular use of fire by hunter–gatherers roughly doubled the total energy use (somatic and extrasomatic) of human populations, bringing it to around 2 HEE or 20 MJ per day per capita.

In general, except where fires got out of hand, this consumption of wood and discharge of gases had little ecological impact on material flows in primeval ecosystems, representing but a minute fraction of the total matter cycling within the systems. There would have been no shortage of wood for burning, and no major environmental disturbances would have arisen through the release of the products of its combustion.

After the use of fire, the next ecologically significant development affecting the metabolism of society dates back only about 12,000 years. It was the introduction of farming. This development resulted in an increase of at least ten-fold, and in the long run many hundred fold, in the proportion of the energy fixed by photosynthesis in human ecosystems that actually flowed, as somatic energy, through human organisms. However, farming itself did not have much effect on the per capita rate of resource use and waste production by humans. With the development of pottery there must have been some increase in the use of fire, and hence in the use of extrasomatic energy and materials in the form of clay and wood; but even this development did not have major impact on societal metabolism.

The introduction of metallurgy six to eight thousand years ago represented a qualitative change in the technometabolism of human populations, involving material inputs initially of copper, and then of tin, iron, and zinc ores, and outputs in the form of metal artefacts and slag. It also involved increased use of wood, and later coal, to provide extrasomatic energy for smelting the ores and softening or melting the metals. However, for several thousand years the per capita use of metal was not very great. It is true that soldiery in particular was associated with the use of relatively large amounts of metal, but taking the population as a whole the quantity of metal 'consumed' per head per year was very modest. In England even in Elizabethan times most homes contained little more in the way of metal objects than a pewter mug or two and an iron bowl for cooking. Iron implements were used for farming purposes, but the larger of these, such as ploughs, were often shared among several families.

The next change of major importance in societal metabolism came with the industrial transition and the introduction of machines using fossil fuels as a source of energy to drive their moving parts. The effect of this development and its countless technological repercussions on the metabolism of human societies has been immense, both qualitatively and quantitatively (Figure 7.1).

Extrasomatic energy

Almost all aspects of the use of non-renewable resources today involve the utilisation of extrasomatic energy, including the removal of these resources from the Earth's crust, the extraction of minerals from ores, the transport

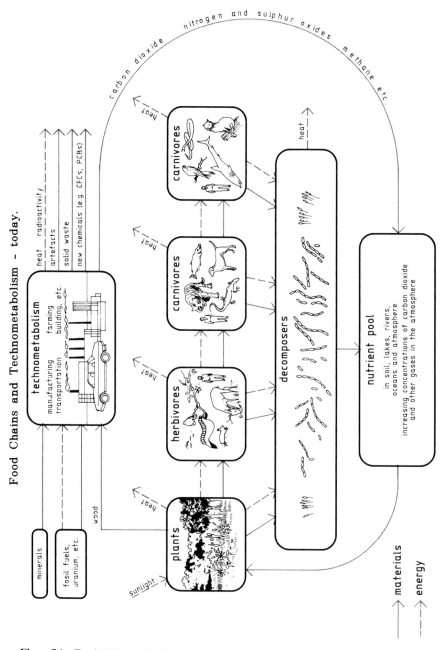

Figure 7.1 Food chains and technometabolism for humans in ecological Phase 4

of raw materials, the manufacture of commodities, their transport to retail outlets and, in many instances, their use by consumers. In fact, the changing pattern of energy use is the best single indicator of the overall scale of human industrial activity and of the intensifying technometabolism of society.

At present humankind is using over 350,000 PJ extrasomatic energy per year, which is about 10,000 times more than was used by the total human population when farming was introduced around 400 generations ago, and most of this increase has occurred since the industrial transition. Figure 7.2 shows the increase in extrasomatic energy use by humans since 1800.

By far the greater part of this use of extrasomatic energy, and of the associated ecological impact on the biosphere, is due to human activities in the developed countries. In North America today, the average person uses nearly 100 times as much extrasomatic energy as the average hunter-gatherer, and about 20 times as much as his or her ancestors of, say, 10 generations ago. Figure 7.3 depicts the per capita consumption of extrasomatic energy at different times in history for humankind as a whole and for selected countries in the modern world.

The question naturally arises: for what purposes is all this extrasomatic energy being used? Table 7.2 summarises for the United States in 1973 and the United Kingdom in 1979, the patterns of energy use, in terms of percentages used for four different broad categories of purpose.

The main sources of extrasomatic energy throughout the high-energy phase of society have been fossil fuels, although the relative contributions of coal, oil and natural gas have changed considerably over the past 60 years. Hydroelectricity has increased slowly during the period, and very recently nuclear energy has made a contribution in some countries. The changing pattern on a global level is reflected in the figures in Table 7.3.

Material inputs

It is not easy to provide an accurate picture of the changing rates of use of different mineral resources either by humankind as a whole or by separate societies. However, it stands to reason that increasing industrial productivity involves increasing use of resources.

The figures available for the per capita production of pig iron the world over show a steady increase during the past 120 years, from around 6 kg per capita for the year in 1860 to 122 kg per person in 1978. It is difficult to calculate the per capita consumption in individual countries, because of complications due to the importing and exporting of iron and iron-containing products. However, it is apparent that the annual per capita use of iron in the high-energy societies amounts to between 2 and 3 kg each day, or 50–80 tonnes in an average lifetime. With respect to the use of

157

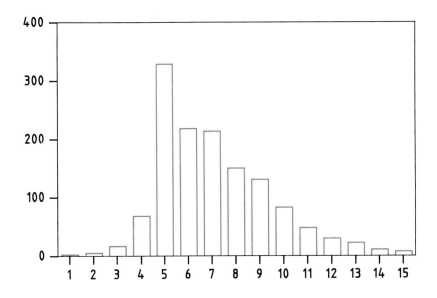

1	World average	-	10.000 BC
2		-	1650 AD
3		-	1900 AD
4		-	1987 AD
5	1987	-	North America
6		-	Australia
7		-	USSR
8		-	United Kingdom
9		-	Japan
10		-	Spain
11		-	Latin America
12		-	China
13		-	Africa
14		-	India
15		-	Nepal

Figure 7.3 Per capita extrasomatic energy use (GJ/year)

metals in general, although relatively sophisticated metallurgy was practised five thousand years ago, more primary metal has been consumed by society during the past 25 years than during the whole of previous history.

Table 7.2 Extrasomatic energy use by categories of purpose

Use	Extrasomatic energy use (%)	
	USA 1973	UK 1979
Residential/ domestic	19	35
Commerce	15	37
Industry	40	22
Transport	26	6

Table 7.3 World energy consumption by source

Energy	Energy consumption (%)		
	1925	1950	1979
Solid fuels	82.9	61.0	28.6
Liquid fuels	13.3	27.7	45.2
Natural gas	3.2	9.7	18.0
Hydroelectricity	0.7	1.7	6.0
Nuclear energy	–	–	2.2

Table 7.4 Per capita use of mineral materials in the USA in 1972

Material	Amount (kg)
Sand and gravel	4091
Stone	3864
Cement	364
Clays	273
Total non-metallic minerals	8592
Iron and steel	545
Aluminium	23
Copper	11
Lead	7
Zinc	7
Other metals	16
Total metals	609

Some figures for the per capita rate of use of various non-renewable resources, including iron and steel, in the USA in 1972 are shown in Table 7.4.

Needless to say, the control and use of material resources, and of the material benefits derived from them, are far from evenly distributed within the populations of most high-energy societies. Even more striking are the disparities that exist in the intensities of resource use between populations

Table 7.5 Percentage of consumption recycled

	USA 1974	UK 1978
Iron	24	69
Lead	40	65
Copper	23	37
Aluminium	8	29

in the developed and the developing regions of the world. The industrially developed world, which contains about one fifth of the total human population, uses 90 per cent of the non-renewable resources produced. This means that on a per capita basis the populations in these countries are using about 20 times as much non-renewable resources as are populations in the Third World. The United States, which has 5 per cent of the world's population, uses 27 per cent of the materials extracted. Per capita, this is 36 times more than in the developing world.

Clearly, a critical question is: How long will the deposits of the important minerals in the Earth's crust used in the technometabolism of the industrialised world last, either at the present rate of use, or at the present rate of increase in use? The answers to these questions are not easily determined, and much caution is necessary in interpreting estimates of existing reserves. Among other factors to be taken into account is the extent to which resources are used, or might be used, over again. In fact, recycling is already an important feature of the flow path of some minerals in developed countries. The rate of recycling for four metals in the United States in 1974, and the United Kingdom in 1978 is shown in Table 7.5. Recycling of minerals clearly alleviates problems arising from increasing scarcity of suitable deposits in nature. On the other hand, all recycling processes are costly in terms of extrasomatic energy.

Another major cause of uncertainty is the degree of accuracy in the various estimates of remaining resources of different minerals. Such estimates may vary by as much as 600 times. The range of some recent estimates for the 'lifetimes' of the reserves of six important metal resources at the present rate of consumption is as follows: aluminium, 53–146 years; copper, 30–61 years; lead, 29–50 years; zinc, 18–32 years; nickel, 42–92 years; and tin, 32–82 years.

Metabolic outputs

From the ecological standpoint, the possibility of resource scarcity is far less dangerous for humankind than that of civilisation 'choking in its own wastes', or severely damaging the productive processes of the biosphere. If resources which are not actually essential for human survival, health and well-being become increasingly scarce, some changes would be necessary in our patterns of consumption and in our societal arrangements; but the human species would survive, and there is little reason to doubt that people would find ways of enjoying life. Severe degradation of the biosphere as a living system capable of supporting humanity would be an infinitely more serious matter.

Broadly, the wastes produced by the high-energy societies are of two kinds. First, there are the organic waste products which are an aspect of the biometabolism of society. They include sewage and unused food, as well as other discarded products of primary production, such as timber and organic fibres. This aspect of societal metabolism is not, of course, peculiar to the high-energy societies. The main differences between the Phase Four situation and earlier societies lie in the quantities of organic wastes produced and in the fact that in many modern situations little of it is returned to the soil, so that the natural nutrient cycles are interrupted. An extreme example is the case of Hong Kong where, for example, in 1971 between six and seven thousand tonnes of organic solids in sewage was discharged into the ocean every day, while artificial fertilizers for use on the land were imported from the other side of the world (Figure 7.4).

The other kind of waste produced is that which results from industrial activities and the use of machines – an aspect of the technometabolism of society. It includes the by-products of extrasomatic energy use itself, such as carbon dioxide, carbon monoxide and radioactive wastes, as well as other waste products of industrial processes and the residues of various commodities, chemical and otherwise, which are used in society. There is now an enormous literature on this subject, and we will deal here only with a few salient examples which draw attention to some of the key ecological issues of our time. The following topics have been selected for brief comment: *acid rain; carbon dioxide in the atmosphere; threats to the ozone layer; and chemicalisation of the biosphere.* First, however, let us indulge in a brief historical digression.

A historical perspective

The recognition of pollution of the environment as undesirable, and the application of cultural adaptive measures aimed at rectifying the problem, are not new and are by no means an exclusive feature of modern high-energy societies. The Hittite code from 15th or 16th Century BC imposed a fine of 6 shekels of silver for people who polluted water in pots or tanks; and air pollution was well recognised as undesirable in England around 1300 AD, when King Edward I is said to have demanded the death penalty for those found guilty of burning coal, presumably because of its undesirable effects on air quality. Nearly a century later, Richard II introduced milder measures, in the form of taxation, to control the use of coal; and early in

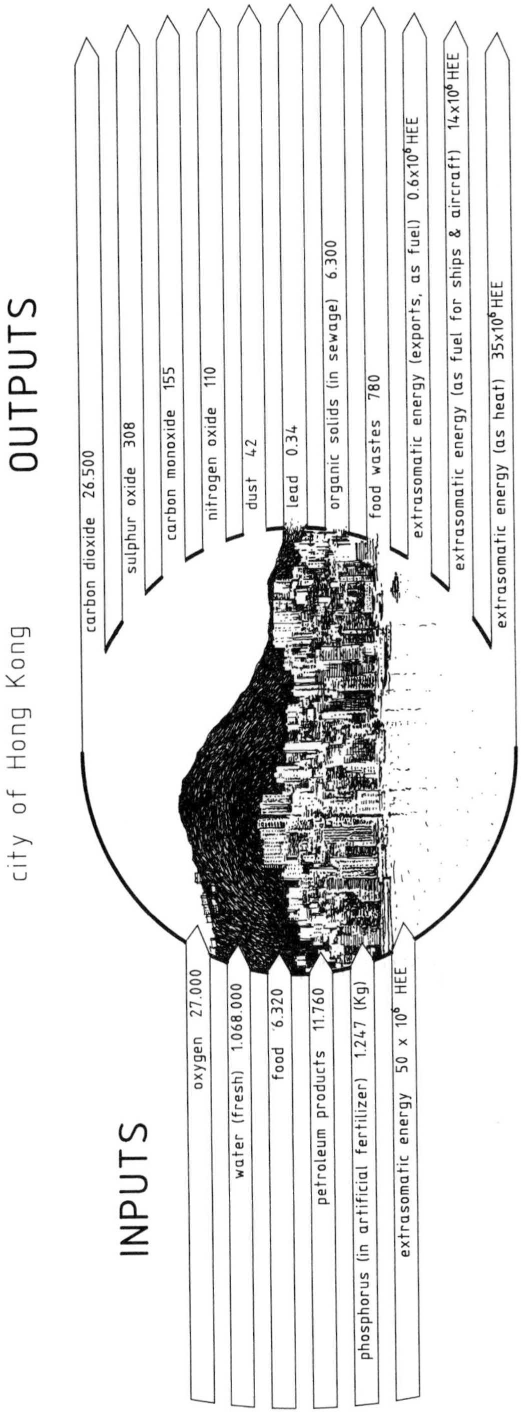

Figure 7.4 The daily metabolism of the city of Hong Kong 1971

Note: except where otherwise stated, the units are tonnes.

INPUTS

oxygen 27.000

water (fresh) 1.068.000

food 6.320

petroleum products 11.760

phosphorus (in artificial fertilizer) 1.247 (Kg)

extrasomatic energy 50 × 10⁶ HEE

city of Hong Kong   OUTPUTS

carbon dioxide 26.500

sulphur oxide 308

carbon monoxide 155

nitrogen oxide 110

dust 42

lead 0.34

organic solids (in sewage) 6.300

food wastes 780

extrasomatic energy (exports, as fuel) 0.6x10⁶ HEE

extrasomatic energy (as fuel for ships & aircraft) 14x10⁶ HEE

extrasomatic energy (as heat) 35x10⁶ HEE

the following century Henry V set up a commission to oversee the use of coal in the city of London.

In 1661, John Evelyn, who later became one of the founding members of the Royal Society, wrote his famous and extraordinarily interesting pamphlet on air pollution in London, entitled *Fumifugium: Or the Inconvenience of the Aer and Smoak of London Dissipated.* He addressed the pamphlet to King Charles II, and in it he blamed the air pollution for 'corrupting the Lungs, and disordering the entire habit of their [the inhabitants of London] Bodies, so that Catarrhs, *Phthisicks, Coughs* and *Consumptions* rage more in this one City, than in the whole Earth besides'. He called for firm measures aimed at removing the industrial sources of the pollution from the precincts of the city. No such measures were taken. His pamphlet was reprinted a hundred years later, but again no action was taken.

Early in the 19th century Parliament in Britain established a Select Committee to study and report on smoke abatement and over the ensuing decades many more committees were set up to consider the problem and to make recommendations. However, it was not until the notorious smog episode of December 1952, when four thousand people died, that the government was finally galvanised into introducing effective legislation banning the burning of coal in open fires in the London area.

As a consequence of more efficient methods of combustion, the use of 'clean' fuels and the installation of smoke-remover equipment and of taller chimneys, the smoke and sulphur dioxide concentrations in the atmosphere have declined in London, and no serious 'acute' pollution episodes have been reported since the early 1960s. London's notorious 'pea-soupers' have become a thing of the past. Since that time regulations aimed at controlling air pollution have also been introduced in many other cities in the developed world. However, in other parts, especially in the developing countries, the atmospheric concentrations of sulphur dioxide and sulphurous particulate matter are increasing. The total global emissions of sulphur dioxide by human society grew at a rate of around 5 per cent per year in the 1970s and reached around 200 million tonnes a year at the end of that decade.

Motor car engines are mainly responsible for the so-called photochemical oxidant smog which results from the release into the atmosphere of nitrogen oxides which react with certain hydrocarbon compounds to form substances that are toxic for human beings and plants. When photochemical smog was at its worst in Los Angeles, citrus fruits could not be grown within 50 km of the city. Photochemical smog is especially important in towns with high traffic densities and warm sunny climates, but it also occurs in Canadian and northern European cities. Controls have been brought into effect in some cities in North America, such as San Francisco and Los

Angeles, and in Japan, reducing the concentrations of noxious substances by up to 40 per cent.

It has been estimated that the annual loss to the grain harvest due to ground-level ozone alone (in the troposphere) resulting from the burning of fossil fuels is around 1 million tonnes.

So far we have discussed undesirable consequences of air pollution which occur locally in the vicinity of the site of release of the noxious agents. However, the scale of societal metabolism is now such that ecologically harmful effects are sometimes observable many hundreds of kilometres away from the site of origin of the pollutants. Indeed, as will be discussed below, it is now apparent that the continuing discharge of waste products of industrial society into the atmosphere will bring about significant and irreversible changes in the climate of this planet as a whole, with unpredictable consequences for humankind.

Acid rain

A pollution issue that has caused considerable concern in recent years on the regional level concerns the impacts on the health of ecosystems of parts of Europe and North America caused by the release into the atmosphere of the products of combustion of fossil fuels. The effect seems to be due, at least in part, to the conversion of the oxides of sulphur and nitrogen to strong mineral acids, and their eventual precipitation. Other pollutants may also play a part. The pollutants may be transported in the atmosphere for 1000 km or more before they reach the ground.

This phenomenon has led to extensive regional acidification of watercourses in southern Scandinavia, in parts of the eastern side of North America and in many other areas. Pollution of the atmosphere is also interfering with bioproductivity in terrestrial ecosystems, and is producing severe and progressive damage to forests over a wide area of Europe. It has been reported, for example, that the area of forest in West Germany showing serious damage from atmospheric pollution in 1987 was about 38,000km^2, or 52 per cent of that country's forests. Forests are dying even high up in the central alpine region of Switzerland, where 53 per cent are dead or severely damaged.

Carbon dioxide

Before the high-energy phase of human existence, certain gases in the atmosphere, notably water vapour and, to a lesser extent, carbon dioxide played a key role in keeping the temperature of the earth at levels suitable for life as we know it. If these gases had not been there, the energy radiated onto the Earth's surface from the sun would have been reradiated, mainly in the form of heat, back into space, and the average temperature on Earth would have been $-18°C$. But water vapour and carbon dioxide, unlike oxygen and nitrogen, absorb some of this heat and then re-emit, it thus blocking its escape into space. The end result of this process, referred to as the greenhouse effect, is a world with an average temperature of $+15°C$.

Cultural developments characteristic of the high-energy phase of human history have resulted in important modifications in the carbon cycle (see page 20), brought about mainly through the use of machines powered by the combustion of coal, oil or natural gas. These fossil fuels contain carbon which was fixed by photosynthesis over many tens of millions of years; it is now being released into the atmosphere in what is, relatively speaking, an extremely short period of time.

The changing pattern of release of carbon dioxide into the atmosphere by human society since the time of the domestic transition is depicted in Figure 7.5, while the increase since the industrial transition is shown in Figure 7.6. The latter figure indicates a fifty fold increase between 1860 and 1975. This development has resulted in an overall increase in the carbon dioxide concentration in the atmosphere since 1860 of about 17 per cent – that is, from around 290 parts per million to over 390 parts per million at the present time. The annual increase in the rate of use of fossil fuels, and hence in carbon dioxide production, has hovered around 4.3 per cent, except during the Depression in the 1930s and the two world wars. It is noteworthy, however, that following economic pressures and some consequent reduction in use of oil, involving some improvements in efficiency of energy use, a fall of 10 per cent in CO_2 emissions was reported for the period 1979–1985. Since that time, however, there has been a steady increase in carbon dioxide production by human society.

Mention must be made of the fact that technological devices using fossil fuels as an energy source are not the only source of extra carbon dioxide in the atmosphere. Deforestation, such as is occurring on a massive scale in tropical and subtropical regions of the world today, also makes a substantial contribution. This is due to the fact that, whether the trees are burned or left to decay, their carbon content is converted in a relatively short time to carbon dioxide and released into the atmosphere. Also, certain industrial processes, such as the manufacture, of cement release carbon dioxide beyond that which results from the combustion of fossil fuels.

Predictions of future changes in the carbon dioxide concentration in the atmosphere depend on assumptions made about the rate of increase in use of fossil fuels in years to come. Assuming, conservatively, an average growth rate of 2 per cent in the future, it is estimated that carbon dioxide would reach 450 parts per million by the year 2025, and 600 parts per million by 2030 – that is, double the pre-industrial level.

This increase in the amount of carbon dioxide in the atmosphere is expected to result in an increase in mean global temperature. In 1896, the

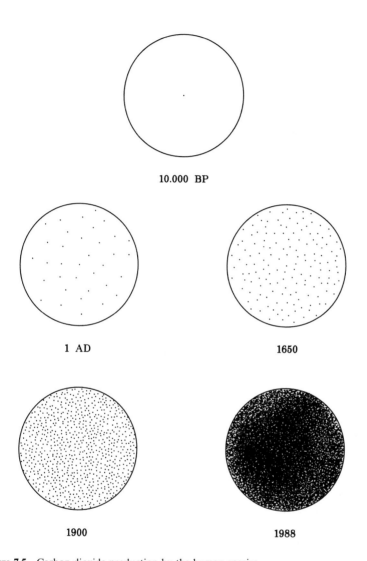

Figure 7.5 Carbon dioxide production by the human species

Swedish chemist Arrhenius calculated that doubling the concentration of carbon dioxide would result in a global mean increase in temperature of 5°C, and most recent calculations come to about the same conclusion. Recent trends in the global temperature are consistent with the view that the warming of the Earth is already underway. For example, the 5 warmest

167

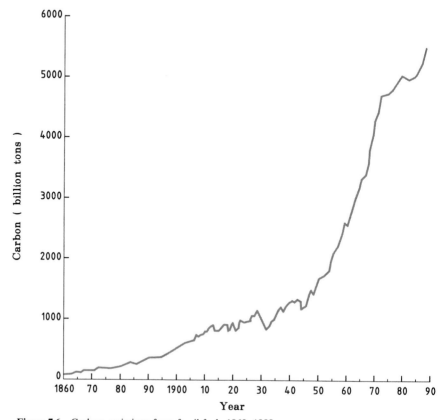

Figure 7.6 Carbon emissions from fossil fuels 1860–1988

years in the last 100 years have all been in the last decade. The global average temperature in the 1890s was 14.5°C, and by the 1980s it had risen to 15.2°. Temperatures levelled off between 1940 and 1970, but there has been an accelerated rise again in the 1980s. However, it is impossible to prove, of course, that these trends are due to human activities.

While there is agreement among scientists that this effect will be manifest, considerable uncertainty exists about the precise degree of warming that might be anticipated for a given increase in carbon dioxide concentration. In general, simulation models suggest that, with a carbon dioxide concentration of 600 parts per million (a conservative prediction for the year 2050) the average global temperature rise would be 3°C to 5°C. Temperatures up to 7°C higher than those at present prevailing would be anticipated in the polar regions.

168

A global temperature rise of 3°C would be unprecedented in human evolutionary history. It would exceed temperatures prevailing in the Antethermal Period around 10,000 years ago, as well as the previous (Eemian) interglacial period of 125,000 years ago. It would approach the warmth of the Mesozoic Period, the age of the dinosaurs, some 200 million years ago.

Human activities are also resulting in the discharge into the atmosphere of other gases which can, through the same mechanism, contribute to global warming. After carbon dioxide, methane (or marsh gas) is the next most important 'greenhouse gas'. It has a bigger effect, molecule for molecule, than carbon dioxide. Methane is produced naturally by fermentation that takes place in the absence of oxygen. The concentration of methane in the atmosphere, which has now reached 1.65 parts per million, has apparently increased between two and three–fold over the past 200 years. It is at present increasing in concentration at a rate of more than 1 per cent per year. There is some uncertainty about the main source of this extra methane, although paddy fields certainly make an important contribution. It is also produced in the digestive tracts of cattle, sheep and other ruminants which have, as a result of human intervention, increased dramatically in numbers over the past couple of centuries. The production and combustion of fossil fuels also results in the release of some methane, although the amount is much less than the amount of carbon dioxide produced. A significant amount is also released from the massive garbage tips of the cities of the modern world.

Rising concentrations of methane in the atmosphere are also bringing about another change, distinct from the greenhouse effect. The methane has created a phenomenon called *noctilescent clouds*, which light up the twilight in certain parts of the world. This effect results from the fact that this gas, on reaching the stratosphere, reacts with oxygen to produce carbon dioxide and water vapour, and the latter condenses to form clouds in the mesosphere. These clouds appear in the summertime at latitudes between Paris and the Arctic Circle and at comparable latitudes in the southern hemisphere.

The chlorofluorocarbons (CFCs), the synthetic products of our industrial society which are responsible for the thinning of the ozone layer, are, volume for volume, many thousand times more potent as greenhouse gases than carbon dioxide. Thus, although in comparison with carbon dioxide the concentration of CFCs in the atmosphere is very low (about 0.6 ppm), their contribution to global warming may well be significant. Nitrous oxide also contributes to the greenhouse effect, but its significance in this regard is at present not well understood.

The increases in concentrations of greenhouse gases in the atmosphere over the last 10 years as a result of human activities have been estimated to be as follows: carbon dioxide, 5 per cent; methane, 11 per cent; nitrous oxide, 3.5 per cent; CFCs, more than 100 per cent.

It is necessary to point out that, while the majority of atmospheric physicists at present consider that global warming due to the production of greenhouse gases is inevitable, there are some who believe that factors such as increasing moisture in the atmosphere will counteract this effect. It appears to be universally agreed, however, that if human society continues to release these substances into the atmosphere some major and progressive climatic change on a global scale is a certainty.

It is expected, on the basis of comparison with earlier periods and of recent improvements in climatic models, that the temperature increase will give rise to considerable changes in global precipitation patterns. This would have severe effects on ecosystem dynamics, on agricultural productivity, and consequently on human societal, economic and political institutions.

The ozone layer

As discussed in Chapter 1, the ozone in the stratosphere absorbs a significant proportion of the ultraviolet radiation from the sun, including especially the most biologically harmful ultraviolet-B (UV-B) rays. For the past 15 years scientists have been predicting that the CFCs released into the atmosphere by modern society would cause progressive destruction of the ozone layer.

The CFCs are used as propellants in spray cans as well as for other purposes such as in refrigerators, air conditioners and freezers and in the manufacture of foam plastics. Despite the warnings, the industrial societies have continued to produce and release vast quantities of CFCs, and it is only very recently, now that the thinning of the ozone layer is becoming apparent, that some action is being taken internationally to reduce, and hopefully one day to halt the production of CFCs. Unfortunately, this action, embodied in the so-called Montreal Protocol, is seen by many as being woefully inadequate. In fact, it has been estimated that, even under the best conditions of the Protocol, the concentration of CFCs in the stratosphere will increase to three times its present level in the next 30 years.

As far as humans are concerned, an increase in the amount of UV-B reaching the ground is predicted to cause an increase in the incidence of skin cancer. As we shall discuss in Chapter 10, there has already been a remarkable increase in the incidence of malignant melanomas in some regions in recent years, and the possibility cannot be ruled out that this may be due to thinning of the ozone layer that has already taken place.

The direct and indirect effects on other forms of life and on bioproductivity could be far-reaching. The plankton near the surface of the oceans, which play so vital a role in the oceanic food chains, will be particularly vulnerable, and many crops grown by humankind are also likely to be adversely affected. In fact, the yields of some crops (e.g. soy beans) may already have been reduced due to this cause.

Chemicalisation of the biosphere

The waste products of modern industrial society discussed above are those which have given rise to most expressions of concern and controversy. However, they represent only a very small fraction of the chemical compounds produced by high-energy societies and released into the environment. It has been estimated that in 1978 about 30,000 different chemicals were manufactured in quantities greater than one tonne per annum and 1500 of these were produced in amounts in excess of 50,000 tonnes per annum. On the basis of predictions of future industrial growth, an increase of 20–25 per cent was estimated in emissions of major conventional pollutants between 1978 and 1985. These chemical substances may be transported across the world by various means, and it is clear that already a significant proportion of the world's human and terrestrial animal populations are exposed to the cumulative effects of low levels of chemical pollutants from a wide range of different sources.

A high proportion of these substances eventually find their way to the oceans, where their long-term effects are as yet unknown. It is clear that already a significant proportion of the world's human and animal populations are exposed to the cumulative effects of low levels of chemical pollutants from a wide range of different and distant sources. Especially important among these substances are heavy metals (e.g. lead and cadmium) and numerous synthetic pesticides, including the organochlorine insecticides like dichlorodiphenyltrichloroethane (DDT) and Dieldrin.

The problem is that undesirable effects of the chemical products of modern civilization on ecosystems or on humans are often not discovered until vast quantities of the substances have already been released into the environment. The case of the polychlorinated biphenyls (PCBs), which are used in electrical equipment and for various other industrial purposes, is a good example. These are synthetic oily compounds which were first made in 1929. Their production peaked between the late 1950s and early 1970s. After that time there was a sharp decline in production when it was discovered that they were causing serious and widespread environmental problems.

The PCBs are harmful to animals in which they accumulate in fatty tissue and readily pass through the lipid parts of cell membranes. It is reported that they reduce the efficiency of the immune system, cause birth defects, promote cancer and, in humans, induce hypertension and stroke.

It has been estimated that 65 per cent of the world's PCBs are still in use, or in storage or deposited into landfills. If these compounds are allowed to leak into the oceans, the extinction of all marine mammals is considered to be inevitable.

Radioactivity

It is well appreciated in our society that the use of nuclear chain reactions as a source of extrasomatic energy results in the production of highly radioactive waste-products and entails significant risks for humankind. The ongoing debate on whether these risks are worth taking – weighed against the perceived advantages of nuclear power – is unresolved. At present there are about 350 nuclear generators in 30 different countries in the world, and these together produce about 15 per cent of all electricity used.

The radioactive by-products of nuclear power generation give rise to two major kinds of problems, one relating to the *disposal* of the end-products of the process under normal conditions, and the other to the possibility of *accidents* in nuclear power stations.

The quality of the wastes produced by the nuclear industry is very variable, but most are highly radioactive and harmful for living organisms, and many will remain so for tens of thousands of years. Waste production begins at the first step in the nuclear fuel cycle – with the mining of uranium. It has been estimated that radioactivity from mill tailings in the USA could be the cause of 4000 cancer deaths each year. The highly radioactive wastes that are produced at the end of the whole process are usually put into stainless steel tanks. Since the dumping of nuclear wastes in the oceans is now prohibited by international agreement, these tanks are stored on land. At one storage site in the USA, between the years 1945 and 1973 about 422,000 gallons of liquid waste containing 500,000 curies of radioactivity had leaked out of the tanks. In the UK high-level wastes are stored at a plant in Cumbria, and the aim is eventually to solidify the waste material in glass, a process known as vitrification. There is controversy among scientists, however, about the long-term effectiveness of this technique.

The other problem, the discharge of highly radioactive material into the environment as a result of accidents at nuclear plants, is also cause for serious concern. According to official estimates published in the USA in 1974, the chance of a major accidental release of radioactive material from a nuclear reactor is 1 in 1 billion years of reactor operation. There is, however, much criticism of such estimates and the assumptions on which they are based. In fact, since 1957 there have been at least four major accidents at nuclear installations: at Kyshtym in the USSR in 1957; at Windscale in the UK in 1957; at Three Mile Island in the USA in 1979; and at Chernobyl in the USSR in 1986.

In the explosion at Chernobyl, which tore through a 1000 tonne 65 cm-thick steel lid and surrounding concrete, at least 30-50 million curies of radioactive substances escaped, including especially iodine-131, caesium-134 and caesium-137. Apart from two individuals killed at the time of the explosion, 30 others died within the following months, mainly from radiation burns and radiation sickness. Several hundred others suffered extreme physical distress as a consequence of the effects of radiation.

Significant radioactive fall-out from the Chernobyl explosion occurred over much of Europe. In Scotland, for instance, sheep became contaminated and hundreds of thousands of lambs, which would have been sold for meat, had caesium levels in their bodies greater than that permitted by the British Government. And to the south, Turkey, Greece and Italy also received disturbingly high fall-out of radioactive iodine and caesium.

Authorities differ in their predictions about the number of extra human cancer deaths that are likely to result from the Chernobyl episode. Estimates range from 2000 (in the European Economic Community alone), through 39,000 to over 1 million.

TECHNOADDICTION

Let us conclude this chapter by noting a biohistorical principle of great importance – the *principle of technoaddiction*. In human history it has frequently been the case that, when new techniques have been introduced into a society, they have not been really necessary for the satisfaction of the survival and health needs of the population. Sometimes they have been introduced simply for curiosity, and sometimes because, in one way or another, they have benefitted a particular individual or group within the society. With the passing of time, however, societies reorganise themselves around the new techniques and their populations gradually become more and more dependent on them for the satisfaction of basic needs. Eventually a state of complete dependence is reached. Clearly, already by 7000 BC, the population of Çatal Hüyük had become almost entirely dependent on farming for their survival, despite the fact that a small part of the food supply still came from hunting. The dependence of the populations of high-energy societies on machines driven by fossil fuels and electricity are more recent examples.

FURTHER READING

Cole, H.S.D., Freeman, C., Jahoda, M., and Pavitt, K.L.R. (eds) (1973). *Thinking about the future: a critique of the limits to growth*. Chatto and Windus, London.
Derry, T.K. and Williams, T.I. (1960). *A short history of technology: from the earliest times to AD 1900*. Clarendon Press, Oxford.
Graham, F. (1970). *Since silent spring*. Houghton Mifflin, Boston.

Grigg, D.B. (1980). *Population growth and agrarian change: an historical perspective.* Cambridge University Press, Cambridge.

Howard, R. and Perley, M. (1982). *Acid rain: the devastating impact on North America.* McGraw-Hill, New York.

Keepin, B. (1986). Review of global energy and carbon dioxide projections. *Annual Review of Energy.* 11. pp.357–392.

Odum, H.T. and Odum, E.C. (1976). *Energy basis for man and nature.* McGraw-Hill, New York.

Pearman, G.I. (ed). (1988). *Greenhouse: planning for climate change.* E.J. Brill, Leiden.

Rowland, F.S. and Isakson, I.S.A. (eds.) *The changing atmosphere.* John Wiley and Sons, New York.

Scott, M., Edmonds, J., Kellogg, M. and Schultz, R. (1990). Global energy and the greenhouse issue. *Energy and Environment.* **1**(1), pp.74–91.

Taher, A.H. (1982). *Energy a global outlook: the case for effective international co-operation.* Pergamon Press, Oxford.

United States National Academy of Sciences. Panel on Stratospheric Chemistry and Transport (1979). *Stratospheric ozone depletion by halocarbons: chemistry and transport.* National Academy of Sciences, Washington DC.

CHAPTER 8

WARFARE AND WEAPONRY

One of the most outstanding characteristics of human populations since the time of the formation of the earliest cities has been *warfare* – that is, the organised and deliberate killing by human groups of members of other human groups. Through the ages warfare has increased, if not in ferocity, certainly in intensity and scale, and it has been almost entirely initiated and carried out by males of the species.

At the root of this phenomenon lies the tendency of humans to form themselves into distinct groupings, based sometimes on biological or racial factors, sometimes on geographical location, but more especially on cultural differences, especially language, religious beliefs and political affiliations. These groupings have, to varying degrees, been transient, sometimes eventually splitting up into new groupings, sometimes merging with each other, and sometimes disappearing altogether.

While humans are usually concerned for the well-being of members of their in-groups, this concern is seldom extended to members of out-groups, who are usually viewed with suspicion. Not infrequently this suspicion develops into overt hatred and hostility, and the extent to which this occurs and to which it persists in different human situations is determined largely by cultural forces.

The actual motivations for organised violence among humans are multiple. The following seem to be especially important: political motives, aimed at achieving dominance over, or independence from, other groupings; greed, and desire for material wealth; religious fervour, leading to the slaughter of non-believers in the name of one's god or gods; simple self-preservation – for example, when population pressure or other factors cause a shortage of resources, or when individuals fear that they and their families will be wiped out by a perceived enemy; the collection of prisoners to be used as slaves or to be sacrificed in religious rituals; transgenerational transmission of hatred and fear between groups; and response to cultural glorification of the idea of violence for its own sake. Often the motivation is a combination of two or more of these factors.

It is significant that the motives for fighting commonly vary considerably even among the participants on one side in any particular conflict; those of the military leaders are often quite different from those of the ordinary members of the fighting force.

Culture came to accept warfare as a normal aspect of human affairs early on in the history of civilization, and the warrior soon became the hero figure of society – an image encouraged, no doubt, by the ruling classes. Moreover, the acceptance of warfare as a natural and inevitable aspect of life led to the creation of a range of special societal institutions concerned primarily with preparation for, and the waging of war.

UBIQUITY OF WARFARE

Warfare became thoroughly institutionalised as an aspect of societal behaviour soon after the formation of the first cities in Mesopotamia. To what extent it had been a feature of pre-urban communities before that time it is unclear. Certainly the remains of pre-urban settlements in the Tigris and Euphrates valleys, and of many neolithic settlements of central Europe suggest that their inhabitants were peaceable, and did not feel themselves to be threatened by physical attack from strangers; and the archaeological work at the remarkable neolithic settlement of Çatal Hüyük in Anatolia suggests that warfare was not a feature of the life experience of its population.

On the other hand, it is clear that from very early times violent hostilities were an important aspect of life in some farming communities. The walls of Jericho, first built around 8000 BC, are often cited as evidence of this fact. Towards the end of the neolithic phase in Europe – that is, just before the introduction of metallurgy, the relative peace was shattered by the aggressive 'Battle-axe People', intent on warfare and on political domination; and recent evidence indicates that around 2500 BC early farming people in the south of England built and attacked fortified settlements. More recently, tribal warfare was a commonplace among the tribes of the highlands of Papua New Guinea. It was of a strongly ritualized nature, and each episode usually resulted in only one or two deaths, if any. At the same time, however, the people of the villages along the coastal strip to the east of the Papua New Guinea Highlands lived at peace with one another.

There has been speculation and debate about the role of militarism in the formation of the early cities in Sumer. There is no evidence of fortifications around the settlements of farmers in the region immediately before the cities formed. However, some authors suggest that the initial formation of the cities was the result of the local people clustering together, perhaps under transient military leaders, as protection against attack from bands of aggressive nomads. Certainly the first cities were in existence well before soldiering came to be a recognised profession. In the early days of Sumerian civilization there was no standing army, although the king may have had a small bodyguard. The male citizens of each city were organised into a fighting force when the occasion demanded. At first this occurred when plundering bands of barbarians invaded the area; but, as the region came to be more sharply divided into city states, each owing allegiance to a different patron god, and as water and land became increasingly scarce, warfare between these states became common.

By the beginning of the 3rd millennium BC, military formations with a distinctly professional appearance were in evidence. Foot soldiers were uniformly equipped with bronze or copper helmets, big rectangular shields and long spears, and were depicted in sculptures as being drawn up in a six-deep phalanx; other troops, with helmets but no body-armour, carried long lances and were arranged in double file. It is not clear whether these were full-time soldiers, but we do know that around 2388 BC Sargon, King of Akkad, found it necessary to have a standing army of 5400 men. Hammurabi of Babylon also had a large force of professional soldiers and, according to Egyptian sources, the Hittite army late in the second millennium BC numbered 17,000 infantry plus 3500 chariots.

As civilization spread into, or developed in other parts of the Eurasian continent, it took on somewhat different characteristics in different places. Eventually four quite distinct and lasting cultural regions came into being: the Middle East, Europe, India and China. Let us very briefly consider the history of warfare in each of these regions. There also existed a fifth region of human habitation that was of immense consequence for all four zones of civilization; it was the vast steppe-lands extending across the northern part of the Eurasian continent north of the Himalayas and, at the eastern end, to the north of the Gobi Desert. The grasslands of this immense area proved to be a prolific source of invaders, wave after wave of whom migrated into the Middle East, Europe, India and China.

In the Middle East the two original centres of civilization were Meso-potamia and Egypt. In the case of the former especially, the multiplicity of rulers and the frequency of warfare, both between the city states and resulting from invasions from outside, led to the appearance and disappearance of numerous empires. The first of these came into existence around 2375 BC under Slugalzaggisi of Umma and, a generation later, the more enduring Akkadian Empire of Sargon was formed; and then between 500 and 600 years after this Hammurabi established the Babylonian Empire. These were followed by a long series of different transient kingdoms or empires associated with different cultural or racial groupings that included the

Assyrians, Hittites, Persians, Hyksos, Partheans, Bactrians, Greeks, Romans and, considerably later, the Moslems.

In Europe the situation was rather different, because at the time of the Roman invasion there was essentially no background of urbanisation and there were no city states. Nevertheless, there had already been considerable movement and intermixing of groupings, no doubt on occasion involving some violence – as in the case of the movements of Battle-axe People who migrated across Europe from the east in the second millennium BC, entering Britain at about the same time as the Beaker-folk. At the time of the Roman invasions, Celtic groups were dominant in Western Europe. Later, during the decline of the Roman influence, many different groupings of humans made themselves felt throughout the region through their aggressive actions. Some originated within the region, and some came from farther afield. They included, to mention just a few by name: the Sueves, Angles, Jutes, Saxons, Goths, Visigoths, Vandals, Francs, Vikings, Normans, Moors, Picts, Scots – and, emanating at least in part from the East, the Avars and Huns.

After the time of the Carolingian Empire, and especially after the period of Charlemagne's rule (768–814 AD), the tribal movements became less common and a succession of competing and, to a greater or lesser extent, transient kingdoms, empires and principalities came into existence, and these were frequently at war with each other. However, every now and again fresh waves of migrating warriors entered the area, including Turks, Tartars and Mongols originating in the Eurasian steppes.

Warfare in Europe thus became commonplace. Some wars were short-lived, and some lasted for many decades, and there were a few civil wars among them. Over the centuries there was a general tendency for the scale of warfare to increase – with ever-larger armies and navies and ever-higher numbers of casualties. It was political conflicts between European states that provided the starting points for the two greatest wars of all time – World War I and World War II of the 20th century.

In India the cities of the Harappan civilization were in full flower between 2500 and 2000 BC; but archaeological investigations have yielded little evidence of weapons or of armour, and this has been interpreted as indicating that warfare was not an important feature of these communities. Harappan society was not, it seems, a military empire, but rather a kind of priestly state. After a period of decline, these cities were completely destroyed about 1500 BC by the invading barbarians who called themselves Aryans, and who spoke an Indo-European language. The Aryans grouped themselves into a number of rival and warlike coalitions and by around the 8th century BC a series of monarchies had come into existence in this part of India. Somewhat later some big kingdoms were formed further to the east in the Ganges Valley (Kosala and Magadha). At the end of the

4th century BC, Chandragupta Maurya used military force to unite the populations of the Ganges and Indus Valleys; and this empire was further expanded by his grandson Asoka. This empire extended from what is now Afghanistan to the province of Madras.

Asoka, however, turned out to be exceptional among military monarchs. After one of his successful expeditions he suddenly developed a deep sense of disgust at the cruelties and horrors of war, and decided thenceforth to cease all military activities. He became a devout Buddhist and put a great deal of effort into a range of charitable works and to establishing hospitals and public gardens. He was especially concerned about the welfare of the aboriginal people of India and he particularly made provision for the education of women.

After Asoka's reign, India was subjected to a series of invasions, coming mainly from the steppes to the north. These resulted in political fragmentation which lasted until the time of the Gupta Empire, which was in existence from 320 to 570 AD, during which time conditions were relatively peaceful. Subsequently the region split up again, this time into a number of different kingdoms, some Moslem and some Hindu, and there was frequent conflict between them. Early in the 16th century a Turkoman chieftain called Baber, a descendant of Jengis Khan, assembled an army in Afghanistan and invaded Hindustan, where he became emperor. His descendants extended this empire so that eventually all of India came under Mogul control. This Mogul regime persisted as an effective entity, although not without perturbations and considerable military activity, until 1707, after which date the region became fragmented again and suffered a series of relatively small-scale invasions from Iran, Afghanistan and Nepal.

India then became subject to a different kind of invasion – the spread of European trading companies. By 1761, the East India Company of Britain, with the help of its own private army, had become dominant in India, and it remained so until it handed over its authority to the British Crown in 1858. The eventual relinquishment of British power over India and Pakistan in the present century was achieved without war.

Warfare became firmly established early on in the history of Chinese civilization. Noble worriors were much in evidence in the Shang Empire of the 14th to the 11th centuries BC. This dynasty itself was eventually overthrown by armies of the Chou dynasty around 1000 BC. However, throughout this period warfare between princely states was a chronic feature of Chinese civilization, until around 200 BC when the formidable Qin Empire came into existence. This regime was radically different from those that preceded it, and was highly militarised, bureaucratic and ruthless. It was responsible for the construction of the Great Wall (some parts of which were already in existence) as protection against the continual threat from people of the steppes to the north. The first emperor, Qin-Shihuang, became the political and military master of all China. As an individual, he was greatly concerned about life after death, and he arranged to have an army of 7000 terracotta soldiers and many horses, beautifully and realistically shaped, buried with him at the time of his death. Discoveries in this tomb include many weapons which show a striking degree of technological sophistication, including cross-bows made of wood with elegant metal triggering mechanisms.

This conception of the Emperor as the all-powerful did not, however, persist. The Qin Dynasty was eventually displaced by the Han Dynasty and later by the Sui (598–618), Tang (618–907) and Sung (906–1250) Dynasties. There appear to have been some periods of relative peace during the reigns of the different dynasties, although the Tang Dynasty in particular was an age of military expansion towards the west.

Then came the great Mongolian conquest, and Kublai Khan was made Emperor of China at Shanghai. This alien regime, known as the Yuan Dynasty, lasted from 1280 to 1365, and was eventually overthrown by native revolt and replaced by the Ming Dynasty which persisted until the 17th century, when further military invasions from the north once again disturbed the peace.

THE STEPPE LANDS

From the biological standpoint, the fact that the Eurasian steppe lands were a source of continual waves of invaders, moving to the south-east, south and south-west, over at least three thousand years remains something of an enigma. The inference seems to be that, although the conditions in the steppe country were especially conducive to population growth, the potential for increasing local food supply in the region was rather limited. While the grasslands in the summer were lush, the winters were undoubtedly cold. Subsistence was based mainly on the maintenance of large herds of cattle and sheep. It seems that the conditions of life in the region were conducive to good health, successful reproduction and the formation of relatively large families; and the rugged lifestyle produced men who were particularly strong, vigorous and effective as warriors. Whatever the biological explanation, the migratory movements of these people were already underway between the 17th and 15th centuries BC, and they hardly ceased thereafter during the next two to three thousand years. Especially notable in Europe were the Huns, who invaded around 375 AD and the Avars who came just over 300 years later and who settled in the western extremity of the European steppe in Hungary (later, around 895 AD, the Magyars arrived in this region, also coming from the north-east). Finally, the great series of Mongol invasions, begun early in the 13th century by Genghis Khan and continuing late into the 14th century under the leadership of his successors, conquered and subdued populations in China, eastern Turkestan, Afghanistan, Persia, Mesopotamia, Asia Minor, Syria, Poland, Russia, Hungary, Bulgaria and Korea.

THE SCALE OF WAR

Cultural evolution in Eurasia over the past 5000 years has been associated with a progressive increase in the number of people actively participating in the wars that have taken place, as well as in the number of people killed. Even more striking has been the massive growth in the destructive power of weapons.

Numbers of participants and casualties

In the very early days of organised warfare between the city states of Mesopotamia, the numbers of individuals actively participating in the combat process was probably not great – perhaps sometimes less than 100 and seldom more than a few thousand.

In Europe, in the 1st century BC, the armies involved in Caesar's campaign in Gaul are said to have confronted three million enemy soldiers, killing one million of them and taking another one million prisoner. At the battle of Troyes in 451 AD, when Attila the Hun was finally defeated by an army of Franks, Visigoths and Romans, 150,000 men are thought to have been killed. The armies of Jenghis Khan were quite small, considering the extent of their military successes. While he had a personal guard of 10,000 men, the total army of ordinary soldiers probably numbered no more than 120,000.

Napoleon took about 600,000 men with him to Russia in 1812. One hundred and fifty thousand of them had been lost even before he reached Moscow, and only a very small proportion of the total number, perhaps no more than 4–5000, returned home. In the Taiping rebellion in China, which started in 1850 and lasted for 14 years, forty million people were killed.

In the 1914–1918 World War, about 53 million men were mobilized into the armed forces, and about 13 million were killed. During the 4 months from August to November in 1914, 640,000 French soldiers lost their lives. The army of the United Kingdom lost over 400,000 men in the battle of the Somme, 50,000 of them on the first day.

World War II differed from previous conflicts in that aerial bombing of important cities resulted in much higher civilian casualties. The armed forces (armies, navies and air forces) of the warring nations numbered about 30 million and the total number of individuals killed, military and civilian, was probably between 35 and 40 million.

181

To the time of writing, a further world war has so far been avoided, although serious regional military conflicts have taken place resulting in hundreds of thousands of deaths.

Weaponry

The tool-kit of humans has, since primeval times, included some weapons. In hunter–gatherer situations these were used mainly in hunting animals for food and, to some extent, for protection against large predators, and it is unlikely that they were often used in combat between human groups. Broadly, these weapons were of two classes. First, the *close-range* weapons, which included clubs, hand axes and spears, consisted basically of an extension of the human arm and were used for directly striking the quarry. The *long-range* weapons were missiles, such as sticks or stones, which were thrown at the quarry, initially by the human arm, but later by other means, as in the case of the sling and the bow and arrow.

After the beginning of urban civilization most weapons were designed especially for killing other members of the human species. They also fall into the same two classes. Long-range weapons are of prime importance in the current human situation.

Along with the development of weapons, there was a concomitant development of armour, usually made of leather or metal, the purpose of which was to provide individual soldiers with some protection against the weapons of the enemy.

Of the close-range weapons used in warfare, the spear is the most ancient. In one form or another it had been used by humans for hunting for tens of thousands of years, originally with a handle of wood and a spearhead of stone. When techniques of metallurgy were developed around 3000 BC spearheads, and sometimes spear shafts, were made of copper or bronze. The soldiers of Sumeria (from 3000 BC) and the Old Kingdom of Egypt (from around 2700 BC) were equipped with metal spears. Later, the lance was developed as the cavalry version of the piercing spear.

The other important short-range weapon used in warfare, invented and developed specifically for that purpose, is the *sword*. This weapon is adapted for cutting or thrusting into flesh, and consists of a handle or *hilt* with a cross-guard, and a pointed blade which may be straight or curved. One or both of the edges of the blade are usually sharp. Soldiers often became emotionally attached to their swords and even gave them names. Famous examples from history and legend are Charlemagne's sword 'Joyeuse' and King Arthur's 'Excalibur'.

The discovery, probably made early in the 13th century AD, that a mixture of saltpetre (i.e. potassium nitrate), sulphur and charcoal is highly explosive represented an extremely important development in the history of warfare.

Some authors suggest *gunpowder* originated in China. Certainly, the Chinese had used inflammable mixtures in warfare for centuries as, indeed, had Europeans; but there is no direct evidence that they used explosives.

There is evidence of the use of gunpowder in warfare around 1250 AD by the Moors, who placed 0.5–1 kg of the explosive mixture into an iron bucket, which had a small touch-hole at the bottom. They placed a pile of stones on top of the gunpowder, which was then ignited, so that the stones were propelled through the air, ideally towards the target.

The first *cannons* were introduced at the beginning of the 14th century and were made of bronze. They were replaced by iron cannons half a century later. It is said that the first event of importance in Europe in which the power of artillery played a leading part was the capture of Constantinople in 1453 by the Ottoman Turks. The gunpowder invention was also applied to the development of hand weapons, but these proved relatively ineffectual for quite a long time – partly because of the necessity to keep a match alight in the combat situation (to fire the gunpowder), and partly because of the difficulties in keeping the gunpowder dry. The clumsy process of using a ramrod for stuffing the lead bullets into position from the end of the barrel also contributed to the problems. Proper *rifles* were not used for military purposes until the Thirty Years War (1618–1648). Later technological developments, including breech loading and many other technical advances greatly increased the accuracy, range and general effectiveness of both hand firearms and artillery.

Associated with these developments, important changes began to take place in the 'art of warfare'. By the time of the First World War, some of the combat was no longer on a face-to-face basis, or even on a one-to-one basis. A single touch of the trigger of a machine gun might kill a dozen men; and one artillery shell could destroy large numbers of individuals who were completely out of sight of the shooter. This fundamental change in the nature of armed conflict had proceeded further by the time of World War II, when bombing by air became important and long-range weapons, including rockets of various kinds, were introduced. The situation now exists that deliberate hostile action by a very small number of individuals many thousands of miles away from their targets could result in the deaths of millions of human beings.

Modern weaponry

As we have already noted, various technological advances in human history have led to a progressive increase in the lethality and destructive capacity of weapons used in warfare. The invention and use of gunpowder, although at first not very effective, was a particularly significant step in this regard. Cultural processes in the high-energy societies have resulted in further highly portentous developments in the production of devices designed for destroying humans. Among the range of highly sophisticated instruments of mass destruction that exist today in the arsenals of powerful nations, *nuclear weapons* are by far the most destructive.

During the last part of World War II, Germany and the United States were competing to be the first to produce nuclear weapons. Then, 3 months after the capitulation of Germany, at 8.15 a.m. on the 6th August 1945, a nuclear bomb was dropped from an American aircraft onto the city of Hiroshima in Japan. At least 140,000 people, that is about 40 per cent of the population of the city, were immediately killed or died soon afterwards. The buildings of the city were flattened over an area of 13 km^2. Three days later, another bomb was dropped on the Japanese city of Nagasaki, and 26 per cent of its population of about 280,000 was killed outright.

Since that time, governments of opposing ideologies have directed immense financial resources and human effort on research into and development of nuclear weapons, with the result that bombs now exist with an explosive power one thousand times that of the bomb which was dropped on Hiroshima. A single American B-52 strategic nuclear bomber can now carry more explosive power on a single trip than has been used in all the wars in human history.

At the time of writing, the USA, the USSR, the United Kingdom, France and China are known to possess nuclear weapons. India has detonated a nuclear explosion, and Israel and South Africa are believed to have nuclear arms. However, the arsenals of the United States and Russia completely overshadow those of other nations. Together, these two powers possess weapons with explosive power equivalent to 12,000 million tonnes of trinitrotoluene (TNT). The explosive power of the nuclear arsenals of the world is now equal to about one million of the bombs that were dropped on Hiroshima. This is equivalent to at least 3 tonnes of TNT per man, woman and child of the world population.

The individual weapons range in strength from the equivalent of around one hundred tonnes to twenty million tonnes of TNT, depending on the particular use for which they are designed. Broadly two categories of nuclear weapons are recognised – the strategic (or intercontinental) and the shorter-range tactical weapons.

The growth in the explosive power of bombs during the present century can be illustrated by the following analogy. If we imagine the explosive power of the biggest bombs in World War I to be represented by a pea, then the most powerful weapons (other than the atomic bombs used at Hiroshima, Nagasaki) used in the Second World War would equal the size of a large plum. The Hiroshima bomb would be equivalent to a sphere of about 0.5 metres across, and the most powerful bombs now ready for use would have a diameter of 5 metres.

It is impossible to predict precisely the ecological and human impacts of a nuclear war, and in any case these would obviously depend to some extent on the scale of that war and on the geographical distribution of the nuclear explosions. Nevertheless, it is clear that, even if only one tenth of the existing nuclear weapons were used, the numbers of people killed by fire, blast and fall-out would be astronomical[1]. Most commentators consider it likely that a nuclear war between the major world powers would leave some survivors, especially in the southern hemisphere. However, major uncertainties exist about the effects of such a war on the bioproductivity of ecosystems as a consequence of radiation and of climatic changes resulting from smoke from widespread fires. It could well be that the biosphere as we know it today would collapse, and no longer be capable of supporting a human population. Even if this did not occur, it is clear that life for any surviving groups of humans would be very different from that which we experience today.

So it is that in the lifetime of many of us alive today, and for the first time in 3000–4000 million years of life on Earth, a single species, through its unique and peculiar aptitude for culture, has developed the means to destroy most, if not all of its kind within a few days, and to cause unimaginable devastation in the biosphere as a whole.

Before concluding this chapter, mention must also be made of the enormous amount of effort and resources that have been devoted in modern high-energy societies to the development of other sophisticated and extremely potent methods of killing people. Thus, apart from the advances in nuclear armaments, great progress has been made in the development and production of chemical and biological weapons. We will not, however, discuss these weapons here since, horrific though they may be, their impact on civilisation, on the human species, and on other life forms would be small in comparison with that of a nuclear war.

The share of the industrial work-force employed in military-servicing industries in selected countries in 1989 was as follows: Israel 22.6 per cent, Malaysia 18 per cent, USA 11 per cent, USSR 9.7 per cent, UK 9 per cent, France 6.3 per cent, Argentina 5.0 per cent, India 3.0 per cent, Norway and Singapore 2.7 per cent, Spain 2.0 per cent, Pakistan 0.8 per cent, South Korea 0.7 per cent. Human society as a whole spends over US $1 million per minute on the development and manufacture of homicidal devices. In 6 hours, more money is spent on the manufacture of arms than was spent

---

[1] The explosive power of this number of nuclear weapons (1/10 of the total in number in existence) would be 100,000 times as great as that of the Hiroshima bomb. If they caused 100,000 times as many casualties, the number of people killed outright would be three times the total population of the world.

CHAPTER 9

CHANGES IN HUMAN SOCIETY

In this chapter we will take a brief look, from a biohistorical standpoint, at some of the momentous changes that have taken place in the structure of human societies over the past several thousand years.

It is reasonable to regard the introduction of farming as the first critical step in this series of changes in the nature of human society. Nevertheless, despite the larger numbers of people living together in a single farming community as compared with primeval society, the farming economy itself does not necessarily demand any important change in societal organisation, beyond the need for some simple arrangements to determine who is responsible for working a particular portion of land and who has the right to keep and use the food grown on it. However, while farming does not demand major deviation from the primeval social pattern, it certainly allows such deviation. In fact, the range of patterns of societal organisation, of land tenure and of distribution of material wealth in early farming communities has been very wide.

There is, however, one common denominator and underlying determinant of social organisation in farming communities, and that is kinship. In all farming societies, the family network, whether organised along patrilineal or matrilineal lines, forms the basis of the economic system, and economic co-operation is mostly between members of families, and most social interaction is based either on family connections or on shared residential area. As in the case of primeval societies, almost all social interactions are on a face-to-face basis.

Of much greater biosocial significance were the changes that occurred when people came to live together in much larger groups, made up initially of several thousand individuals, in the early towns and cities. One of the biologically novel aspects of this new situation was the fact that *Homo sapiens* became the only species of mammal in which a high proportion of the members of certain populations did not participate in direct subsistence activity – that is, they were not directly involved in acquiring food from the ecosystems of which they were a part.

Already by 7000–6000 BC there was at least one place in existence, Çatal Hüyük, where several thousand people lived together in a township in homes built of mud bricks. Most of the cities that emerged between 3500 and 3000 BC in the so-called 'cradle of civilization' in Mesopotamia had populations numbering from 5000–20,000, although it has been suggested that in 2000 BC the city of Ur may have had a population of 34,000, with a much larger number of people living in suburban areas beyond the walls of the old town.

The Harappan civilization, which came into existence in the Indus valley in the last part of the 3rd millennium BC, included a number of cities, of which Harappa and Mohenjo-daro were the largest. They were destroyed at the time of the Aryan invasion of India about 1500 BC. At about this time cities were also developing in China in the valley of the Yellow River.

Although there is some evidence that very large ceremonial buildings were built in Peru as long ago as 1200 BC, it seems that true cities did not develop on the American continent before the beginning of the 1st millennium AD. Excavations suggest that the Mayan city of Dzibilchaltan in Yucatan contained as many as 17,000 structures, most of which would have been dwellings, suggesting that the population was around 28,000. The largest city on the continent was almost certainly Teotihuacan, the capital of the Aztec empire, which was situated in the region of modern Mexico City. Its population may have reached 300,000.

The populations of the cities of Europe and the Middle East did not, with a few exceptions, exceed 100,000 before the 17th and 18th centuries. Athens, in the days of Pericles and Socrates, probably had about 100,000 inhabitants. One of the exceptions was Rome: estimates of its population around the first century AD range from 250,000 to one million. Constantinople, at the time of Justinian in the middle of the 6th century AD, may also have had a population of about one million.

During the early part of the Middle Ages, there was a great multiplication of cities in Europe, associated with a considerable increase in the total population of the region. For example, 2500 townships are believed to have been sprung into existence between the 12th and 13th centuries in the area known today as Germany. Throughout the Middle Ages and the time of the Renaissance, most of the larger cities of Europe had populations of between 25,000 and 60,000, although Venice and Milan may have exceeded 100,000. During the 17th century there were big increases in the populations of some cities, and by the end of the 18th century, Paris had a population of over 670,000, Naples of over 430,000 and London of over 800,000.

The cities of the Western world grew rapidly at the time of the industrial transition. In Britain the population of the new industrial city of Manchester increased from 35,000 in 1769 to over 300,000 in 1851.

The proportion of the world's population living in cities has increased dramatically in the present century. In 1920 14 per cent of the human population lived in urban areas, and in 1980 the proportion was 40 per cent. It is predicted that by the year 2000 more than half of the total population will be city dwellers.

The size of cities has also been increasing. In 1900 no city had a population of as much as 5 million. In 1960 there were six cities with 5 million or more inhabitants, while in 1980 there were 26, and it is predicted that in 2000 AD there will be 60. The world's 15 fastest growing cities are all in developing countries.

The sheer size of present and future cities is without precedent in human history. At the time of writing the population of Mexico City is about 20 million. By 2000 it will be 30 million.

Cities are, of course, of immense ecological significance for the planet, since it is in them that most of the extrasomatic energy is used by humankind, and that by far the greater part of the pollutants that threaten the integrity of the biosphere are produced.

SOME BIOSOCIAL CONSEQUENCES OF URBANISATION

It is self-evident that cultural developments which resulted in, and resulted from, the formation of cities had profound effects on both the biology and the social organisation of human populations. Some of these effects have already been mentioned in the last chapter in which we discussed the role of cities in the institutionalisation of warfare; and in Chapter 10 we will consider some of the biological consequences of urbanisation. In the present chapter we will comment briefly on some of its implications for social organisation. Before doing so, however, it is worth recalling that, despite the multiplication and growth of cities and townships over the past several hundred years, and despite the overwhelming role of cities in human affairs, until very recent times the great majority of humans have not lived in them.

From the biological standpoint, one of the most consequential of the culture-created changes that followed urbanisation was the shift from relative homogeneity to marked heterogeneity in human populations. This change came about as the result of three key societal developments. They were: *occupational specialism*; *political stratification* (social stratification in terms of power); and *wealth stratification* (stratification in terms of material possessions). As a result of these changes, and for the first time in human history, enormous variability came to exist in the life conditions of different human beings living in a single community. As a result, different groups of humans experienced quite different patterns of health and disease and of enjoyment and distress.

This fundamental change in the biology of human populations became evident early on in the history of civilization, and it persists to the present day. In the early Sumerian cities of five thousand years ago there were leather workers, cabinet-makers, bakers, potters, metal workers, basket-makers, shop keepers, housewives, brewers, weavers, gardeners, artists, music-makers, soldiers, scribes, priests and members of the ruling royal family. The life conditions of these various specialists differed not only from one group to another, but also from the life conditions which had prevailed in the evolutionary environment of the human species. In some cases, the evodeviant conditions were aspects of people's personal environments (e.g. polluted air or high noise levels) and in others they consisted of unnatural behaviour patterns. The following ailments, taken from a list of common names of about 130 occupational diseases, are examples of phylogenetic maladjustment resulting from the evodeviant life conditions experienced by workers in different occupations that came into existence as a consequence of urbanisation: brass-founder's ague, chimney sweep's cancer, grocer's itch, housemaid's knee, woolsorter's disease, baker's asthma, blacksmith's deafness, coal-miner's phthisis, flour worker's dermatitis, gold smelter's cataract, lighterman's bottom, metal-fume fever, mule-spinner's cancer, nun's bursitis, painter's cramp, potter's rot, stonemason's disease and weaver's bottom.

Occupational specialisation has remained a feature of civilization to this day, and despite the fact that a great deal of attention has been paid to the problem of occupational disease, many jobs in modern society are still associated with health hazards. Repetitive strain injury in musicians and word-processor operators, the overconsumption of calories as a consequence of frequent business lunches in executives, and lung cancer in asbestos workers are examples.

Although the organisation of society in the early cities when they first came into existence may have been moderately egalitarian, it was not long before marked social stratification became a feature of urban communities. The situation differed significantly from that in primeval society not only because the hierarchical structure of urban populations was much more complex, but also because it was more permanent. Unlike in hunter–gatherer communities, an individual's place in the hierarchy was seldom decided spontaneously according to his or her propensity for leadership in different circumstances, but was determined mainly by birth, and it was unlikely to vary a great deal from hour to hour or day to day. It is true that the whole social arrangement could be overturned by invasion or revolution, but otherwise it was relatively fixed. An individual might be born as a slave, a member of the lower or middle classes, a member of the nobility, or a king or queen.

The relationship between wealth and power in early civilization has been the subject of one of the numerous cause-and-effect debates in the social sciences. Some authors have assumed that it was the growth of private property and differentials in material wealth that led to political stratification. Others have taken the opposite view and have assumed that the uneven distribution of material wealth and the rights to property were an expression of political stratification, rather than a cause of it. Whichever of these viewpoints is correct, or whether perhaps the relationships between power and wealth went hand in hand from the very start, the end-result was a stratified society in which political power and material wealth were closely associated.

Although there has been considerable variability throughout history in the means by which permanent or semi-permanent hierarchies have been formed and in their durability, they have remained an established feature of civilization throughout its history. At present they are found in all walks of life – commercial, industrial, military, governmental, religious and academic – and a positive correlation still exists in all societies the world over between material wealth on the one hand and place in the power structure on the other.

One of the important consequences of urbanisation from the biosocial standpoint was that it brought about a fundamental change in the in-group and out-group structure of society[1]. In the hunter–gatherer setting, the in-group and out-group situation was relatively simple. Individuals usually belonged to a single in-group, the band, which was made up largely of members of the extended family. Out-groups were other bands, which were for most of the time out of sight and probably also out of mind. It is possible that populations of other animal species were regarded in somewhat the same way as out-groups of human beings were perceived in later societies. With urbanisation and societal specialisation and stratification, the individual's world became full of different out-groups to which he or she did not belong – some of them to be feared, and some to be despised. For the first time, the distinction between 'us' and 'them' became a characteristic feature of the daily experience of the average person.

Because individual human beings do not seem to have any particular innate concern for other human beings who are not members of their in-groups, and because there is a tendency to treat out-groups with suspicion,

---

[1] The expression in-group is used here to denote a group of people with which an individual identifies, and the members of which behave supportively to each other. Out-groups are all those groups of people which are perceived by an individual to be external to the in-group or in-groups to which he or she belongs.

and because this tendency can so readily develop into overt hostility, the new in-group–out-group structure of early urban society created a potentially explosive state of affairs. Society responded to the new situation by compensating for this absence of appropriate innate regulatory mechanisms by introducing formal regulations, or laws, and by institutionalising punishments for disobeying them. These laws were usually presented as being the instructions of a deity. The Code of Hammurabi of Babylon of around 1750 BC, and the Hebrew Code of Moses from around the same time are particularly well-known examples, although they are both essentially revisions of codes originally put together several hundred years earlier.

Fragments from the Code of Ur Nammu, dated around 2500 BC, show that the law of 'an eye for an eye and a tooth for a tooth' had already given way to a system in which a money fine was substituted as a punishment. In this respect, the Code of Hammurabi was somewhat retrogressive, in that the principle of retaliation played a larger part than in earlier codes, and the death penalty was invoked more widely, especially for crimes against the upper class. In the Babylonian Code, death was the punishment for house-breaking, brigandage, rape, incest, causing abortion, faulty building resulting in a fatal accident, black magic, kidnapping, connivance in a slave's escape, sheltering a runaway slave, receipt of stolen property and certain kinds of theft. It is interesting to note that, while the higher the class of the individual wronged, the bigger the punishment, the punishment for a given offence was also greater for a member of the upper class than it was for a member of the lower class.

Thus we see that compensatory cultural adaptive mechanisms eventually gave rise to new ways of controlling social behaviour, rather different from those that had operated for tens of thousands of generations before the advent of urbanisation. Over the millennia formal legislation became increasingly complicated, and modern society would be inconceivable without its elaborate set of laws and various prescribed punishments for their infringement.

Ownership and wealth

The concept of ownership is presumably as old as the human species. Indeed, it is very much older, in that in many animal species individuals will take possession of geographic territories or items of food and vigorously resist efforts of other individuals to appropriate them. In the case of humans, however, the notion of ownership has become extraordinarily elaborated by culture. In the primeval situation ownership was necessarily restricted to a few objects, usually artefacts, that were small enough to be carried around from place to place, and also, ephemerally, to morsels of food; and judging from the behaviour of recent hunter–gatherers, the feeling of ownership was not particularly strong, and there was much giving and taking. And in any case, there were few possessions which, if given or taken away, could not be easily replaced by an hour or so's workmanship.

An important feature of ownership in the human species has been the existence of two kinds of goods: *essentials* – that is, articles which are needed for providing the biological necessities of life, like food and protection from the elements, and which contribute to Darwinian fitness; and *non-essentials* – that is, objects which are kept for their magical or supernatural properties, for their symbolic significance for status, or for their sheer enjoyment value – arising, for instance, from their aesthetic or nostalgic appeal. One of the most notable changes which accompanied urbanisation was a substantial increase in the importance in the economy of non-essential or luxury commodities. This development made a major contribution to the growth of trade between different communities that were often long distances apart. In the early cities in Sumer, for instance, timber was imported from the Zagros Mountains to the east and from the Kbanon to the west; metals, such as copper, silver, lead, tin, and gold were imported from the Taurus Mountains in Syria, from Elam, Anatolia and Oman (at the southern end of the Persian Gulf); and lapis lazuli , the blue stone so cherished in Mesopotamia and Egypt, was brought from northern Afghanistan. In turn, the Sumerians provided manufactured goods, mainly in the form of textiles, which were produced in large quantities in the royal workshops.

The introduction into the economy of all sorts of manufactured goods – textiles, utensils of many kinds, earthenware, metalware, jewellery, ornaments and furniture – brought about significant changes in the meaning of ownership and material wealth. Some of these items had practical functions, but more importantly the quantity and quality of possessions became symbols of status, and the notion that to have a large number of possessions is a good thing became firmly entrenched in culture. The pattern was thus set for the whole of the early urban period and, indeed, for the rest of human history. The main difference in modern high-energy societies is the vastly greater range of available and wanted manufactured commodities.

Another profoundly important development in the early Mesopotamian cities was the extension of the concept of ownership so that it applied not only to land, material objects and animals, but also, to other members of the human species. Slaves were quite plentiful in these societies. It is likely that most of them were collected during raids into the hills flanking the Tigris and Euphrates Valleys, but others were captured in the frequent scuffles between the cities. The concept of ownership even came to apply to the members of a married man's family. In Ur, for example, a man could avoid bankruptcy – that is, he could avoid being sold into slavery himself –

by selling his wife or children to pay off his debts. However, although both slavery and the perception of a man's wife and children as a part of his chattels persisted throughout the early urban phase of human history, neither was universal. It is sobering to recall that in North America the final abolition of slavery did not occur until the lifetime of the grandfathers of some of us alive today.

A highly significant cultural development associated mainly with early urbanisation was the introduction and increasing importance of a cash economy. The desire to exchange things is as old as humankind, but it is not older. There is no other species which engages in the exchange of material objects, although separate giving and taking is, of course, common among animals. When such exchange took place in relatively simple economic situations in hunter–gatherer or early farming societies it was usually by the process of barter. However, in other societies, including some early farming societies, an alternative system was introduced involving a third element – *money*. Shells, beads, or in the case of the early cities, precious metals were used for this purpose. Money need have no intrinsic value itself in order to perform its societal function; it is no more than a symbol that can be given in exchange for material goods or for services and that can be used by the recipient for the same purpose.

As mentioned above, metals were used in the early cities as a form of currency. They had the advantage of being durable, but they had the disadvantage that the necessary weighing and dividing up was a tedious process; and so, in time, the idea arose of minting metal coins of a definite weight. As far as we know, the first coins were struck during the 7th century BC, either in the Greek coastal cities of Ionia or by the kings of Lydia. Later, the use of coin money was taken up by the Semitic people, the Celts, the Romans and the people of India. By the 6th century BC the new money economy was becoming well established in Greece, and bankers and commercial go-betweens were becoming important components of society. By the 3rd century BC, a new type of money had appeared – the Bill of Exchange, payable to any bearer. This development was to become a major influence in economic affairs 2 millennia later.

CORPORATE ORGANISATIONS

A dominant feature of modern high-energy society, and one of great ecological and biosocial significance, is the existence of *corporations*. These are groups of human beings who act as a body or unit and who are organised in such a way that they collectively contribute to the attainment of a particular goal or set of goals.

Although corporations are especially characteristic of the modern world, where they impinge on almost every aspect of the life experience of the average individual, they have existed, although to a much lesser extent, for several thousand years. Examples are the Catholic Church during mediaeval times and the military and administrative dimensions of the Roman Empire. Indeed, the very first city states in Mesopotamia had some of the important characteristics of corporations. Large corporations did not, however, exist in hunter–gatherer and early farming societies.

In a number of ways, corporations are rather like humans. Each of them has a set of values, sometimes inherited from a bygone era, a set of goals which reflect these values, and a typical behaviour pattern, which in turn reflects the values and goals. Another human-like characteristic is a strong drive to compete. This tendency is especially evident among industrial and commercial organisations, but it is not limited to them. It also occurs among government departments, which may compete with each other for status or influence, with the result that the criteria for policy formulation are often quite unrelated to the needs of the community which the government is supposed to serve. Corporations sometimes exhibit behaviours reminiscent of certain psychopathological conditions, such as paranoia, schizophrenia and megalomania. Most important of all, corporations have a strong drive for survival.

There is also a tendency for corporate organisations to go through a life cycle, from a youthful phase to one of senility. Sometimes they die, but seldom without a struggle. Others, however, seem to be immortal. And corporations, like people, metabolise and depend on an input and outflow of energy, inputs of material resources and the discharge into the environment not only of intended products but also of various kinds of waste material.

A particularly disturbing feature of corporations is that, depending on their origins and perceived goals, they are often completely lacking in compassion or aesthetic sensibility; and they may also lack concern about the natural environment and the survival and well-being of future generations of humankind. As Edward Thurlow wrote almost 200 years ago: 'Did you ever expect a corporation to have a conscience, when it has no soul to be damned and no body to be kicked?' On the other side of the coin, as Kenneth Galbraith has pointed out, corporations do often seem to strive to be loved by people, although such love is seldom forthcoming except from members of the corporation itself.

Returning to the question of values and goals, these vary greatly from one corporation to another: those of a steel manufacturing firm will be very different from those of an army, which again will be different from those of a sect of the Christian Church. The other values and goals vary according to the societal function of the organisation, especially as these are perceived by the executive section of its membership. The success of one organisation might be measured in terms of the numbers of human lives destroyed (e.g. in the case of an army at war) while another by the number of lives saved (e.g. in a famine-relief organisation).

The values and goals of corporations depend largely on the perceived purpose for which they were initially brought into being, and it is not uncommon to come across corporations clinging onto this historical legacy long after the original purpose or function has ceased to be appropriate. The built-in momentum and inertia of corporations often makes change in direction difficult. Lack of flexibility in this regard is more characteristic of government departments and academic institutions, and less so of profit-dependent organisations, the survival of which is dependent on maintaining economic profitability in a changing world. Thus, profit-dependent organisations are generally more opportunistic and adaptable, responding to shifts in market preferences and perceiving, and indeed inducing, new societal wants and modifying production accordingly. Such adaptability has been characteristic, for example, of the petrochemical and electronics industries over recent decades.

Some social scientists have put a great deal of emphasis on the 'rational' nature of corporations, particularly with respect to their internal functioning and efficiency. In fact, it seems that a progressive trend toward rational internal behaviour is inevitable in most corporate organisations, at least in those on a sound economic or political base. On the other hand, it is clear that there is no guarantee of rationality on the societal level: there is no automatic mechanism that ensures that the behaviour of corporations is rational in terms of the health needs of the biosphere or of people, or even in terms of the perceived needs of the economy as a whole. This is the case in capitalist free-enterprise societies because the state as a whole is not a corporation, and consequently it has no built-in tendency toward internal rationality. It has also been the case in the planned economies of some communist countries, perhaps because, although the state is effectively a corporate organisation, planning on this scale has not been sufficiently enlightened to produce rationality at the overall societal level. On the global level, ecological and economic rationality would seem to be a long way off.

Influence in society

While it is clear that the maintenance and functioning of the high-energy societies would be impossible without some corporate organisations, it is pertinent to question whether adequate safeguards exist for ensuring that corporations are properly under human control and that they are always acting in the best interests of the biosphere and of humanity. Certainly, many corporate organisations in the developed nations wield enormous power. They exert strong influences on the economic system, on societal organisation, on the prevailing value system and on the daily experience and aspirations of ordinary individuals. Indeed, the role of industrial and commercial corporations as trend-setters and in creating new wants, mainly through advertising, has been the subject of much discussion among the critics of corporate power. This issue is of significance not only for individual human beings, because of the influence that corporations have on their wants, values, sources of enjoyment and thinking patterns, but also for society as a whole and its ecological relationship with the biosphere. The more material commodities people want, the more will be produced, and the greater the intensity of societal technometabolism.

Concern has been expressed especially about the sheer overwhelming power of the large profit-dependent *multinational corporations*. It has been estimated, that 200–300 global industrial and commercial corporations control 80 per cent of all productive assets in the non-communist world, and some authors predict that the multinationals will become the chief organising structures of future society.

An especially important aspect of the behaviour of corporations in the context of the theme of this book is the active part which they play in the ecological or environmental debate. On the one hand, some non-profit-dependent organisations established for the purpose of working for the conservation of the natural environment publicly promote ideas and policies aimed at protecting natural areas from the impacts of industrialisation and provoke discussion about the concept of the 'no-growth' society. In Australia, for instance, the Australian Conservation Foundation actively plays this role. Large industrial and commercial organisations have also joined the public debate on such matters, and the viewpoints they take reflect, as would be expected, their in-built values and goals. Some of these large economic organisations have considerable financial resources at their disposal, and they often use these to glamorise, through the mass media, their contribution to 'progress' and in some cases, to attempt to ridicule the environmentalists. There are many examples of this kind of corporate counter-reaction including, for instance, the defensive response of the petrochemical industry to Rachel Carson's assertions in the 1960s about the undesirable effects of pesticides on the natural environment. She was publicly described by the president of one large corporation as 'a fanatic defender of the cult of the balance of nature'. This statement was no doubt intended as ridicule. In retrospect it is the individual who uttered these words who is seen to be ridiculous – as well as highly irresponsible. The tobacco industry has played, and is still playing, a similar anti-reformist role in the campaign against smoking.

People within corporate organisations

Corporations could not operate without the active contribution of the individual human beings whom they attract and who offer their services in return for financial or status rewards.

Broadly, the people serving corporations can be seen as consisting of two classes, the *agents* of the organisation and the *workers*. The agents are those who have executive roles and who, usually nowadays in group situations, take part in the decision-making process – that is, in the formulation of corporate policies. The workers are those who carry out defined tasks according to the prescribed instructions emanating from the agent groups, thus contributing in a mechanical way to the outcome of the organisation's activities. While the dividing line between these two classes is not a sharp one, the distinction is useful for the purposes of this discussion. Needless to say, a corporation must exert effective control over both its agents and workers, offering incentives and rewards for behaviour which is appropriate in terms of the interests of the organisation, and imposing disincentives for inappropriate behaviour.

In the following comments emphasis will be on the agents, in their role as facilitators of corporate power. The workers, of course, are just as essential as servants of the corporate machine, but they usually have less influence on its policies, although they may well affect its efficiency in economic or other terms.

Once individuals are absorbed into corporate organisations at the agent level they usually strive to serve it as well as they are able. This means not only that they work to promote the organisation's interests, but also that they often modify their lifestyles in ways seen to be appropriate by the organisation. They seek the approval of their peers and seniors within the organisation, and tend to identify with it and to show loyalty towards it. They thus become *occupationally committed* to the organisation to which they belong and, by doing their prescribed jobs as well as they are able, they further its aims and objectives. Already early in this century Max Weber, while accepting the desirability of internal efficiency in organisations, expressed concern about the effects of bureaucratisation on the individual employee. He did not like the trends which he discerned and felt that they spelled 'the destruction of the individual personality and subjected it to a dehumanising regimentation'. In 1956 William Whyte's 'The Organisation Man' expressed similar concerns; his book might as well have been written in 1991 – little has changed.

Sometimes a potential conflict exists between the values of the person joining a corporation and those of the organisation itself. An individual might accept employment in a munitions factory, although believing that the making of armaments is ethically wrong. Various resolutions to this moral predicament are possible. First, the individual can leave the organisation. Failing this, he or she may modify their values, so that these are consistent with those of the organisation. As George Orwell wrote :- 'put a pacifist in a munitions factory and in a week he will think of how to make better bombs'.

Alternatively, the individual may put into effect one of various psychological mechanisms for coping with the situation. An example is *compartmentalisation*, which occurs when individuals learn to accommodate to the values of their organisation when at work, while embracing their own personal, and different, values in private life. This mechanism seems to be more effective in some people than in others. How often have we heard spokespersons for large corporations explain that they are speaking as representatives of their organisations, and that the views that they are putting are not necessarily their own? Indeed, it is theoretically possible for a corporation to flourish and to grow in power, while all its executive members personally disapprove of its objectives and activities. The implications for humanity of this aspect of the decision-making processes of modern society are far-reaching.

Another important psychological device for resolving potential conflict of values is the use of *information denial*. Someone who is working for a large corporation that is causing damaging pollution of the biosphere might hold values to the effect that we should protect the integrity of the natural world and live in harmony with nature. This individual might cope with the situation by vigorously denying the findings and interpretations communicated by scientists concerning the likely impact of the pollutants on the biosphere. It is not uncommon, for example, to hear an executive agent of the tobacco industry flatly deny that there is any evidence of a causative link between smoking and lung diseases.

In other words, people who find themselves working for corporate organisations behave in a very human way. They identify with their organisation as if it were an in-group, and they behave within it in a manner consistent with its expectations and goals. If their personal values conflict with those of the organisation, they adapt either by changing their values or by using one of several psychological defence mechanisms that enable them to receive with a clear conscience the various rewards that membership of the corporation offers. These rewards may include not only indirect subsistence support and material gain, but also the approval and praise of peers and a sense of personal involvement, belonging, security and status. The adaptiveness of the human organism thus appears to be working to the advantage of the individual in the given situation, even if it involves accepting values and criteria for success that would be anathema in a different cultural setting. Clearly, it also works to the advantage of the corporate organisation. The crucial question is whether human adaptability of this kind and expressed in this particular way is a good thing for human society as a whole and for future generations of humanity.

In summary, through cultural evolution there has come about a new situation in which large numbers of individual human beings act out their parts and express their common behavioural tendencies as members of corporate organisations – which, as relatively autonomous bodies, have an immense influence on ecological and biosocial interrelationships. These corporations tend towards rationality within themselves, in terms of their particular aims and objectives; but there is no tendency for their behaviour to be rational with respect to the needs either of the biosphere or of people; either in the short- or the long-run. In the market economy the 'invisible hand', however effective it might be in regulating small-scale enterprises in the interests of the community, plays an insignificant part in controlling the activities of large profit-making corporate organisations. There is, in fact, no automatic regulatory mechanism to ensure either that only those organisations exist which operate in the best interests of humanity, or that the activities of organisations are appropriate in terms of the ecological needs of the biosphere.

Comment

Clearly, when great numbers of people come to live together in urban situations, some new kinds of organisational arrangements are necessary which are different from those which sufficed in hunter–gatherer or early farming societies. For the long-term survival and well-being of humanity, these arrangements must be consistent with the health and well-being of all sections of the community, as well as with the health of the ecosystems of the biosphere. Unfortunately, the haphazard development of civilisation has resulted in there being no mechanism in existence to ensure that these two conditions are met, with dire consequences for millions of human beings and for many local ecosystems – and recently for the biosphere as a whole.

FURTHER READING

Barnet, R.J. and Muller, R.E. (1974). *Global reach: the power of the multinational corporations*. Simon and Schuster, New York.
Chandler, T. and Fox, G. (1974). *3000 years of urban growth*. Academic Press, New York.
Davis, K. (1965). The urbanisation of the human population. *Scientific American*, **213**(3), pp.41–53.
Kramer, S.N. (1967). *The Sumerians*. University of Chicago Press, Chicago, IL.
Mellaart, J. (1975). The origins and development of cities in the near east. In *Janus: essays in ancient and modern studies* (ed. L.L. Orlin), pp.5–22. Centre for Coordination of Ancient and Modern Studies, Ann Arbor, MI.

Mumford, L. (1966). *The city in history*. Penguin, Harmondsworth, Middx.
Redman, C.L. (1978). *The rise of civilization: from early farmers to urban society in the ancient Near East*. W.H. Freeman, San Francisco.
Whitehouse, R. (1977). *The first cities*. Phaidon, Oxford.

CHAPTER 10

BIOLOGICAL IMPACTS ON HUMAN POPULATIONS

In this chapter we turn our attention to some of the more significant biological effects that cultural processes have had on human populations since the domestic transition. We will focus especially on changes in life conditions and their implications for patterns of health and disease and of enjoyment and of distress in human populations, bearing in mind the principle that significant deviation from the biological conditions characteristic of the natural habitat of the species are likely to give rise to signs of maladjustment (see page 64).

POPULATION DENSITY AND INFECTIOUS DISEASE

Biologically, one of the most significant impacts that cultural developments have had on humans since the domestic transition, and especially since the urban transition, has been the spectacular increase in the numbers of people per unit area of land; and perhaps the most important consequence of this change has been the effect it had on the interrelationships between human beings and their various microbial and animal parasites and pathogens.

Even before the extreme crowding which occurred with urbanisation, the introduction of the farming economy created a new situation which favoured the spread and perpetuation of certain human parasites and pathogens. This was not only because population densities were considerably higher than in primeval society, but also because people were leading relatively sedentary lives. These changes meant that pathogenic organisms, or the eggs of parasites discharged into the environment by an infected individual, were more likely to be picked up by other individuals than had been the case in the hunter–gatherer situation. The human parasites which spend part of their life cycles in other animal hosts were also favoured by the increase in the density of human populations. In particular, the farming lifestyle appears to have resulted in increased prevalence of two diseases

203

which eventually became the two biggest single causes of death in human populations – malaria and schistosomiasis.

It has been suggested that it was the introduction of slash-and-burn agriculture into tropical and subtropical regions that allowed malaria to become an important cause of ill health and death in human communities. This change in the economy brought humans into close contact with populations of mosquitoes breeding in stagnant pools of water, and this situation, combined with the relatively high density and immobility of the population, was particularly favourable for the maintenance of the life cycle of the malarial parasite. Schistosomiasis occurs everywhere in the world where large-scale irrigation is practised, and there is good evidence that it was already common in Mesopotamia, Egypt and the Indus Valley by two or three thousand years before the time of Christ. This disease is due to infection with one of several species of blood fluke, belonging to the genus *Schistosoma*, which spends part of its life cycle in the body of certain species of snail. It has been estimated that about 200 million people in 72 countries suffer from schistosomiasis today.

The close physical association in some early farming communities between people and domestic animals increased the chances of individuals becoming infected with those particular micro-organisms and parasites which are normally carried by these animals but which are potentially pathogenic for people. Examples of such diseases are brucellosis, bovine tuberculosis, and infection with dog hookworm.

The increase in mortality in farming societies due to these various infectious diseases did not, however, completely outweigh the biological advantages of the protection that village life afforded against the hazards of the hunter–gatherer lifestyle. This, together with the fact that the farming economy provided nutritional support for a greater number of people per unit area, resulted in an increase in the total human population. By the time of the development of the early Mesopotamian cities, there were probably about one hundred million on the Earth.

The formation of true cities, in which the majority of inhabitants were not involved in direct subsistence activity (i.e. hunting and gathering, farming or fishing), represented a most important development in the biological history of humankind. Humans became aggregated together in larger numbers and at a higher population density than ever before. One of the consequences of this was a further increase in susceptibility to infectious diseases and to attack by external animal parasites, like flees, lice and mites. As a result, infectious diseases, including forms spread directly from human to human, like smallpox, and forms involving intermediate hosts, like typhus and plague, became very common. Indeed, infectious disease became by far the most important cause of death in the early urban societies, and remained so until various cultural adaptive processes in the latter part of the 19th century and the first part of the present century greatly reduced their prevalence.

Perhaps the best documented epidemic of antiquity was that which affected Athens at the time of the Peloponnesian Wars. In the summer of 430 BC, large armies were camped around Athens, and the people from the countryside swarmed into the city, which became extremely overcrowded. The disease, which is generally considered to have been smallpox, struck suddenly. Its symptoms were distinctly unpleasant, and included severe headache, redness of the eyes, followed by inflammation of the tongue and pharynx, with sneezing and coughing followed by vomiting, diarrhoea and excessive thirst. The individuals who died usually did so between the 7th and 9th days. At the height of the fever, the body was covered with reddish spots, some of which ulcerated. Severe cases that recovered often suffered from necrosis of the fingers, toes and genitals; some lost their eyesight and in many cases there was complete loss of memory. The epidemic had a big effect on political events, and it eventually brought the current hostilities to an end. The Peloponnesians left the region in a hurry, and in Athens itself people became completely demoralised and a period of lawlessness ensued.

Infectious disease thus became firmly established as a feature of Western civilization, and it played a major role in human affairs well into the 20th century. Sometimes it caused terrible epidemics; but some forms, like tuberculosis, infantile diarrhoea and other causes of childhood mortality were endemic. The case of the children of Queen Anne (1665–1714) is often mentioned in this context: there were 18 of them altogether, and of these the only one to survive infancy died at the age of 11. The most important of the infectious diseases throughout the early urban phase were dysentery, enteric fever, typhoid, typhus, bubonic plague, smallpox, tuberculosis and, late in the period, cholera.

One of the most notorious epidemic diseases of civilization is bubonic plague, which is due to infection with a bacterium, *Pasteurella pestis*. This organism is a natural parasite of certain rodents, in which it seems to cause little trouble. However, sometimes the black rat, *Rattus rattus*, becomes infected and this species is very susceptible to the bacterium and suffers a high mortality rate. The disease is normally spread from host to host by fleas, and humans are usually infected by being bitten by fleas which have been feeding on infected rats. The first known outbreak of bubonic plague in Europe was the epidemic of 542 AD in Constantinople where people were dying at the rate of about 10,000 a day. This particular epidemic may well have played a decisive role in European history, because it effectively put an end to Justinian's efforts to re-establish the Roman Empire.

The epidemic of bubonic plague that became known as the Black Death and which had such important social repercussions in Europe, spread rapidly into the continent from an area just north of the Black Sea in 1345, and estimates of the death rate for Europe as a whole range from 25 to 75 per cent of the total population. This epidemic died out in 1351, but there were many somewhat less devastating and more local epidemics during the following 400 years. After this time the disease disappeared from Europe, presumably as a result of certain ecological changes in the human habitat, possibly involving a reduction in size of the reservoir of natural rodent hosts for the plague bacillus, or perhaps as a consequence of the replacement of the black rat, *Rattus rattus*, by the brown rat, *Rattus norvegicus*, which is less susceptible to plague. The last outbreak of plague in Europe occurred in France at Marseille in 1720, and there was a serious epidemic in Moscow in 1771. A major reactivation of the disease occurred in China in 1894.

Whatever the explanation of the disappearance of bubonic plague from Europe, it was definitely not the result of any trend towards decreasing population density or any improvement in human life conditions. It is true that complex societal, political and economic changes were occurring in Europe from the 15th century onwards, but these were not associated with better conditions of life for the masses.

While the high incidence of infectious disease in the early urban period of human history was itself a biological response to culturally-created conditions, in turn it had widespread cultural repercussions. The story of the Spanish invasion of Mexico under Hernando Cortez early in the 16th century AD provides an example. The virus disease, smallpox, was introduced to the American mainland in April 1520 when one of the Spanish expeditions landed at present-day Vera Cruz. This expedition included an African slave who was suffering from smallpox. The disease spread very rapidly among the Amerindian population which was extremely susceptible, having had no previous contact with the smallpox virus. By September of that year, smallpox had reached the towns around the lakes in the Valley of Mexico and had invaded Tenochtitlan, the Aztec capital. It is estimated that about half of the population of this city and of the surrounding region died within 6 months. This happened at a time when the Aztecs had seemed to be gaining the upper hand in the conflict with the forces of Hernando Cortez. According to the interpretation of one Spanish witness: 'When the Christians were exhausted from war, God saw fit to send the Indians smallpox, and there was a great pestilence in the city' (see D.R. Hopkins, 1983, p.207). Most of the Spaniards were immune to the disease and they were able to exploit this differential resistance to their military advantage. Smallpox also played a key role in the Spanish conquest of the Incas in Peru, 13 years after the fall of the Aztecs.

This was not by any means the only military campaign in which infectious disease played a role. Indeed, until very recent wars, micro-organisms have caused more deaths among warriors than combat itself. There is evidence from the Holy Bible that this was so in the Middle East two or three thousand years ago. More recent examples are provided by the following figures: Crimean War (1854–1856) – about 60,000 men on both sides killed or died of wounds, about 130,000 died of disease; American Civil War (1861–1868) – about 220,000 men killed or died of wounds, about 400,000 from infectious disease; South African War (1899–1902) – of the British forces, 7534 were killed or died of wounds, 14,382 died of infectious disease. The influenza epidemic immediately after World War I killed at least 21 million people, and probably many more, compared with the 8–10 million soldiers killed in action.

It is clear that under the new conditions created by cultural processes, including increased population density, the biological adaptive mechanisms which come into play in the human body when it is invaded by alien organisms were not adequate to prevent high death rates from epidemic and endemic contagious diseases. Nor were cultural adaptive measures very effective. These were hindered by lack of understanding of the nature of infectious disease; and it is not surprising that in this vacuum, apart from trying out all sorts of magic potions aimed at prevention or cure, people turned for help to the supernatural. The Romans, for example, appealed through various rituals to the Goddess of Fever. In England in 1666 there was a general feeling that the Great Plague was a punishment from God for neglecting religion and for generally low morality, and a Bill was introduced into Parliament aimed at curbing atheism in the country. Although this Bill was eventually dropped, moves were taken to prevent the publication of any literature which was critical of the teachings of the Church.

However, despite the lack of understanding of the nature of infectious disease, simple observation had given rise to the strong suspicion in some quarters that these illnesses were contagious, and isolation and quarantine procedures were introduced in some places from an early date. The books of Leviticus and Deuteronomy in the Holy Bible describe this practice in relation to leprosy, and in mediaeval times many cities in Europe established quarantine procedures for people moving into their precincts.

It was not until the latter part of the 19th century that really effective cultural adaption against infectious disease came into play. The Public Health Movement in Britain was especially important in this regard. Interestingly enough, this cultural adaptive response was not based on a proper or full understanding of the nature of infectious disease, but rather on the simple observation that high rates of disease and mortality were associated with certain kinds of life conditions – namely the conditions of crowding, poor ventilation, accumulation of organic refuse around dwellings and general uncleanliness that typified working class areas in the rapidly growing cities during the industrial transition. The prevailing theory at the time, the miasmatic theory, was that these diseases were due to noxious gases emanating from decomposing organic matter. Although the theory was wrong, it led eventually to governmental action aimed at improving the living conditions of workers, cleaning up their residential areas and ensuring proper sanitation and ventilation. The end result of this movement, together with some improvements in nutrition, was a significant reduction in the prevalence of infectious disease in the big cities of the Western world.

Another factor contributing to the reduction in the infectious disease was artificial immunization or 'vaccination'. According to some authorities, the art of inducing specific immunity by artificial means goes back over two thousand years. Evidence from ancient manuscripts written during the last millennium BC has been interpreted by some as indicating that Brahmin priests travelled through the Indian countryside in springtime, the smallpox season, reciting prayers to the goddess of smallpox and inoculating susceptible individuals as they went. Two thousand years later a somewhat similar activity carried out by national and international medical teams resulted in the elimination of smallpox as a disease of humankind.

The technique supposed to have been used by the Brahmin priests, and certainly used in other regions of Eurasia up until the 18th century AD, involved the introduction into the tissues of susceptible persons of the fully virulent smallpox virus taken from individuals who were suffering naturally from the disease. Material was taken from an active smallpox pustule and introduced into a very small artificially inflicted wound in the skin of the person being immunised. Although an occasional individual inoculated in this way developed a severe case of smallpox, and a few of them died, the majority developed only a small number of pox lesions locally around the site of inoculation; but this was sufficient to confer on them complete immunity for life.

Smallpox inoculation of this kind was introduced into England in 1721 and became widely used in rural communities and small towns within a few decades, a fact which contributed to the unusual population growth at that time. For some reason it was not practised to the same extent in the large cities, where epidemics of smallpox, mainly affecting young children, remained common. There was more opposition to inoculation on the continent and in France, for instance, opposition weakened only after the death of Louis XV in 1774. Inoculation was widely practised in the English colonies in America early in the 18th century.

Late in the 18th century an English doctor, Edward Jenner, noticed that milkmaids seemed to be immune from smallpox, and he suspected that this was because their occupation caused them to become infected with cowpox, from which they always recovered after only minimal pox lesions (usually on their hands and fingers). Jenner carried out experiments in which he deliberately inoculated individuals with cowpox and subsequently showed them to be resistant to smallpox. He published his results in 1798, and in an amazingly short time his 'safe' method of immunization, which became known as *vaccination*, was widely used throughout Europe. Indeed, only 5 years after Jenner's book was published, Spanish medical authorities introduced the method in Mexico to protect the surviving Indian populations from further devastation from smallpox (about one million had died in this region from the disease since it was introduced by the conquistadors early in the 16th century).

Although aspects of the vaccination technique have been refined in various ways over the years, it was basically Jenner's procedure which, through the efforts of the World Health Organization, was used in the programme to eliminate smallpox as a human disease, a goal which was achieved in 1977 when the last known case of the disease occurred in Somalia.

The application of the 'vaccination' principle to other infectious diseases had to await the discoveries of Louis Pasteur and other bacteriologists in the late 19th century, and the recognition and isolation of viruses in the present century. The meaning of the word 'vaccine' has now been broadened to include all preparations which consist of other living non-virulent forms or killed virulent forms of disease-producing micro-organisms, or of various components or products of these organisms, which are introduced into the body (by injection, by swallowing or by inhalation) with the intention of inducing a state of specific immunity. Diseases which are routinely protected against in this way in modern high-energy societies include diphtheria, typhoid, measles, German measles, poliomyelitis, whooping cough and tetanus. Vaccines are also available against tuberculosis and cholera as well as certain forms of influenza and many other infectious diseases. Much research is at present aimed at the development of an effective vaccine against malaria.

Vaccination is also widely used for protecting domestic animals against infectious diseases, including, for example, brucellosis in cattle, swine fever in pigs, black kidney in sheep, Newcastle disease in poultry and distemper in dogs.

Also important among the cultural adaptive responses to infectious disease during the present century has been the use of specific chemo-therapeutic agents and antibiotics which are toxic for the invading microorganisms, but not for cells of the host. Of course, countless different concoctions, made mainly from materials of biological origin, had been used for millennia in the treatment of diseases. One of the most successful of these in the Western world, in terms of its fame and the fact that it was in use for nearly 2000 years, was Venice treacle, which contained the flesh of vipers as one of its 50 or more ingredients. It originated in the 2nd century BC and was still in use in India in 1835; and very recently a substance purporting to be Venice treacle could still be purchased in Venice. The mixture was used not only for the therapy of all kinds of sickness, but also for preventive purposes, and was highly recommended for protection against plague in the 17th century. Horn of unicorn was another ancient medicament which retained its popularity for many hundreds of years, although it was usually rather expensive. It was still recommended in the 1677 edition of the London Pharmacopoeia for such diseases as plague, measles and smallpox.

The 20th century has been marked by astounding advances in chemo-therapy and the antibiotic treatment of infectious disease. Let us note, however, that one of the most effective chemotherapeutic agents, quinine, has been in use for hundreds of years for the treatment of malaria. Quinine is an alkaloid which is extracted from cinchona bark, and it acts by interfering with the growth and reproduction of the malarial parasites in red cells of the blood. It was introduced into Europe from America nearly 400 years ago.

The first effective chemically synthesised chemotherapeutic agent was 'Salvarsan', which was introduced by Paul Ehrlich in 1910 for the treatment of syphilis. The next major advance in this area was the introduction of the sulpha drugs in the late 1930s. Even more effective were the antibiotics which, beginning with penicillin, first came into use in the early 1940s. There are now well over 300 different antibiotics available, of varying degrees of specificity and usefulness.

While these chemotherapeutic and antibiotic agents have undoubtedly saved millions of human lives, they are not without their problems. One of these arises from the fact that micro-organisms tend to develop resistance to them, and their widespread and indiscriminate use promotes the emergence of resistant strains. Another difficulty is that some people are, or can become, dangerously sensitive to some of these agents, and in rare instances this has led to the death of patients treated with antibiotics or chemotherapeutic substances.

The end result of these various cultural adaptive responses of the past 150 years in the high-energy societies has been a dramatic decline in the prevalence of the severe infectious diseases which have infested humanity for most of civilization. Instead of being the main cause of death, as they were in the early cities, they now account for only about 2 per cent of the total mortality in these regions. Infectious diseases are more important in the developing regions of the world, where infantile diarrhoea due to microbial infection is still quite common. However, even in these parts their prevalence is much lower than previously.

It is worth emphasising that improved hygiene and nutrition is believed to have made a far greater contribution to the drop in deaths from infectious disease in the developed countries than have artificial immunisation, chemotherapy and antibiotics.

Before concluding this section on population density and infectious disease, mention must be made of the very large number of viruses which are circulating among human populations in the modern world. Fortunately, most of them produce relatively mild diseases, causing inflammation in the respiratory or gastro-intestinal systems. There are probably at least 500 such viruses in existence at the present time, and there is every reason to believe that the number is increasing. These virus diseases are products of civilization, because they could not have survived in the sparsely populated world of hunter–gatherers and early farmers. It has been estimated, for instance, that the measles virus requires for its survival a contiguous human population of around 300,000. In a smaller population there would not be a sufficient number of susceptible individuals to keep the virus going, and the disease would die out. The demographic situation in the modern world is such that whenever a new pathogenic virus appears on the scene, whether as a result of a mutation from another previously existing human virus or by transfer from some other animal species, there is nothing to stop it gaining a foot-hold and becoming established as a new member of the ever-growing band of disease-causing viruses now supported by humankind.

In 1981 a new virus disease, now called acquired immune deficiency syndrome (AIDS), was discovered among male homosexuals in California. AIDS is almost always fatal, although it may lie dormant in the body for 8 or 9 years before causing symptoms. At the time of writing about 400,000 cases have occurred worldwide, and it is predicted that another 1 million will be identified by 1992 (compared with 2.5 million deaths each year for smoking-related illness, 5 million from chronic diarrhoea and 3 million from tuberculosis). AIDS is spread when body fluids of an infected individual gain access to the tissues of another. It is transmitted mainly through sexual intercourse, blood transfusion and the sharing of needles among drug addicts. In North America, Europe and Australia heterosexual activity is responsible for only a very small proportion of cases, while in sub-Saharan Africa and the Caribbean AIDS is primarily a heterosexual disease.

POPULATION DENSITY AND PSYCHOLOGY

Some years ago studies on animal populations showed that in some species unusually high population densities give rise to various behavioural abnormalities. A population of crowded rats, for example, showed an abnormally high incidence of aggression, rape and homosexuality. And, in many species unusually high population density results in certain physiological responses, including enlargement of the adrenal glands, increased rates of abortion, and a weakened resistance to infectious disease.

These findings raise the question whether unnaturally high population densities in humans also promote abnormal behaviour or pathological changes in the organs and tissues of the body. In fact, numerous investigations have been reported designed to show whether relationships exists between population density and various undesirable social phenomena, including crime and mental or physical illness. The results of such studies, however, are difficult to interpret, because high population densities are usually associated with certain other conditions, such as poverty and poor housing. Thus, while in some cases a relationship has been found to exist between high population density and antisocial behaviour or mental illness, there is at present no clear evidence that high population density is itself responsible for these states. Indeed, it is likely that the most important factor determining behavioural and psychological responses of people to high population density is whether or not they *feel* crowded. The extent to which people feel crowded is strongly influenced by their cultural background and expectations. Thus, if individuals feel crowded, but are unable to move to a less crowded situation, then they are likely to experience chronic frustration. Discontent is likely to follow, and this in turn may well lead to behavioural or psychological abnormality.

It should be noted, however, that investigations on the effects of crowding in human populations have usually involved comparisons in which the population densities of even the least densely populated groups have been considerably greater than those of humans in their natural environment. Consequently, the possibility cannot be ruled out that the threshold for any impact that unnaturally high population densities might have on humans might be below the population density of the groups compared in these studies.

DIET

In Chapter 3 we noted the broad characteristics of the diet of humans in their evolutionary habitat. In that setting the species is typically omnivorous, consuming a wide range of different foods of plant origin, including roots, tubers, fruits, nuts and leaves, as well as a variable amount of cooked lean meat, which on average probably constituted 20–30 per cent of the diet by weight.

The introduction of farming, and later the development of cities, resulted in some significant deviations from this natural diet of the species.

Quantitative aspects of diet

It is often assumed that hunter–gatherers, in the words of one author, 'hardly ever had enough to eat'. This is biologically very improbable. It is no more likely to be true for humans than for any other species of animal living in its natural habitat. In fact, hunter–gatherers in general were in a more secure situation than farming people from this point of view, although undoubtedly now and again they would have suffered shortages of food in unusual seasons. In the case of farmers who were mainly dependent on a single crop of wheat or of some other cereal, one or two bad seasons could be devastating. Indeed, recurrent famine has been an outstanding feature of civilization in many parts of the world, especially where relatively large populations have grown up and have been dependent on a narrow range of foodstuffs. The food sources of hunter–gatherers, however, were typically diverse and this meant that the undesirable effects of a very dry or a very wet season would be less severe, because not all food sources would be equally affected by the extreme conditions.

The ancient literature of the Middle East is full of accounts of famine due to drought, warfare or crop disease. A particularly well documented famine is that which occurred in Egypt in Joseph's time, in 1708 BC. It is said that the Egyptian scribes recorded altogether 1829 different famines.

Broadly, we can recognise two 'famine belts' in the Old World. One extends from the British Isles across Europe and Russia to northern China, and corresponds to a region in which crop failures usually occur as a result of excessive dampness, cold, or shortened growing seasons. The other extends from Africa and the eastern Mediterranean eastward through the dry and monsoon lands to China. In this belt famine is usually due to drought.

Although famine does not seem to have been common in the history of Britain, it certainly occurred moderately frequently in other parts of Europe. In France, for example, 75 severe famines were recorded between the years 501 to 1500 AD. In Russia, 9 million people died of famine between 1921 and 1922, 4–7 million died between 1933 and 1934 and nearly 2 million died between 1944 and 1947. At least 2 million people died from famine in China in 1929.

The immediate adaptive response of human populations faced with severe food shortage has usually involved, apart from the consumption of various kinds of organic matter not normally considered edible, migration across the land or across the sea in search of sustenance. Recent examples of this response have been seen in the Sahel and in Ethiopia, where many thousands of starving individuals have moved across hundreds of miles, hoping to find food. In the Irish potato famine in 1845 and 1846, 2 million people left Ireland for North America, Britain and Australia .

The other quantitative deviation from the natural diet is *over-consumption* of calories. The principle of *optimum range* (page 90) thus operates in the case of calorie consumption: too little or too much can interfere with health. Two factors have, in different circumstances, contributed to overconsumption of food. First, in some societal settings, humans often perform much less physical work than was usual in the natural habitat. Consequently, even if they consumed about the same amount of food as their ancestors in the primeval environment, their calorie intake would be in excess of their metabolic requirements. Second, various influences have come into play in the modern high-energy societies that tend to increase the amount of food eaten by sections of the population or, more recently, by most of the population. These influences include the following: the ready accessibility of foodstuffs without the expenditure of major physical work; the efforts, through the culinary art and, recently, commercial interests, to increase the palatability and general attractiveness of foodstuffs; the removal of fibre and the refinement of carbohydrates; regular meal times; boredom; various rituals (e.g. dinner parties, business executive's lunches).

As a consequence of these various factors, individuals in the high-energy societies often consume much more food than is necessary to satisfy their biological requirements and, as a result, forms of ill health which are partly or completely due to over-consumption are especially common. In fact over-eating appears to make an important contribution to a multitude of forms of maladjustment, including coronary heart disease and some forms of malignancy, such as cancer of the breast and of the uterus. It was less of a problem in early urban societies, although the upper echelons in the social hierarchy were often at risk.

While under-consumption of food calories is relatively rare in the modern high-energy societies, it does still occur in some sections of the population as a consequence of sheer poverty. Recent studies suggest that about one in five of the citizens of the USA are undernourished for this reason.

The situation is very different in some of the developing regions of the world where stress and death due to poor nutrition are widespread. It is not easy to assess precisely the degree of ill health and mortality resulting from starvation and malnutrition in the world today, but authorities suggest that at least 500 million, or ten per cent of the world's population, are malnourished, and that at least ten thousand people die every day from this cause. Indeed, in a bad year, 10 million people may die from starvation or malnutrition. Children are particularly affected.

Populations which are near the limits of human tolerance with respect to nutritional intake are especially vulnerable to the undesirable effects of bad seasons. The serious and prolonged drought which occurred in west African countries from 1968 to 1972 had a devastating effect on the populations in the region. This drought affected Mauritania, Senegal, Mali, Upper Volta, Niger and Chad, and before it was finished severe droughts were also occurring further to the east, affecting the Sudan, Somalia, Kenya and Tanzania. Even more recently, a severe chronic drought has affected Ethiopia.

Before leaving the topic of quantitative aspects of food consumption, a few words are necessary on growth rates in children and on the ultimate height of individuals. One of the striking changes in the biology of humankind that has taken place in the developed regions of the world has been a progressive increase in stature. A study in Glasgow showed that in 1960 boys and girls of 13 were, respectively, 4 inches and 3.25 inches taller than their counterparts 40 years earlier. However, from the biological viewpoint, tallness does not seem to be a particular advantage. Certainly, in times of food shortage small stature may well be desirable, because small individuals have lower food requirements than big ones. Indeed, it has been suggested that small body size is sometimes a biological adaptive response coming into play in situations in which calorie intake is severely restricted.

Qualitative changes

Since the domestic transition cultural developments have resulted in a number of significant qualitative deviations in the diet of humankind from that which was characteristic in the evolutionary environment of the species. These deviations are broadly of two kinds. First, as a consequence of a narrowing of the diet or of developments in food technology, there have on occasion occurred important nutritional *deficiencies* – that is the absence or relative absence of certain important components of the natural diet. Second, diets have sometimes been modified as a result of *additions* of extraneous matter, either deliberately added or entering the food incidentally.

Deficiencies

Nutritional deficiencies arise from the fact that for proper functioning the human body requires a range of specific chemical compounds which cannot be synthesised in the body and which are not present together in sufficient quantity in any single natural foodstuff. The natural diet, consisting of a broad range of different plant sources and a certain amount of lean meat provided these specific chemical compounds. However, the tendency during the course of civilization for some populations to become over-dependent on a single food source, or to omit from the diet a major group of foodstuffs, such as fresh fruit and vegetables, has been an important cause of nutritional disease.

Of the 20 or so amino acids that are used in human metabolism, eight cannot be synthesized in the body, and they are therefore essential components of the diet. Certain foodstuffs are deficient in one or other of these amino acids. Corn (i.e. maize), for example, is deficient in tryptophan, and plant foods in general, but especially wheat, are relatively deficient in lysine. With respect to the vitamins, heavy dependence on white flour (if not artificially supplemented with vitamins) or on polished rice, has resulted in thiamin and riboflavin deficiency, with symptoms of beriberi; and heavy dependence on maize (corn) as a food source has resulted in niacin deficiency and consequent maladjustment in the form of pellagra.

One of the best known specific nutritional deficiency diseases in Western civilization is scurvy, due to lack of vitamin C. Before the importance of fresh fruit or vegetables in the diet was recognised, scurvy was a common occupational hazard for sailors on long voyages. It was also common among soldiers, and often played a decisive role in the outcome of military engagements.

Another important disease in European cities was rickets, which is associated with a deficiency of vitamin D. Evidence for the prevalence of rickets in the Netherlands and in northern Germany is provided by paintings from the 15th and 16th centuries, which often depict small children with a swollen belly, bent limbs and a squarish shaped head typical of this disease. Vitamin D can, in fact, be synthesized within the body, provided that the skin is exposed to sufficient direct sunlight. The wearing of clothes, the habit of living indoors and air pollution from industry all interfere with such synthesis. At the beginning of the industrial era, the poorer people could not afford such luxuries as eggs and milk products, which were the only common foods containing vitamin D in quantity, and in the 19th century as many as 75 per cent of the children in some European cities were seriously affected with rickets. The disease is not uncommon among children in some European cities even today.

It is worth noting that vitamin deficiency diseases have not always been due to the lack of availability of appropriate food sources, or even to economic disadvantage; sometimes they have been due simply to cultural attitudes. There is evidence, for instance, that in England in the 17th century a considerable amount of vitamin A deficiency occurred among the children of the wealthy, because it was not the custom of the nobility to eat green vegetables or butter, both of which were considered to be inferior foods.

As a consequence largely of improved understanding of the nutritional needs of the human species, specific deficiency diseases, so important in the earlier urban societies, are relatively rare in the modern high-energy societies. However, deficiencies of iron, leading to anaemia, and of thiamine (vitamin B1) still occur in populations in the USA today. Moreover, in Third World countries, nutritional deficiency diseases, such as beriberi, rickets and kwashiorkor are still very common among children. Indeed, the degree of *protein energy malnutrition* (PEM) among children in some areas is sufficient to interfere with mental development.

In the high-energy societies today the most serious dietary deficiency is the lack not of a specific nutrient, but rather of plant fibre. This deviation from the natural diet of humans is the consequence of developments in commercial food technology associated with the refinement of carbohydrates. While fibre is not an essential nutrient, the human digestive system is nevertheless adapted through evolution to diets containing plant fibre. Its artificial removal from the diet has a number of consequences, one of the most important of which is associated with the fact that plant fibre is relatively resistant to the digestive processes, so that it passes through the alimentary canal largely unchanged. Nevertheless, it takes up space in the gastro-intestinal system and in the natural diet it contributes significantly to the volume of the gut contents. This is especially important in relation to the stomach, because after a meal containing plant materials the non-digestible fibre accounts for a significant part of the stomach contents, thus contributing to the feeling of repletion. In the case of a relatively fibre-free meal made up largely, for example, of refined carbohydrates, the same feeling of repletion would be associated with a much higher content of food energy in the stomach.

The intestines of humankind are also adapted, through evolution, to a high-fibre diet. Removal of the fibre from plant foodstuffs results in a slowing down in the rate of passage through the alimentary canal of its contents, contributing to constipation and probably also to cancer of the colon, haemorrhoids and various other disorders.

In concluding these comments on nutritional deficiency diseases, let us note that the discoveries in medical science and biochemistry in the latter part of the 19th century and the early part of the present century of the vitamins and their role in health and disease represent one of the most interesting and impressive stories in the annals of scientific research. They have contributed immensely to human health and well-being. However, it is salutary to bear in mind the fact that no knowledge of the existence, identity, chemistry or biological function of the vitamins or any other nutrient is necessary for the avoidance of the nutritional deficiency diseases. All that is required is, first, appreciation of the principle of evodeviation, and second, the knowledge that the diet of *Homo sapiens* in the evolutionary habitat included a wide variety of different kinds of fresh vegetables, fruit, nuts and roots, and a certain amount, perhaps 20–30 per cent of the diet, of cooked lean meat.

Additions

Potentially harmful chemical compounds or micro-organisms can become incorporated into drinks and foodstuffs either inadvertently or deliberately. A good example of inadvertent contamination of the diet is provided by the situation which existed in Rome at the beginning of the first millennium AD. It was the practice in those days, especially among the nobility, to store fruit juice and other drinks in lead containers, and we can therefore assume that many people were regularly consuming small amounts of lead. Chemical analysis of human bones from this period confirm that this was happening. The symptoms of mild lead poisoning include tiredness, constipation, slight abdominal discomfort or pain, altered sleep patterns, irritability, anaemia, pallor, and, less frequently, diarrhoea and nausea. The nature of these symptoms is such that the people affected might well have come to accept them as 'normal' assuming, perhaps, that they were merely the natural consequences of growing older. However, if most of the members of the population, especially of the ruling class, were suffering from symptoms such as these, the impact on society as a whole might well have been considerable.

In the high-energy societies of the present century incidental contamination of human food with various chemical products of industrial processes has proved a serious problem. Especially important is contamination with various pesticides, such as dichlorodiphenyltrichloroethane (DDT), used in the treatment of crops or of harvested plant food. Another common contaminant is polychlorinated biphenyl (PCB) which is used for various industrial purposes. Like DDT, it is a chlorinated hydrocarbon and persists in the environment for a very long time, and it also accumulates in the internal organs of animals, including humans.

In the developed countries, there has been growing awareness of the risks associated with the chemical pollution of foodstuffs, and in some of them much progress has been made towards the regulation of the use of potentially noxious substances. Nevertheless, the situation is still far from satisfactory. At the time of writing, for example, concern is being expressed about the contamination of various grains with ethylene dibromide, a substance with pesticidal properties which is still widely used in the USA for spraying crops, and which until 1981 was used in Britain for directly fumigating grain. It is also added to leaded petrol as a 'scavenger' to prevent lead accumulating in the moving parts of the engine. Ethylene bromide has been shown to be one of the most potent carcinogenic agents known in experimental animals.

The situation is even less satisfactory in the developing regions of the world. Thus, while in the USA public outcry led to legislation banning the use of some pesticides and regulating the use of others, no such legislation exists in many Third World countries. Moreover, corporate organisations in the USA which manufacture biocides that are banned in that country are still exporting them on a massive scale to developing regions of the world where legislation controlling their use does not exist or is ineffective. Poisoning with pesticides is a significant cause of human deaths in some of these countries.

Another important class of incidental contaminants of food is living organisms. Some of these, especially bacteria and fungi, may hasten decomposition of foodstuff and hence affect its taste; and some of them produce toxic products. An example of the latter is the bacterium, *Clostridium botulinum*, which produces an extremely potent toxin, very small amounts of which can cause death in humans. Other contaminating organisms in food may cause diseases by multiplying in the intestines. This happens in the case of food poisoning due to *Salmonellae*. However, ill health due to the contamination of foodstuffs with micro-organisms is not common in modern high-energy societies.

Turning to deliberate additives, countless different substances have been, and still are, added to human food for specific purposes – to improve its flavour, for example, to make it more visually attractive, or to act as a preservative. The most widely used of all these chemical additives is sodium chloride or 'salt', which humans have added to food since ancient times. The majority of people in modern high-energy societies consume ten to fifteen times more salt than is necessary to satisfy their metabolic requirements. It is added to vegetables during cooking and to soups and sauces, and it is often shaken liberally onto food on the plate; and most canned and processed foods on sale in supermarkets contain added salt. Indeed, one conventional slice of bread provides sufficient salt to satisfy an individual's physiological needs for one day. There is now a strong body of medical opinion that holds that this deviation from the natural diet of humankind is responsible for much of the high blood pressure that exists in populations in the high-energy societies.

Another sodium compound that has been used extensively to alter the flavour of food is monosodium glutamate, or 'gourmet powder'. It has been used especially in Chinese cooking, but was also, until recently, added to many commercial infant foods. It has been estimated that the average per capita consumption of monosodium glutamate in Hong Kong is in the region of 1 gram per day. For some time it has been appreciated that occasional individuals are particularly sensitive to this additive and are prone to suffer from Kwok's disease, also known as the 'Chinese restaurant syndrome'. The signs and symptoms of this conditions include a tightening of the muscles of the head and neck, headache and giddiness. Recently, it has been reported that the inclusion of monosodium glutamate in the diets of young mice, rats and monkeys causes abnormalities in the developing brain. It is noteworthy that within a year of the first publication of these experimental results the manufacturers of baby food in North America put a voluntary ban on the use of monosodium glutamate in their products, and they were followed a year later by British firms.

Other substances are added to food to make it look more attractive. For example, in the mid-nineteenth century millers and bakers tried to boost their sales by adding *alum* to flour to make bread appear whiter. Around 1850, a London chemist by the name of Accum analysed some of the bread sold in that city and showed that it was adulterated with alum, and he published his findings in a pamphlet. The defensive backlash from the vested interests – the millers and bakers – was severe, and Accum was eventually forced to leave the country. Many years later his claims were confirmed and legislation was introduced aimed at preventing adulteration of bread with any substance not approved by the authorities. During the present century various bleaches have been added to bread made from white flour in order to make the bread appear even whiter. Concern was voiced in some quarters when it was demonstrated that when agene, one of the bleaching agents that was commonly used for this purpose, was fed to dogs it caused them to suffer fits.

The distinction between 'ingredients' and 'additives' in food is not a sharp one. For example, herbs and spices may be added to a stew, but whether we should regard these as additives or as ingredients is an academic question. In the present context we are especially interested in distinct chemical compounds that are added to food by the commercial component of the food-processing chain rather than by the cook or the consumer. These agents include preservatives, anti-oxidants, colouring agents, flavouring agents, sweeteners, sequestrants, filling agents, stabilizers, emulsifiers and other 'improving agents'. The battery of flavouring agents alone which are incorporated in commercial food products today includes well over a thousand different chemical compounds.

Other important qualitative changes

Reference was made above to the refining of carbohydrates. This process can be said to have its beginnings in palaeolithic times, when grain was collected and separated from the husks by grinding. The next important step was the introduction 3000 years ago in Egypt of sieves designed to separate the grain from the bran (the outer coating of the grain once the husk has been removed). The grain was used for making bread, and it is probable that at that time whiter bread was preferred because it was likely to contain less grit than the coarser, browner products. Certainly in Greece and in Rome the upper classes consumed off-white bread made from flour from which some of the bran had been extracted; and from that time onwards, until very recently, the consumption of white bread became associated with high social status.

Various advances have been made over the centuries in the technology of the refining of flour, both in the grinding system and in the sieving process, resulting in progressively whiter and more branless flour. However, even until the middle 19th century the best quality 'white flour' was a wholemeal flour produced by stone grinding, from which the coarse particles of bran had been removed by sifting through fine linen and woollen cloths. This flour still contained much finely ground bran as well as most of the germ. It was the introduction of fine silk sieves and the steel roller mills in the latter half of the 19th century that made the big 'breakthrough' which resulted in the almost complete removal of the bran. The bran content of wholemeal flour is around 2 per cent, and with the new technology it dropped to 0.1 per cent; and out with the bran and the germ went most of the proteins, mineral salts and vitamins. In Britain in the 1930s community-based organisations like the Bread and Food Reform League and its descendant, The Food Education Society expressed concern about these trends on nutritional grounds and called for a return to the old methods of flour production. However, because of its low nutritional value, white flour keeps much better than wholemeal flour – it simply will not support the forms of life which would otherwise multiply in it and cause its degradation. This characteristic is much to the economic advantage of the millers and bakers who, understandably, vehemently resisted moves to replace white bread with bread made from wholemeal flour.

The other important example of carbohydrate refinement is seen in the preparation of the soluble disaccharide known as sugar. There has been an enormous increase in the consumption of sugar over the past five or six generations in the Western world. In Britain, about 25 times as much sugar is now consumed on a per capita basis than was the case in the middle of the 19th century, and it now accounts for about one fifth of the total calorie intake of the population. Before 1850, sugar consumption in Britain had been minimal. After that it rose steeply, and it had reached 80 grams per day per capita in 1870, and it continued to rise to a 100 grams in 1900; after that date, except during the periods of the two World Wars, the amount consumed continued to rise until 1958 when it became stationary at about 164 grams per day per person.

This change in sugar consumption is depicted in Figure 10.1, which also shows changes already discussed in other dietary constituents.

In what ways, we may ask, are humans responding to the deviations from the evolutionary diet of the species resulting from the refining of carbohydrates? Is the change giving rise to signs of maladjustment? Although some uncertainty still exists in this area, an increasing number of biomedical scientists consider that the removal of fibre from the diet is responsible for many forms of ill health in modern society. The least controversial case is that of dental caries, which is generally accepted to be the consequence of the consumption of sugar and white flour. The teeth of people in populations who are not on a Western diet show very little sign of dental caries, although the condition becomes common when refined carbohydrates are introduced into their diets.

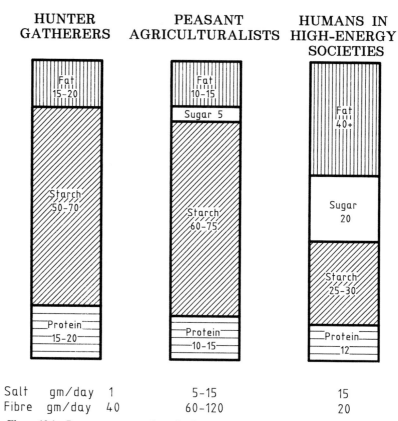

Figure 10.1 Percentage energy from food components and intake of salt and fibre in different societies

In the case of dental caries, the evidence strongly suggests that the purified carbohydrate is the cause of the pathological condition, through its effect on the bacterial flora on the teeth. In other pathologies associated with the consumption of refined carbohydrates it is less clear whether the concentrated carbohydrate itself causes the abnormality, or whether the pathology is due rather to the lack of fibre in the diet. As mentioned earlier in this chapter, the refinement of carbohydrate, involving the removal of fibre from plant foodstuffs, often results in individuals consuming more food-energy than would otherwise be the case. Moreover, the lack of fibre in a diet rich in refined carbohydrate has a marked influence on the physical consistency of the contents of the intestine, and this affects the ease and rate at which material travels through the alimentary canal. Consequently, pathological conditions associated with the consumption of refined carbo-hydrates may in some cases be the result of a generally high intake of energy, and in others the result of modifications in the consistency of the gut contents.

Other conditions for which refined carbohydrates are blamed by some authorities include diverticular disease of the colon, cancer of the colon and rectum, ulcerative colitis, varicose veins and haemorrhoids, coronary heart disease, duodenal ulcer, appendicitis and gallstones.

Another notable deviation in the diet in people of modern high-energy societies as compared with that of hunter–gatherer populations relates to the consumption of animal fats and cholesterol. First, the total amount of animal fat consumed per capita in affluent Western countries is higher than that in most hunter–gatherer populations. This is in part the result of higher levels of meat intake, but it is mainly due to the fact that the proportion of lipid to protein in meat from domestic animals is much higher than it is in the leaner wild animals. Second, the ratio of saturated fats to polyunsaturated fats is much higher in domestic animals than in wild animals. The average meat-eating individual in modern high-energy society therefore consumes considerably more saturated fats than hunter–gatherers eating the same amount of meat. It is generally believed among medical scientists that high levels of saturated fat in the diet contribute to heart disease.

In many societies some individuals, for religious or other reasons, live on a purely vegetarian diet that contains no animal products. This, of course, is a deviation from the diet of humans in their evolutionary environment, and the question therefore arises whether it might give rise to signs of maladjustment. In fact, it is apparent that humans can remain healthy on a vegetarian diet if special care is taken to ensure that it contains plants with a high content of the essential amino acid lysine.

AIR QUALITY

Culturally-induced modifications in the quality of the air that people breath go back, no doubt, to the first deliberate and regular use of fire by our ancestors of several hundred thousand years ago. However, except in the case of occasional cave-dwellers, the amount of smoke inhaled was probably not sufficient to interfere with health in the typical hunter–gatherer situation. It would not have been until people kept fires burning within dwellings that serious problems would have arisen. While clearly no information is available from prehistoric times on the effects of this environmental change on human health, it would be surprising from the biomedical standpoint if it did not give rise to pathological changes in the lungs of some individuals. In recent times, villagers in Papua New Guinea have customarily kept a fire alight in their homes at all times of day and night, and the incidence of respiratory disorders apparently resulting from smoke inhalation is relatively high.

Air pollution became a more important problem in human settlements with the introduction of coal as a domestic fuel. As discussed in Chapter 7, complaints about air pollution in London go back to the beginning of the 14th century. However, the first serious effort to deal with the air pollution problem due to the burning by coal in that city was made after the notorious smog episode of December 1952, which resulted in the death of about 4000 people.

The main air pollutants resulting from the use of fossil fuels and of significance for human health are the sulphur oxides (SO_2 and SO_3), nitrogen oxides (NO and NO_2) and carbon monoxide (CO). Sulphur dioxide was the chief irritant in the London smog episode in 1951. Its main effect, especially when in the form of acid-sulphate aerosols, is to aggravate asthma and pre-existing heart disease. The main source of the nitrogen oxides is the internal combustion engine, and their main role in air pollution is as essential components in the chemical reactions which lead to the formation of photochemical smog. The main source of carbon monoxide in the air of modern cities is also the internal combustion engine. The use of fossil fuels also results in the release into the atmosphere of a range of hydrocarbon compounds of variable molecular weight. These include various aromatic polycyclic hydrocarbons which are known to be carcinogenic, and it is likely that these substances contribute, even if only to a small extent, to the incidence of lung cancer in urban environments.

Another important air pollutant in the air of high-energy cities has been lead. This comes mainly from tetraethyl lead, which is added to petrol used in motor vehicles in order to prevent premature detonation. The lead content of air in modern city streets is commonly between 1 and 10 $\mu g/m^3$. The average is around 2 to 4 $\mu g/m^3$. As a consequence, city dwellers regularly inhale lead, and concentrations of this element in the blood of 10–15 $\mu g/100$ ml are not uncommon. Higher levels are found in people who are frequently exposed at close hand to the exhaust fumes of motor vehicles. Obvious symptoms of lead poisoning are associated with considerably higher levels, such as 60–80 $\mu g/100$ ml of blood. Nevertheless, smaller amounts are likely to result in a certain degree of maladjustment. If everyone in the city were to suffer from the symptoms of mild lead poisoning, life might well go on much as usual, and people would not realise that there was any interference with their health and well-being. Apart from these more immediate effects of mild lead poisoning, investigations have led some authors to conclude that chronic lead poisoning interferes with mental development of children living in cities. It has even been suggested that it

Table 10.1   Noise levels in various locations

Level/location	dB(A)
just audible	10
leaves resutling in the breeze	20
soft whistle	30
quiet restaurant	50
freeway traffic (50 metres away)	70
busy city street	90
heavy traffic in city street	100
low flying jet aircraft overhead	100
discotheque	120
jet aircraft taking off within 50 metres	120

may contribute to juvenile delinquency. Recently legislation has been introduced in some countries restricting the use of lead in petrol.

It is important to appreciate that, as in the case of so many potentially harmful environmental factors, there is considerable variability among individuals in their sensitivity to chemical pollutants in the atmosphere, and the reactions of a single individual to a given pollutant may vary over time.

NOISE

Another obvious change in the human environment associated with machine use is a local increase in noise levels in various locations, including factories, busy streets and airports. Some typical figures for noise levels in dB(A)[1] in a variety of locations in the modern world are shown in Table 10.1.

Noise levels in the natural or evolutionary environment are usually about 30 dB(A) – or about 40 dB(A) when people are talking. In a busy city street today the noise level may be up to 100 dB(A). It is therefore valid to ask whether this deviation from the natural life conditions of the human species gives rise to any signs of maladjustment. The answer is in the affirmative. It is known, for instance, that 90 dB(A) will cause a temporary reduction in the acuity of hearing, and frequent exposure to such levels over long periods of time produces a permanent impairment.

The extent to which noise gives rise to psychological disturbances depends to a considerable extent on how it is perceived by the hearer. Some individuals in modern technological societies find the extreme levels of noise in discotheques, even as high as 120 dB(A), to be pleasurable. Others

---

[1]   The decibel (dB) scale is logarithmic. The 'A' relates to the level of only those sounds which are at the frequency response of the human ear.

find both the levels and the kind of noise in these places to be a cause of distress.

High noise levels can also affect health and well-being indirectly, by competing aggressively with other sensory inputs and thereby interfering, for example, with enjoyable conversation or the contemplation of objects of beauty.

COMMENT

Patterns of health and disease in human populations, or in sections of such populations, are largely a function of the life conditions experienced by members of these populations or subpopulations – that is, they are a function of people's personal environments and their behaviour patterns in those environments. Consequently, changes through history in human life conditions have been associated with changes in patterns of health and disease.

While statistics are not available for the early farming communities and early cities, it is clear that the main cause of ill health and death in those days was infectious disease. However, in some places and at some times, malnutrition and famine made an important contribution.

The transition to the high-energy phase of human society has been associated with further striking changes in health and disease patterns. Life expectancy has greatly increased and in many developed countries is now around 75–76 years (male–female average). This change has been mainly the result of the spectacular reduction of deaths from infection.

The main causes of death in these societies are cardiovascular disease, accounting for nearly 50 per cent of deaths, and cancer, accounting for about 25 per cent. While all human beings must die eventually from one cause or another, the evidence strongly suggests that most cases of both cardiovascular disease and cancer are the direct consequence of certain aspects of life conditions which are particularly characteristic of the modern high-energy societies. They are, therefore, theoretically avoidable.

FURTHER READING

Blum, R.H. (1969). A background history of drugs. In *Society and drugs: social and cultural observations* (eds. R. H. Blum *et al.*), pp.3–23. Jossey-Bass, San Francisco.

Brothwell, D. and Sandison, A.T. (eds.) (1967). *Diseases in antiquity: a survey of the disease, injuries and surgery of early populations*. Charles C. Thomas, Springfield.

Bull, D. (1982). *A growing problem: pesticides and the third world poor*. Oxfam, Oxford.

Rees, A.R. and Purcell, H.J.(eds.) (1982) *Diseases and the environment*. John Wiley, New York.

Burkitt, D. and Trowell, H.C. (eds.) (1975). *Refined carbohydrate foods and disease: some implications of dietary fibre*. Academic Press, London.

Carefoot, G.L. and Sprott, E.R. (1969). *Famine on the wind: plant disease and human history.* McGill-Queens University Press, Montreal.

Diesendorf, M. and Furnass, B. (eds.) (1977) *The impact of environment and lifestyle on human health.* Society for Social Responsibility in Science (ACT), Canberra.

Drummond, J.C. and Wilbraham, A. (1958). *The Englishman's food: a history of five centuries of English diet.* 2nd edn. Jonathan Cape, London.

Dubos, R. (1965). *Man adapting.* Yale University Press, New Haven.

Fenner, F., Henderson, D.A . Arita, I., Jezek, Z., and Laynyi, I.D. (1988). *Smallpox and its eradication.* World Health Organization, Geneva.

Hopkins, D.R. (1983). *Princes and peasants: smallpox in history.* University of Chicago Press, Chicago.

Hunter, D. (1971). *The diseases of occupations.* 4th edn. English University Press, London.

Langer, W.Ł. (1964). The Black Death. *Scientific American,* **210**(2), pp.114-21.

McCance, R.A. and Widdowson, E.M. (1956). *Breads, white and brown: their place in thought and social history.* Pitman Medical Publishing Company, London.

Rutter, M. and Jones, R.R. (eds.) (1983). *Lead versus health: sources and effects of low level lead exposure.* John Wiley, Chichester.

Trowell, H.C. and Burkitt, D.P. (eds.) (1981). *Western diseases: their emergence and prevention.* Edward Arnold, London.

Ziegler, P. (1969). *The Black Death.* Collins, London.

Zinsser, H. (1935). *Rats, lice, and history.* George Routledge, London.

both farmers and hunter–gatherers had engaged in *direct subsistence behaviour*, being actively involved in acquiring food directly from the natural environment, many city dwellers received their food from other human beings, usually in return for services rendered – either to the farmers themselves or, more often, to other sections of the community. These people were thus performing *indirect subsistence behaviour*, in that the activities which they carried out, and which resulted in their receiving sustenance, did not require any direct involvement in the processes of acquiring or producing food from its biological point of origin.

Another significant change was the fact that, unlike in the primeval situation, the subsistence behaviour of different individuals in towns and cities took on many quite different forms – including various kinds of craftwork, the construction of buildings, riding horses, driving vehicles, fighting, and playing the roles of priests, administrators, merchants and shopkeepers. Clearly, the indirect subsistence behaviour of different sections of the population produced quite different end-products. It is noteworthy that in modern high-energy societies different individuals may actually engage in very similar subsistence behaviours, and yet by so doing contribute to very different societal consequences. For example, the indirect subsistence behaviours of clerks in motor car factories, government departments, universities, department stores, ammunitions factories, hospitals and nature conservation organisations are very alike – but the end results of their activities, along with those of their colleagues, are extraordinarily different.

From the time of the earliest cities, some occupations were more pleasant than others. Indeed, for a very small minority of the population indirect subsistence behaviour involved no more than maintaining an inherited place at the top of the societal hierarchy and giving commands. It is not surprising that individuals in the more desirable positions strove to retain them and did their best to ensure that their children were similarly privileged; and, for this and a number of other reasons, occupations during the early urban period were largely hereditary. This is still the case, but to a lesser extent, in the high-energy societies of the 20th century.

The basic reward for indirect subsistence behaviour, or 'work', has always been the satisfaction of nutritional needs and other survival needs (e.g. shelter, clothing) of the individual and his or her family. However, in most urban societies, some individuals have received more in the way of material rewards than have others. In general, material rewards have, rather unfairly, tended to be greater in the occupations which are more enjoyable. Thus, indirect subsistence behaviour in some sections of society has resulted not only in the provision of essential goods necessary for satisfaction of the universal health and survival needs, but also of non-essential or luxury goods. While for most of the history of civilization only a minority of the population has been in this class, in the modern high-energy societies by far the greater part of the population receives material rewards far beyond those which are necessary for survival and health.

Different occupations are associated with very different life conditions. There is much variability with respect to material aspects of the immediate environment of workers – variability, for instance, in the level of noise and in the quality of the air in the immediate environment. There is even greater variability in *patterns of physical behaviour*. Some individuals spend nearly all day in a sitting position at a desk, while others perform a great deal of vigorous muscular work. The former may suffer some ill-effects from lack of physical activity such as obesity and an enfeebled cardiovascular system. On the other hand, muscular work performed in work situations may give rise to signs of biological maladjustment if it is excessive or if it involves continual and repetitive use of certain muscle complexes.

Occupations also differ markedly in the way they affect a range of important intangible aspects of human experience. They vary, for example, in the extent to which they involve personal creativity, the use of learned manual skills, co-operative small group interaction, and variety versus monotony. They also differ in the degree to which they are enjoyable and conducive to a sense of personal involvement, purpose, challenge, belonging, and responsibility.

Before leaving the subject of subsistence behaviour, it is necessary to draw attention to the notion of unemployment – which is a relatively recent product of civilization. Although the existence of an 'unemployed' section of the community goes back at least several hundred years, it has become an especially important characteristic of the high-energy societies of the 20th century. The economic arrangements and occupational structure of these societies are such that there is not sufficient work to keep all able-bodied men and women occupied in either direct or indirect subsistence activities for 35 or so hours per week. Society's response to this situation has taken the form of permitting the majority of the population to work for around 35 hours a week, while denying the rest of the potential work force the opportunity of doing any work at all. The subsistence needs of this unemployed group are provided for, through governments, by taxes levied on those who do work.

LEISURE EXPERIENCE

There was no sharp division in hunter–gatherer society between work and leisure. Like other animals in their native habitats, humans simply lived and responded in a spontaneous manner to the needs or pressures of the moment. As in the case of other species, they almost certainly enjoyed most of the activities in which they became involved – whether hunting, gathering,

Table 11.1   Leisure activities through the ages

Active	*Passive*
dancing	observing dancing
making music and singing	listening to music and singing live, or on radio, records, cassettes or television
arts and crafts: painting, pottery, sculpture, woodwork, needlework, photography	visiting art galleries
acting in theatre	attending theatre
story telling, writing, making television programmes	listeneing to stories, reading, watching television
participating in conversation	listening to conversation of others
cultivation of ornamental gardens and keeping plants in pots	visiting ornamental gardens
participating in solitary or team athletic contests, ball games etc.	watching sports contests, live or on television
hunting (mainly males)	
solving crossword puzzels, jigsaw puzzels, mathematical puzzels etc.	
collecting stamps, antiques, matchboxes, etc.	
	observing violence: gladiatorial combats, bear-baiting, bull-fights, dog-fights, cock-fights, some television shows.
driving cars	
shopping	

sitting and talking, dancing, playing games or making tools, utensils or ornaments. The notion of 'work' is thus a product of civilization.

Nowadays, 'leisure-time' is a term used to describe that portion of an individual's time budget when he or she is not engaged in work for wages and is not asleep at night. There has been tremendous variability in the way people spend their leisure-time throughout human history; and in the modern world there is much variation from one society to another, and indeed within societies. Culture and, as a function of culture, the state of technology, are the main determinants of the specific ways through which humans seek enjoyment in non-work situations. It is not possible to present here a systematic account or description of the leisure-time activities of the human species. Instead, in order to illustrate both the diversity of leisure-time activities and the role of culture in determining them, Table 11.1 presents a short list of some of the leisure activities which people have enjoyed through the ages and up to the present day.

FAMILY AND COMMUNITY EXPERIENCE

Throughout human history and prehistory the most common and enduring feature of social organisation has been the *nuclear family* – consisting of a mother, a father and their children. This was the building block of hunter–gatherer societies and, with rare exceptions, of early farming and early urban societies. In these societies the nuclear family, as a residential and economic unit, was commonly part of an *extended family*, which covered three or more generations, to include a parent or the parents of the mother or the father, and sometimes other relatives. Moreover, close social, and often economic, relationships were maintained with an even wider extended family, which embraced uncles, aunts and cousins. Apart from other advantages, this arrangement provided a convenient framework for the *reaction* of *mutual avoidance*, which is an adaptive response that comes into play when personality clashes occur between members of the nuclear family or other small group. When tensions mount between two individuals, one or other of them temporarily seeks the company of another member, or members, of the extended family, later to return to the nuclear unit (or other small group) when the tension has died down. Any societal arrangement that impedes the reaction of mutual avoidance in family or work situations is interfering with a most effective mechanism for reducing interpersonal conflict at the small-group level.

There has been a growing tendency in some high-energy societies in recent years for nuclear families to disintegrate, resulting in a significant increase in the number of single-parent families. In Britain, for example, the number of such families increased from 570,000 in 1971 to 740,000 in 1984, and in 1986 one in eight families with dependent children was headed by a single parent, usually the mother. Nevertheless, the nuclear family still remains the most common social unit at the residential level in these societies. However, unlike the situation throughout most of human history, it is no longer assumed that boys and girls will learn, and later practice, the occupational skills of their fathers and mothers. Another change has been the fact that many of the adult females now have a specialised occupation in society other than that of housewife. In Britain, 60 per cent of married women now have jobs outside the home, compared with 20 per cent 30 years ago.

As a result of increased geographic mobility and other societal changes in modern Western societies, the extended family, as a relatively coherent social unit, has weakened and has lost much of its importance. When contacts are maintained, they often involve writing letters, or conversations on the telephone, rather than face-to-face interactions. In some regions of the world, however, such as Japan and Latin America, the extended family is still very much in evidence.

With respect to community experience beyond the extended family, there has clearly been a great deal of variation from place to place and from time to time in human history. In general, however, most individual human beings, from hunter–gatherer times onwards, have been part of a face-to-face community, sharing a geographical 'home-range', and also to some degree sharing certain social responsibilities within that community. This was the case not only in hunter–gatherer societies and in village situations, but also in pre-industrial and early industrial townships and cities. Among other advantages, this experience provided the individual with the opportunity to give and to receive emotional support and to exchange relevant and interesting information; it also provided some variety in daily experience, the opportunity for co-operative small-group interaction and a sense of personal involvement and belonging. The term *Gemeinschaft* was introduced late in the 19th century by F. Tonnies for societies of this kind that are characterised by face-to-face relationships, family ties and shared beliefs and concerns.

The industrial transition resulted in important changes in societal organisation and in the social experience of individuals, as a result of which the community more based on geographical location has become much weaker in the high-energy societies. Gemeinschaft has been replaced by *Gesellschaft*, in which social groupings are not based on a geographical locality or on family ties, but are held together instead by practical, often financial, concerns, and the interrelationships within them are relatively formal, impersonal and less often face-to-face. In the new situation individuals frequently find themselves interacting with organisations, rather than with individual human beings (except as representatives of organisations). The rise of Gesellschaft has been associated with a decline in 'community spirit'.

LEARNING EXPERIENCE

The human aptitude for and dependence on culture means that learning plays a more important part in human behaviour than is the case in any other species. Indeed, culture itself has wrought great changes over the ages in the learning process. These changes are fundamentally of two kinds. First, there have been changes in the *method of learning*. Second, cultural developments have affected *what is learned*.

With regard to the method of learning, we can recognise two main approaches in pre-industrial times. The first is the 'natural' method – the only method of learning in hunter–gatherer society. This is spontaneous or informal learning. As children grow up, they learn to some extent simply by trial and error, but more especially by observing, listening to and mimicking other individuals, including adults and other children. In this way they become acquainted with the social norms of the society in which they live, with the state of knowledge of that society, and they become proficient in the techniques involved in subsistence behaviour and in other behavioural patterns appropriate to their habitat.

The second method is *non-spontaneous* or *formal learning*. This is epitomised by school classrooms. It is known that these existed at least as long ago as 2000 BC in the cities of Mesopotamia, where boys sat in rows at tables while professional pedagogues taught them the various skills required of the scribes and administrators of the time. According to surviving documents, the boys were strictly disciplined, and could be punished for not paying attention, for looking out of the window, for arriving late and for being improperly dressed. In these situations, fear appears largely to have replaced fun as a motive for learning.

Formal learning in school-type situations has persisted to the present day, although only in the last 50–100 years has it come to include the majority of young people in society, male and female. Previously schooling in Western societies was experienced only by a small minority of boys in the population, mainly the sons of families of the privileged classes.

At the present time nearly all children in the high-energy societies attend school from the age of about 5 until they are 13 or 14 (primary level). About 80 per cent remain at school until they are 17 or 18 (secondary level), and about 30 per cent continue with this type of formal learning at tertiary educational institutions for another 3 or 4 years. A small proportion of individuals return to the classroom in later life.

In the developing countries as a whole, about 86 per cent of young people attend school at the primary level, about 31 per cent at the secondary level and about 7 per cent at the tertiary level. The proportion of males attending educational programmes at the tertiary level is about 6 per cent higher than that of females in the high-energy societies, and about 40 per cent higher in developing regions.

In the modern world a third type of learning has become significant – it is *informal learning through the media*. In the early part of the present century the printed word in newspapers (and to some extent in books and other literature) was the main vehicle for this form of learning. In more recent times radio and television have become important sources of information and of various cultural messages and, together with newspapers and magazines, they have a profound influence on people's understanding of the world in which they live. In Britain, members of the lowest socio-economic category watch television for an average of 35 hours each week, compared with 23 hours a week for the highest socio-economic group. Ninety-seven per cent of families in Britain own a television set, and more than half these families have two sets or more.

Needless to say, the differences in *what is learned* by individual human beings from one time, place or subculture to another since the beginning of civilization have been enormous. This applies not only to *instrumental learning* – that is, the learning of mental or motor skills, but also to *explanatory learning* of the kind that is responsible for people's general *understanding* of the world and of human situations. In turn this understanding is a major determinant of people's general outlook – that is, their assumptions, motivating values, aspirations, intentions and opinions and their perceptions of what kinds of behaviours are approved of, or disapproved of, in their society. The actual behaviour of an individual is largely a function of his or her outlook.

The cultural inputs into the basic learning experience that are responsible for the individual's general understanding have a number of different, although often closely interrelated origins, including general cultural tradition (information passed on from generation to generation as a consequence of accumulated experience), religious teachings, areas of scholarship (e.g. history, literature, philosophy, sociology, economics, physics, chemistry, biology) and, increasingly, various kinds of vested interests in the form mainly of commercial, industrial and political corporate organisations. Because these various inputs have in the past been, and to a very considerable extent still are, so different from place to place, it is not surprising that there is so much variability in people's understanding of human situations, and hence in their outlook and behaviour.

CONSUMER BEHAVIOUR

The term *consumer behaviour* is used here to include all activities of individuals that are associated with, and that often result in, the purchase of commodities – especially manufactured goods, but also various services, like transport and tourism. Such consumer behaviour, as a significant aspect of the lifestyle and aspirations of the average individual, is particularly characteristic of contemporary high-energy societies, and it is a key component of the set of processes which are responsible for the continuing intensification of the technometabolism of human populations (see Chapter 7). Here we will briefly consider the causes and consequences of consumer behaviour as an aspect of human experience.

The various influences lying behind consumer behaviour are broadly of two kinds: societal factors and individual biopsychic factors. The societal factors are inherent in the present economic system in which industrial and commercial organisations play so crucial a role. They include the making available and displaying of a wide range of goods for purchase, the advertising of these goods and, for example, the commercial promotion of certain days in the year as special times for buying and presenting gifts.

The biopsychic factors tending to promote consumer behaviour can be seen as expressions of a number of the common behavioural tendencies of humankind. The following are especially important: the tendencies to seek approval and status, to avoid ridicule; and to seek novelty. Another important human behavioural characteristic in this context is the tendency to seek the attention of others. In present day society, a common means of attracting this attention is to display newly purchased goods. Yet another influential biopsychic factor is the tendency to strive to avoid feelings of deprivation; thus a major factor promoting consumerism is the observation by some people that other people possess goods which they do not possess themselves.

Loneliness, the general absence of arousal and other causes of mental depression are also important factors contributing to consumer behaviour. A common response in the affluent societies to feelings of depression or to sheer boredom is an expedition to a shopping centre. Window-shopping alone may to some extent alleviate the condition, but the biggest relief is experienced through the actual acquisition and taking home of new goods. Consumer behaviour thus plays a most important melioric role in helping to protect individuals from the undesirable effects of environmental stressors. Indeed, it is a reasonable hypothesis that consumer behaviour in modern Western society compensates to a considerable extent for the relative decline of various intangible meliors – meliors associated, for example, with creative behaviour, a sense of responsibility, and a sense of personal involvement.

It is important to appreciate, then, that for many people in the present cultural setting consumer behaviour is necessary in order that they gain in-group approval, achieve self-esteem and status, and do not feel deprived. These are basic universal health needs, and culture has determined that in high-energy societies the main criteria for their satisfaction are in terms of material possessions. Any successful transition to an alternative arrangement which is less costly in resources and energy and which involves lower levels of consumption of material goods would demand a fundamental change in the dominant outlook of society and, in particular, in the criteria for approval, success and status.

RELIGION

One of the characteristics of human society associated with the aptitude for culture is the fact that, until very recent times, the majority of individuals in all human populations have shared belief in a spiritual or supernatural dimension of reality, and in spirits or gods (or in a spirit or a god) who have the power to influence human affairs. Many of these belief systems, or *religions*, have provided explanations about the origins of life and of

---

Meliors are defined as those experiences that have the opposite effect to stressors, promoting a sense of enjoyment in contrast to a sense of distress.

humanity, and have assumed the existence of life after death in either spiritual or reincarnated form. Religions have always involved attempts to communicate with the assumed spiritual being or beings through the spoken word, through thought or silent prayer, and through rituals of various kinds. It is probably only within the last two or three generations that in some societies a high proportion of the population, sometimes following the official government line, would claim not to hold any religious beliefs.

In general, the patterns of religious belief and ritual among recent hunter–gatherers are relatively simple as compared with those of farming and urban societies. They usually involve belief in a range of spirits associated with different components of the landscape – hills, rocks, trees, creeks and so forth – and participation in simple ceremonies aimed at eliciting the help, or avoiding the wrath of these spirits.

After the domestic transition, belief in a Mother Goddess, giver of life and food, became very widespread and seems to have persisted in farming communities for several thousand years. The excavations at Çatal Hüyük in southern Anatolia show clearly that the worship of a Mother Goddess was a central aspect of the life experience of the people in the region eight to nine thousand years ago. And the numerous clay or stone female figurines found in Europe dating back to the Upper Palaeolithic era have been interpreted by some people as evidence of a Mother Goddess cult well before the domestic transition.

The advent of cities was associated with significant changes in religious belief systems. For one thing, the Mother Goddess was displaced by male deities. In Mesopotamia, for example, each city state had its own male god, and wars between the city states were perceived as being wars between their rival gods. The kings were seen as the earthly representatives of these gods. In contrast, in Egypt the Pharaoh was himself regarded as a god.

Early in the 2nd millennium BC a religious movement emerged in the Middle East which eventually had far-reaching consequences for the religious beliefs of a large proportion of the world's population. This movement was associated with a Semitic tribe – the Israelites, Hebrews or Jews and the set of religious beliefs to which the movement gave rise is known as *Judaism*. Judaism, as formulated over the period of nearly two thousand years before the birth of Jesus, lies at the root not only of present-day Judaism, but also of Christianity and Islam. Initially, it taught that the Jews should worship only their own god, and should not pay homage to the gods of other peoples. Later, it decreed that there is only one god.

Around 600 BC *Zoroastrianism* became an important religion in Persia and although it did not survive as an entity in its own right, it had marked influences on Christianity, Islam, Buddhism and Hinduism. It was based on the words of the prophet Zoroaster, who taught that there was only one god, and who explained the existence of good and evil in terms of the birth, at the beginning of the creation, of two spirits, one of whom was associated with a way of life based on truth, justice and respect for life, while the other supported falsehood, destruction, injustice and death.

Following the teachings of Jesus of Nazareth in the 1st century AD, Christianity became established, at first as a movement within Judaism, but later as a separate and competing offshoot from it. As a consequence of the processes of cultural accumulation and elaboration, Christianity became thoroughly institutionalised. Today the various bodies of the Christian church claim to have, together, well over one thousand million members.

Islam which dates back to the 7th century AD, is based on the teachings of the prophet Mohammed, as set forth in the *Koran*. Muslims, the followers of Mohammed, see him as the last and most perfect of a series of messengers from God, which included Jesus of Nazareth. The Koran accepts the writings of the Old Testament of the Holy Bible. Islam, like Judaism, is rigidly monotheistic. It is practised by most Arabs and by arabised Africans, as well as in Turkey, Iran, Pakistan, parts of India, Malaysia, Indonesia and China. The total number of Muslims is four or five hundred million. Perhaps its most fundamental tenet is its emphasis on egalitarianism in humankind, irrespective of race, colour or social position. Except where Islam is highly politicised – that is, where it is regarded as an integral part of the political and legal system – the religion is less institutionalised than the various branches of Christianity.

Hinduism, the belief system of the great majority of the inhabitants of India and of some sections of the populations of Pakistan and Ceylon, has very ancient origins. It arose initially as a synthesis of various sacrificial cults brought into India by the invading Aryans around 1500 BC with the various religions of the indigenous peoples. Hinduism is based on the Veda, which consists of a number of very ancient sacred writings. It involves the worship of a complex set of gods, many of which differ, as do the religious practices, from region to region, and even from family to family. However, one god among these – Vishnu (incarnated as Krishna or Shiva) is dominant. Hinduism, however, concedes that there is some validity in all religions. Hindus believe in the transmigration of souls.

Buddhism dates back to the teachings of Gautama Buddha who was one of numerous ascetic teachers who were wandering in India in the 5th and 6th Centuries BC, and who rejected both violence and the materialistic way of life. Buddhism also rejected the authority of the Vedas, and offered a way of release from the endless sequence of births and deaths believed in by Hindus. This belief system spread not only in India, but also in most regions of the Far East. Today about 90 per cent of the inhabitants of Burma and Thailand are Buddhists, as are 60 per cent of people in Ceylon and Japan, and 17 per cent of Chinese. There are also Buddhists in India, Pakistan and the Philippines.

Although all the main religions of the modern world had quite simple beginnings, they have all (some more than others) been subject to the complicating influence of cultural elaboration, which seems to be an inevitable outcome of the human aptitude for culture. As a consequence of the activities of different individuals or groups of individuals in different places and at different times, this process of elaboration has given rise within each of the main religions to countless different sects, each with its own particular version of perceived religious truth, and each with its own special set of assumptions and beliefs. Also, every now and again, movements develop within the main religions which aim to 'get back to basics', to dispense with some of the superimposed cultural trappings that have accumulated over the centuries, and to highlight the teachings on which the religion was originally based. These reformist movements have led, of course, to further fragmentation within the religions.

It seems that the main implications of early religions for human behaviour lay in the perceived necessity to please omnipotent spirits or gods, giving rise to an impressive range of different kinds of sacrificial rights and other religious ceremonies. But today all the main religions have a powerful ethical component aimed at influencing human behaviour in directions which the religions deem to be good and to be in the interests of humankind. Judaism is still based on the moral code of Moses and the Ten Commandments, which date back to about 1600 BC. In Christianity, there is great emphasis on the virtues of love and charity towards other human beings, even strangers – thus compensating, to some extent, for the lack of innate concern in humans for the well-being of members of out-groups. The Koran teaches a definite code of behaviour, which must be practised if individuals are to survive the final Day of Judgement. This code, however, has been greatly elaborated in some Muslim sects, and sometimes includes, for example, their insistence on purdah and female circumcision, neither of which are demanded in the Koran.

Buddhism puts a great deal of emphasis on non-violence and on the *avoidance* of evil thought and behaviour. There is less emphasis than in elemental Christianity on positive acts of goodness. Buddhism advocates a middle path, between the extremes of self-denial and self-mortification on the one hand and self-indulgence and sensual pleasure on the other. By assiduously following the prescribed 'eight-fold path' individuals are freed of the necessity for rebirth, and are ready for Nirvana.

Because of the human tendencies to identify with in-groups, to accept the cultural assumptions and values of these in-groups, to behave with loyalty towards them, and to be suspicious of out-groups, the different religious belief systems have provided a basis for considerable social fragmentation. The 'us and them' dichotomy has been applied to groupings with different religious beliefs. Despite the emphasis in most religions of such sentiments as love, kindness, charity, tolerance and egalitarianism, throughout the history of civilization conflict between the main religious groupings, and between sects within these groupings, has frequently been the cause of prolonged and bitter violence and of untold human suffering. The crusades are only one example. Many of these transgenerational conflicts between people adhering to different belief systems are still with us today, and many tens of thousands of innocent individuals live under constant fear of injury or death because of this cultural insanity. Perhaps the only one of the main religions to have shown itself to be convincingly above this kind of behaviour is Buddhism.

COMMENT

The purpose of this chapter and the one that preceded it has been to highlight some of the many important ways that cultural processes have modified the biology and life experience of humans since the domestic transition, and especially during the past few thousand years. Some of the changes have been transient, or relatively so, and some have been local, while others have persisted or have become world-wide; and some of them may be judged as desirable, and others as undesirable.

One aspect of human experience that has not been dealt with, except incidentally, relates to aesthetic appreciation and creativity. We noted in Chapter 3 that one of the outstanding and perhaps unique characteristics of the human species in its natural habitat was the fact that individuals found it worthwhile to spend time shaping, or otherwise modifying components of their environment, simply in order to produce an aesthetically pleasing effect. This effort was sometimes directed towards adding an aesthetic dimension to objects of practical value, and sometimes towards the creation of ornaments and other decorative objects of no practical use. It is also noteworthy that many, if not most, of the major technological advances had an aesthetically-motivated beginning. As far as we can know, the earliest kilns were constructed in the late Palaeolithic period and were used for baking little clay models of different kinds of animals. The finds from Çatal Hüyük and many other places indicate that the first use of metals, notably copper and lead, was purely decorative, and this applies also to gold and silver. And the first use of gunpowder may well have been to manufacture fireworks.

While it is not easy to explain this fascination with, and enjoyment of, patterns in colour, shape and sound that appear 'beautiful' in terms of the selection pressures operating in the evolutionary environment, it does seem to be a universal characteristic of the human species. Although culture has certainly had far-reaching effects through the ages on what is and what is not perceived as beautiful, it is likely that, beneath this cultural overlay, there is an important phylogenetic contribution to aesthetic sensibility.

Another relevant influence of culture has been its effect on the amount and kind of creative behaviour experienced by the majority of individuals in a society. While some such activity appears to have been universal in the hunter–gatherer setting, it is not been a feature of the lives of all individuals in many subsequent societies, including the contempory high-energy societies. Indeed, there is much to be said for the view creative behaviour, based on the application of a learned skill, has a powerful melioric or health-promoting potential. It follows that societies which do not offer incentives and opportunities for behaviour of this kind are depriving the majority of the population of an important natural source of enjoymant and sense of self-fulfillment.

FURTHER READING

Bowen, J. (1972, 1975, 1981). *A history of Western education.* Volumes 1–3. St. Martin's Press. New York.

Burrows, D.J. and Lapides, F.R. (eds.) (1970). *Alienation: a casebook.* Thomas Y. Crowell, New York.

Etzioni, A. (ed.) (1971). *Alienation: from Marx to modern sociology.* Allyn and Bacon, Boston.

Hirsch, F. (1977). *The social limits to growth.* Routledge and Kegan Paul, London.

Illich, I. (1975). *Tools for conviviality.* Collins, Glasgow.

Laslett, P. (1971). *The world we have lost.* Methuen, London.

Leiss, W. (1978). *The limits to satisfaction: on needs and commodities.* Marion Boyars, London.

Scitovsky, T. (1976). *The joyless economy: an inquiry into human satisfaction and consumer dissatisfaction.* Oxford University Press, London.

CHAPTER 12

THE PRESENT AND THE FUTURE IN BIOHISTORICAL PERSPECTIVE

THE HUMAN SITUATION TODAY

We begin this final chapter with a short summary of the outstanding features of the human situation today in biohistorical perspective.

(1) Since farming economies first came into existence around 480 generations ago, by which time the human species had already spread to all five habitable continents of the world, the human population has increased about 1000-fold. Half of this increase has occurred in the last 30 years. At present, the fertility rate exceeds the mortality rate so that a further doubling of the population can be expected in the next 40 years.

(2) This 1000-fold increase in population is causing severe pressures on the ecosystems of the biosphere, resulting especially from activities associated with the production of food and the use of timber and fibre. Vast and increasing areas of the Earth's surface, especially in arid and semi-arid regions, have almost ceased to be biologically productive. According to the United Nations Food and Agriculture Organisation, if present rates of land degradation continue, in less than 200 years from now there will not be a single fully-productive hectare of arable land on this planet.

(3) Of even greater ecological significance is the massive increase in the intensity of resource and energy use and waste production by human society that has followed the industrial transition. This development is imposing ecological pressures of a new kind on the biosphere. Expressed in terms of levels of use of extrasomatic energy, the ecological load imposed by the human species on the biosphere has

243

increased at least 10,000-fold since the domestic transition. Three-quarters of this increase has occurred during the lifetime of the generation of which this writer is a representative, and half of it has occurred during the lifetime of his children.

(4) The chief ecological significance of the 10,000-fold increase in extrasomatic energy use lies in the fact that the main source of this energy is the combustion of fossil fuels, which leads to the release of massive amounts of carbon dioxide, nitrogen and sulphur oxides and other gases.

As a consequence of the continuing release of carbon dioxide and other 'greenhouse gases' on this scale by modern industrial society, major changes in the climate of the planet are inevitable. There is considerable uncertainty about the precise nature of these changes, and therefore about their consequences for the human species, although a significant increase in temperature is likely.

(5) Within the past 50 years human society has invented and produced weapons of unimaginable destructive capacity for use against other members of the species. If used, they would not only result in human carnage on a massive and unprecedented scale, but also in the widespread destruction of other species and ecosystems, possibly leading to the end of life on Earth as we know it. Although there has been marked improvement in recent years in the relationships between the super-powers, which possess the greater part of this weaponry, the threat to the biosphere and humanity will remain so long as nuclear weapons continue to exist.

(6) Apart from waste products resulting from the use of extrasomatic energy, the industrial activities of some human populations are also resulting in the release into the environment of a great range of different synthetic chemical compounds, often in vast quantities. Many of these compounds interfere in one way or another with the processes of life.

(7) With respect to the intensity of technometabolism (i.e. resource and energy use and technological waste production) and the release of chemical pollutants in general, extreme disparities exist between different human populations. About 80 per cent of the carbon dioxide and other greenhouse gases resulting from the combustion of fossil fuels is coming from the developed high-energy societies, which make up only about one-fifth of the world's human population. These countries are also responsible for nearly all of the production of radioactive nuclear wastes and of life-threatening chemical pollutants. The per capita use of extrasomatic energy in these high-energy

countries ranges from about 40–100 Human Energy Equivalents (HEE), as compared with 1 or 2 HEE in some of the least developed countries. Because the main source of this energy is fossil fuels, the per capita production of carbon dioxide is 40–100 times greater in the high-energy societies than in the least developed areas. In Australia, for example, the average human organism is responsible for the release of nearly 60 kg of carbon dioxide into the atmosphere every day.

(8) It is thus apparent that, for the first time in the 4000 million years of life on this planet, changes of enormous ecological significance are now occurring at the level of the planet's biosphere as a whole as a result of the actions of a single species of animal, *Homo sapiens*. The ozone layer in the stratosphere, which has been protecting terrestrial life for hundreds of millions of years from the ultraviolet radiation from the sun, is beginning to disintegrate, and progressive changes in the climate of the planet resulting from the release of greenhouse gases are apparently already underway. Other significant developments include important ecological changes in the oceans, severe damage of the forests of the northern hemisphere due to 'acid rain', and the rapid disappearance of tropical forests.

There is no escaping the fact that these various developments represent a serious threat to the continued existence of humankind on this planet . It is noteworthy that they are all, without exception, outcomes of that special biological attribute of the human species, the aptitude for culture. It is culture, not nature, that is responsible for the release of greenhouse gases on a scale sufficient to modify the global climate, for the production of the chloroflurocarbons (CFCs) which are eroding the ozone layer, and for the chemical pollution of the oceans. It is culture that lies behind the manufacture of weapons of mass destruction and that is responsible for the deep antipathies which exist between different human groups and which result in so much needless violence and distress. And it is culture that has brought about the obscene inequities in the life conditions of different human populations and socio-economic groups throughout the world.

On the other hand, of course, we can point to many 'positive' outcomes of the aptitude for culture, to be enjoyed by at least some sections of the human population, including a great deal of pleasing art, literature, poetry, theatre and music, and the various comforts of modern civilization.

The fact that culture is responsible for so much human distress and for the current threats to the survival of our species draws attention to an interesting and challenging paradox. For, while culture has given rise to these highly unsatisfactory aspects of the present situation, it is only through our aptitude for culture that we can hope to overcome them and move

245

towards a saner, safer, fairer and ecologically sustainable society in the future. Thus, as has so often been the case on a smaller scale in human history, the main hope for humanity now lies in the processes of *cultural adaptation* to culturally-induced threats to biological systems. It is impossible to predict, on the basis of the facts of our understanding of the nature of the threats to humankind or of the processes of cultural adaptation, whether or not humankind will overcome the current threats to its survival. In the past, some such attempts at cultural adaptation have been successful, and some have failed. There is, indeed, no law to the effect that humankind is infinitely, or inevitably, adaptable.

In the present global situation, the threats to the human species are of far greater magnitude than at any time in our history, and the impediments interfering with effective cultural adaptive processes aimed at overcoming them are multiple and powerful. On the other hand there is now much more knowledge available than ever before about the sensitivities of the living systems and about the health needs of humans, and the spectacular scientific advances of recent decades favour the development of new technologies that could play key roles in the transition to a peaceable ecologically balanced society of the future.

There is still hope.

A NEW VISION

A great challenge therefore faces humanity the world over to purge our culture of those components which result in behaviours that are hostile to nature and hostile to other human beings, so that we can move towards a restoration of ecological balance between human populations and the ecosystems of the biosphere and towards long-lasting harmony between peoples. While the initial motivation behind this cultural adaptive response will be the avoidance of global ecological catastrophe, the fact that major societal changes are inevitable provides the opportunity to make important improvements also in other areas – aimed, for example, at eliminating the gross social inequities that characterise global society today. The new society must satisfy the health needs both of the biosphere and of all sections of the human population.

In what essential ways, in terms of economic arrangements, social and political organisation, institutional structure, educational system and general culture, would this new society differ from those in which we live at the present time? And how might the transition to the new system be achieved in the shortest time possible with minimum human distress? In light of current ecological realities, these questions should surely be major topics for discussion in all societies today throughout the world – among political groups, government officials and in the community at large. As a contribution to this discussion the following list is presented of the most essential characteristics, as seen from the biohistorical standpoint, of the ecologically balanced and humanly desirable society of the future:

- Respect for nature, and for humans as a part of nature, will occupy top place in the hierarchy of societal values. This will be associated with a better understanding of nature, of the processes of life and of the human situation in the biosphere. Respect for and understanding of nature will be a major influence on the criteria for approval and disapproval at all levels of society, and will be reflected in all cultural arrangements and human activities, from the level of the global community, through nations and regional communities to occupational groups, families and individuals. The first consideration in decision-making at all these levels will be the needs of the biological systems and processes on which we depend and of which we are a part.

- The human population will be more or less steady, and at a level that does not exert undue harmful pressures on the ecosystems of the biosphere, either locally or globally.

- There will be a very much reduced rate of use of fossil fuels. Any replacement of fossil fuels will be by non-polluting energy sources.

- Weapons of mass destruction will not exist, and conflicts between states will be settled by non-military means.

- The economic system will be sensitive not only to human wants, but also to the health needs of the ecosystems of the biosphere.

- There will be strict controls preventing the release in harmful quantities of synthetic chemicals and other substances, and of radioactive materials capable of interfering with the processes of life.

- Strict control of corporate organisations will ensure that their activities are always in the best interests of the biosphere and of all sections of the human community.

- Cultural arrangements will ensure that new technologies are wisely applied, in the best interests of the biosphere and of humanity.

- Cultural arrangements will ensure that the universal health needs of people in all sections of the community are satisfied. This applies not only to tangible health needs, such as clean air and water, good food and shelter, but also to intangible needs, such as opportunities and incentives for creative behaviour, an aesthetically pleasing environment and a sense of personal involvement, belonging, challenge and responsibility in daily life.

- There will be an uncoupling of the present relationship between high rates of resource and energy use (i.e. a high material standard of living) on the one hand and human health and enjoyment of life on the other.

- High levels of employment will not be dependent upon increasing energy and resource use. As far as possible, all jobs will be rewarding in terms of tangible and intangible human health needs.

- Societal arrangements will ensure the protection of a full range of ecosystems of different kinds and the maintenance of biological diversity.

- Economic and societal arrangements in the rural industries will ensure that economic pressures do not force farmers, foresters or any other occupational group to carry out activities which are likely to promote land degradation or undesirable destruction of natural ecosystems.

- Societal conditions will encourage biosphere-friendly and human-friendly outlets for such human behavioural tendencies as seeking status, approval, novelty and challenge.

- The educational system will promote understanding of the processes of nature and of the human place in nature. It will ensure that, whatever area of specialism in which individuals are educated and work, they will possess good understanding of the human situation, and of human situations, in realistic biological and historical perspective.

Viewed against the background of the existing structure and arrangements of today's societies, many of the items on this list may well be judged by many readers to be Utopian in the extreme – indicating, perhaps, that the author is blind to 'economic realities'. On the other hand, they all make good sense either ecologically or in terms of human welfare; and it is ecological realities, not economic ones, that will determine whether the human species is still in existence on this planet at the end of the coming century.

Extrasomatic energy use

With respect to technometabolism and, in particular, levels of use of extrasomatic energy, it is clear that the main problem at present lies in the fact that the main source of this energy is fossil fuels. The direct use of fossil fuels in, for example, transportation, and their indirect use in electricity results in the release into the atmosphere of vast amounts of carbon dioxide, oxides of nitrogen and sulphur and various other gases. As discussed, one of the most ecologically significant consequences of fossil fuel use is the impact on the Earth's climate due to the greenhouse effect. It has been estimated that if further progressive change in climate is to be prevented, it will be necessary to reduce use of fossil fuels to 40 per cent of present global levels at least, and probably to much lower levels.

Some people advocate the replacement of fossil fuels with nuclear energy which, once the power stations are established, do not release greenhouse gases into the atmosphere. However, the use of nuclear power for the generation of electricity does result in the production of highly radioactive wastes which have a great potential for damaging living systems – a potential which lasts for many thousands of years. This author is among those who considers that it is nothing short of insanity to aim to replace one polluting source of extrasomatic energy with another, the by-products of which remain highly dangerous to life forms for so long.

The nuclear option is especially inappropriate in view of the availability of solar energy. The energy reaching the Earth every day in the form of sunlight is about 25,000 times greater than that which is now used by humankind the world over in the form of fossil fuels. Moreover, techniques exist for harnessing this solar energy and using it to provide heat, electricity, or such potentially useful fuels as hydrogen and ammonia. This solar energy does not result in the production of greenhouse gases, nitrogen and sulphur oxides, or dangerous radioactive by-products. The technology for developing and using solar power exists, and all that is needed is the political will and, resulting from this, the financial support necessary for developing and applying solar energy and the other solar-based energy sources such as wind and tidal power.

The other key question is whether we humans really *need* as much energy as we are at present using in the developed countries today for the satisfaction of our health needs and for rich, self-fulfilling, and enjoyable life experience. In Australia today, for example, people are using, on a per capita basis, more than 60 HEE, which is twice the amount they were using in 1960. Few people would claim that Australians are healthier or enjoying life more than they were 30 years ago.

The essential point is that, because of the nature of the cultural soup in which we are immersed and the associated economic system, ever-increasing use of energy and resources is perceived as being necessary for the satisfaction of human needs. Indeed, if we track down the way this energy is used, it can be seen that it is in fact satisfying, directly or indirectly, very basic health needs – needs which, in other cultural systems have been, or are, satisfied without such extravagant use of energy and resources. These needs includes the acquisition of provisions; transportation to place of work; visiting relatives, friends or the natural environment; achieving approval, status or attention; and avoiding a sense of deprivation. The organisation and economic system of the high-energy societies today is such that the human population has become *addicted* to high levels of extrasomatic energy use, in that these simple needs cannot now be easily satisfied without the high rates of consumption of resources and energy.

Accepting that the ultimate aim must be a reasonable degree of equity world-wide with respect to resource and energy use, it has recently been suggested that about 20 HEE per capita would be a sensible target for all societies in the future. This is slightly less than the current rate for Spain and Israel (both of which have life expectancies higher than that of the USA), half that of modern Britain, about six times that of Shakespearian Britain, and about 20 times that of present-day Kenya and Nepal. It must be stressed, however, that because of the greenhouse phenomenon, most of the 20 HEE of extrasomatic energy would have to come from renewable sources, such as solar energy, wind and tidal power, and firewood (assuming that in this last case the timber used for fuel is replaced by new growth).

Population

There is clearly a limit to the number of people that this planet can support in a state of health and well-being. Many authorities take the view that the limit has already been exceeded. The maximum ecologically sustainable population will depend both on the extent to which farming practices are protective of the soil and on the intensity and form of industrial activity and technometabolism. According to one estimate, for instance, an 'agricultural world', in which most human beings are peasants, should be able to support 5000–7000 million people. In contrast, it is suggested that a reasonable estimate for an industrialised world society at the present North American material standard of living would be 1000 million, while at the more frugal European standard of living, 2000–3000 million people would be possible.

The massive increase in the total human population over recent decades has been largely due to the cultural, or 'artificial', control of the main causes of death of humans. From the biological standpoint it is self-evident that this influence must ultimately be matched with compensating cultural, or 'artificial', control of birthrates, if an ecologically stable situation is to be achieved.

For those who take the view that our aim should be to promote as many human lives as possible, the key question is: How can this best be achieved? Broadly, there are two approaches: (1) to promote massive population growth now, with no artificial control of fertility, while accepting the very real likelihood of mass starvation and pestilence and of major ecological disturbance that could bring a sudden end to the human species, (2) to limit population now by controlling birth rates, and to protect the biosphere so that it can support countless generations of humanity far into the future.

An urgent educational challenge

Let us return to the important paradox mentioned earlier in this chapter. The future of humankind hangs in the balance. On the one hand, the most serious threats to humanity today, both locally and globally, are the consequence of the human aptitude for culture. On the other hand, given the existing state of affairs and the realities of our cultural arrangements, institutions and assumptions, it is only through our aptitude for culture that we can hope to bring the biosphere-threatening excesses of the present-day to an end. It is only through our capacity for culture that we can hope to achieve the kind of reorganisation that will be necessary to ensure the protection of ecosystems, local and global, and the well-being of humans the world over.

It follows that the most immediate and urgent task facing humanity today is to apply our aptitude for culture in a new way – using it, in fact, to control culture itself. We must use it to cleanse our cultural soups of those nonsense ingredients that are resulting in activities that violate the processes of nature on which we depend and that interfere with human health and enjoyment of life. This transformation in culture, and hence in our society, can only come about through a massive educational effort that results in a greatly improved understanding of nature and of the human situation in the biosphere.

This book is written in the firm belief that such improved understanding is an essential prerequisite for a successful transition to ecologically balanced, harmonious and equitable human societies the world over.

FURTHER READING

Barbour, I.G. (1980). *Technology, environment and human values.* Praeger, New York.

Birch, C. (1975). *Confronting the future: Australia and the world: the next hundred years.* Penguin, Ringwood, Victoria.

Boulding, K.E. (1966). The economics of coming spaceship Earth. In *Environmental quality: in a growing economy* (ed. H. Jarrett), pp.3–14 Johns Hopkins Press, Baltimore.

Brown, L.R. (1981). *Building a sustainable society.* W.W. Norton, New York.

Brown, L.R. *et al.* (1984, 1985, 1986, 1987, 1988, 1989, 1990, 1991). *State of the world 1984, 1985, 1986, 1987, 1988, 1989, 1990, 1991: a Worldwatch Institute report on progress toward a sustainable society.* W.W. Norton, New York.

Cobb, J.B., Cobb, C.W. and Daly, H.E. (1989). *For the common good: redirecting the economy toward community, the environment and a sustainable future.* Beacon Press, Boston.

Daly, H.E. (1977). *Steady-state economics: the economics of biophysical equilibrium and moral growth.* W.H. Freeman, San Francisco.

Day, L.H. and Day, A.T. (1964). *Too many Americans.* Delta, New York.

Eckholm, E.P. (1982). *Down to earth: environmental and human needs.* W.W. Norton, New York.

Ekins, P. (ed.) (1986). *The living economy: a new economics in the making.* Routledge and Kegan Paul, London.

Gabor, D., Colombo, U., King, A., and Galli, R. (1978). *Beyond the age of waste: a report to the Club of Rome.* Pergamon Press, Oxford.

Goldsmith, E., Allen, R., Allaby, M., Davull, J. and Lawrence, S. (1972). *A blueprint for survival*. Tom Stacey, London.

Goldsmith, E. (1988). *The great U-turn: de-industrialising society*. Green Books, Hartland, Devon.

Hayes, D. (1977). *Rays of hope: the transition to a post-petroleum world*. W.W. Norton, New York.

Hawker, P. 1984. *The next economy*. Angus & Robertson, North Ryde, New South Wales.

Henderson, H. (1981). *The politics of the solar age*. Doubleday/Anchor, New York.

IUCN, UNEP, and WWF (International Union for Conservation of Nature and Natural Resources, United Nations Environment Programme, and the World Wildlife Fund) (1980). *World conservation strategy: living resource conservation for sustainable development*. IUCN, Gland, Switzerland.

Lonnroth, M., Johansson, T.B., and Steen, P. (1980). *Solar versus nuclear: choosing energy futures*. Pergamon Press, Oxford.

Lovins, A. (1977). *Soft energy paths: towards a durable peace*. Ballinger, Cambridge, MA.

McRobie, G. (1981). *Small is possible*. Jonathan Cape, London.

Meadows, D.H., Meadows, D.L., Randers, J., and Behrens, W.W. (1972). *The limits to growth*. Universal Books, New York.

Milbrath, L.W. (1984). *Environmentalists: vanguard of a new society*. State University of New York Press, Albany

Mollison, B. (1988). *Permaculture: a designer's handbook*. Tagari, Tyalgum, New South Wales.

Passmore, J. (1980). *Man's responsibility for nature: ecological problems and Western traditions*. Duckworth, London.

Pearce, D., Markandya, A. and Barbier, E. (1989). *Blueprint for a green economy*. Earthscan, London.

Robertson, J. (1979). *The sane alternative: a choice of futures*. River Basin Publishing Company, St. Paul.

Robertson, J. (1989). *Future wealth: a new economics for the 21st century*. Cassell, London.

Schumacher, E.F. (1973). *Small is beautiful: a study of economics as if people mattered*. Blond and Briggs, London.

Singh, N. (1978). *Economics and the crisis of ecology*, 2nd edn. Oxford University Press, Delhi.

Trainer, F.E. (1985). *Abandon affluence!* Zed Books, London.

Valaskakis, K. (project director) (1977). *Conserver society project: report on phase II. Vol 1. The selective conserver society*. GAMMA, University of Montreal/McGill University, Montreal.

Ward, B. and Dubos, R. (1972). *Only one earth: the care and maintenance of a small planet*. Penguin, Harmondsworth, Middx.

Zolotas, X. (1981). *Economic growth and declining social welfare*. Bank of Greece, Athens.

APPENDIX I

MAIN SETS OF VARIABLES

Biosphere
- soil
- water
- atmosphere
- mineral resources
- energy resources
- fauna
- flora
- plants
- micro-organisms
- biogeochemical cycles
- irradiation
- climatic process
- photosynthesis
- animal and plant growth
- fluctuations in animal and plant growth
- soil erosion
- changes in soil fertility, salination, alkalination
- host/parasite interactions, and epidemic processes
- population size
- population density
- fertility and mortality rates
- health statistics
- population structure
  . age
  . ethnic
  . economic
  . educational
  . occupational

Artefacts
- buildings
- roads
- machines
- works of art
- furniture
- clothes
- tools
- weapons

253

Humans
- population size, density, distribution and structure
- fertility and mortality rates
- health and disease

Human activities
- farming, fishing
- mining
- manufacturing
- transportation
- commerce
- recreation
- administration
- migration

Culture
- assumptions
- knowledge
- understanding
- beliefs
- values
- attitudes

Cultural arrangements
- economic arrangements
- legislation
- hierarchical arrangements
- political system
- educational programmes

APPENDIX II

GLOSSARY

Adaptation.
Adaptation – the process of modifying to suit new conditions; a process of modification which occurs in response to a threat and which results in an increased capacity to cope with or overcome that threat.

  – a modification in an organism or a population which occurs as a result of a new detrimental influence and which renders it better able to cope with the new conditions, leading to a reduction in any signs of maladjustment that may have resulted from the new influence and resulting in improved chances of survival.

  evolutionary adaptation – the adaptation of a population through natural selection (applies *only* to populations and is only transgenerational).

  innate adaptation – physiological or behavioural adaptive responses which occur in individuals, are genetically determined and do not depend on learning.

  cultural adaptation – adaptation through cultural processes.

  antidotal cultural adaptation – cultural adaptation which is directed at a symptom of a disorder or state of maladjustment, or at an intermediate or subsidiary cause, but not at the unsatisfactory conditions which gave rise to the disorder in the first place.

  corrective cultural adaptation – cultural adaptation in which the aim is to reverse the underlying environmental change which is responsible for a state of phylogenic maladjustment.

Biohistory.
Learning about Nature, the sensitivities and interdependencies of living systems, the human place in Nature and the interplay, past and present, between culture and Nature.

Biomass.
The total mass of living organisms in a defined area, usually measured by weight.

Biophysical state.
The morphological, physiological and psychological characteristics of an individual human, including such factors as height, blood pressure, state of lungs, knowledge, assumptions and feelings.

Bioproductivity.
The production in plants of organic material containing energy in chemical form initially derived from sunlight.

Biosensitive society.
A society which is sensitive to the health needs of biological systems, including human populations and the ecosystems of the biosphere.

Biosphere.
The part of the Earth's surface which includes living organisms, the remains of living organisms and the physical and chemical components of the total system necessary for, or involved in the process of life.

BP
Years before the present.

Carnivore.
An animal which gains sustenance primarily from the tissue of other animals.
Chemicalization.
The accumulation of chemicals in the environment (air, water, land) resulting from the activities of humans.
Common behavioural tendencies.
Those behavioural characteristics of humans which are common in all cultures, past and present. They include, in the social dimension, the aptitude for culture, and the tendencies to identify with an in-group and to seek the approval of members of the in-group.
Culture.
The word *culture* is used in this volume to mean: those abstract aspects of human situations which include accumulated knowledge, beliefs and assumptions, values and technical know-how, and which are passed from one human to another, or from one group to another, or from generation to generation, mainly through the use of learned symbols, as in speech or writing.

Ecological sustainability.
For the purpose of this volume, an ecologically sustainable human situation is defined as one in which the bioproductivity (production of organic matter through photosynthesis) of the ecosystems of the biosphere is indefinitely maintained and in which prevailing conditions satisfy the universal health needs of the human population.
Ecosystem.
A recognizable ecological system, comprising both living organisms and the non-living environment, defined over a particular area; for example, a forest, grassland or lake.
Energy.
Extrasomatic energy – that energy which flows in and is utilised by a human community and which is not expended through metabolic processes within living organisms.
Somatic energy – that energy which is expanded, through the metabolic processes, within living organisms.
Eutrophication.
Describes the existence of high levels of nutrients in an ecosystem. More usually used to describe the high human-induced supply nutrients (particularly phosphorus and nitrogen) to an aquatic system, and the resulting degradation of the system.

Gracile hominids.
Lightly-built slender forms of hominids.
Greenhouse gases.
Gases which, in the atmosphere, have the effect of raising, or maintaining at an otherwise higher level, the temperature of the lower atmosphere (water vapour, carbon dioxide, methane, nitrous oxide, chlorofluorocarbons, tropospheric ozone). More specifically, these gases (excepting water vapour), the concentrations of which are being significantly increased via human activities.

hm
hanometre (10^{-1} metre).
Herbivore.
An animal which gains sustenance primarily from the tissue of plants.
Melior.
An experience which promotes a state of well-being, usually associated with a feeling of enjoyment.
Monoculture.
A large-scale assemblage of organisms of the one species, managed by humans; for example, a plantation forest, or a cereal crop.

Nature.
Things and processes of a kind that existed on Earth before human culture became a force in the biosphere.

Omnivore.
An animal which gains sustenance primarily from the tissue of plants.

Parasite.
An animal or plant that lives in, or on, another animal or plant (the host) from which it obtains nourishment. The host does not benefit from the association, and may be harmed by it.
Pathogens.
A living agent that can cause disease.
Primate.
Placental mammals of the order *Primates*, typically with flexible hands and feet with opposable first digits and good eyesight, including lemurs, lorises, monkeys, apes and humans.

Salinization.
The accumulation of salts, especially sodium chloride, in the soil.
Stressor.
An experience which promotes a state of distress.

Technoaddiction.
The tendency of human populations to become dependent for health and survival on technological devices which were not neccesary for health and survival when they were first introduced.
Technometabolism.
The materials and energy which flow into, through, and out of a human population and which are due to technological processes.

INDEX

259